Continuous Peace

Continuous Peace

4 Steps to *Living the Life of Peace* God Intended

DAWN MARASCO

XULON PRESS

Xulon Press
2301 Lucien Way #415
Maitland, FL 32751
407.339.4217
www.xulonpress.com

© 2020 by Dawn Marasco

All rights reserved solely by the author. The author guarantees all contents are original and do not infringe upon the legal rights of any other person or work. No part of this book may be reproduced in any form without the permission of the author. The views expressed in this book are not necessarily those of the publisher.

Unless otherwise indicated, Scripture quotations taken from:
New American Standard Bible (NASB)
Copyright © 1960, 1962, 1963, 1968, 1971, 1972, 1973, 1975, 1977, 1995 by The Lockman Foundation. Used by permission. www.Lockman.org

New International Version (NIV)
Holy Bible, New International Version®, NIV® Copyright ©1973, 1978, 1984, 2011 by Biblica, Inc.® Used by permission. All rights reserved worldwide.

New International Reader's Version (NIRV)
Copyright © 1995, 1996, 1998, 2014 by Biblica, Inc.®. Used by permission. All rights reserved worldwide.

Amplified Bible (AMP)
Copyright © 2015 by The Lockman Foundation, La Habra, CA 90631. All rights reserved. Used by permission. www.Lockman.org

Amplified Bible, Classic Edition (AMPC)
Copyright © 1954, 1958, 1962, 1964, 1965, 1987 by The Lockman Foundation Used by permission. www.Lockman.org

The Message (MSG)
Copyright © 1993, 2002, 2018 by Eugene H. Peterson Used by permission of NavPress. All rights reserved. Represented by Tyndale House Publishers, Inc Used by permission of NavPress. All rights reserved. Represented by Tyndale House Publishers, Inc.

New Living Translation (NLT) Holy Bible, New Living Translation, copyright © 1996, 2004, 2015 by Tyndale House Foundation. Used by permission of Tyndale House Publishers, Inc., Carol Stream, Illinois 60188. All rights reserved.

Paperback ISBN-13: 9781631299261
Ebook ISBN-13: 9781631299278

Printed In The United States of America

PRAISE FOR
Continuous Peace

Dawn, I have one question. When will this book be published? It is a guide to life. I wish I had this when I was younger. This is the second-best guide for living, the Bible being the first.

Love, Grandma

Dawn's book is an owner's manual for life. She teaches simple coping skills which is something I have always lacked even in adulthood. The world can be a tough place, but Dawn has inspired me to manage my emotions and get on track for a rich, full life… the life that Jesus Christ intended me to have. Her words are therapeutic, and I love the step by step instructions of how to navigate through this life which can often be filled with challenges. She has shown me how to "catch the curveball." I will always be grateful.

Lisa

Continuous Peace is like no other book I have read. It taught me concepts and practical ways that made sense to overcome the anxious thoughts that invade my life. The concepts in this book come from the heart of the author because they come from her life experiences. They are not textbook solutions… they were given to her by the Holy Spirit as He led her through dark valleys into a peace that passes understanding. A *must read* for anyone filled with anxiety and seeking continuous peace.

Becky

Dawn has a way of weaving together scripture, experience, and common sense. Her insights helped me finally break down a lifetime of worry, guilt, and doubt, and helped me find the peace and hope that I had been missing.

Nancy

What I got from the book *Continuous Peace*, and why I couldn't stop reading it, was an invitation to know another woman's intimate walk with the Lord – How she talks to Him, How He answers her, what He has brought her through and what He is doing now. More than a model for a relationship it is an inspiration, and a message that creates a deeper hunger for the same kind of intentional, personal, and powerful relationship with God.

Karen

Dawn's book has changed my life and my walk with God. I have released so many life experiences that were hidden deep within. Learning how to recognize and release them has helped me to find God's peace. Recently, I was faced with some medical fears. Multiple doctor appointments, tests, and surgery screamed for my attention. I determined, *"No! This will not steal my peace."* I took it all to God and released it all to Him, trusting Him to navigate me through it. His peace and His promises filled me and guided me through the storm.

Dana

In reading *Continuous Peace*, the author has managed to combine God's word and teaching with personal counseling in easy to understand concepts and real-life examples. These concepts will help you to grow in faith and find peace amongst the struggles, feelings and emotions encountered in your life journey. Once you read, you will thirst to go back to it time and time again as a reference and learning tool.

Cheri

Dawn's 4 steps show us practically how to live the life of peace God intended. He wants us to be healed and whole! Dawn opened my eyes to the fact that God loves and accepts me exactly where I am and that He loves me too much to leave me there. She taught me to remain in HIM and not in fear, worry, anger, etc.

Praise For Continuous Peace

Dawn's heart is to empower us to strengthen our relationship with God, and to know Him intimately, like she does. She longs for us to be free and to cultivate a peaceful way of living. Her 4 steps to peace can get you there. Do yourself a favor and journey with Dawn. Be willing to be open, vulnerable, and honest. These steps have forever changed my life and I know they will change yours too.

Melissa

Dawn continues to be such an inspiration to me. In her book about peace, one principle continues to help me daily. It is the response that, *"I get to do this"*. I have focused on the "I have to" mentality for so long. I "have to" cook dinner for my family. I "have to" get the kids lunches packed. I "have to" read the same bedtime story. Dawn teaches that, *NO... I don't "have to" do these things*. I need to be thankful that I "get to" do these things. She reminds us that *there are those who would love to do what we call ordinary or mundane.*

Dawn has a way of telling stories that are compelling and captivating. Many times, I sat and cried reading her stories. I was impacted by learning how she applied changes to her everyday life, which helped her to get through life's storms. Grab a box of tissues, a journal, and a pen when you sit down and absorb her amazing teachings.

Jaime

After reading *Continuous Peace*, I now realize that finding God's peace is a journey not a destination. This journey is a process and it takes time, but the outcomes are worth it. When you find yourself in the midst of chaos *and you actually feel peace*, it is unreal.

Mandie

Dawn shares God's love from her heart and her story will help you overcome those obstacles that are keeping you from a life of peace. This can be done as a personal study between you and the Lord, but I feel it would be great as a group study!

Roseann

Dawn shares her personal story of how to find the peace of God in daily living!

Debbie

When I was asked to participate in this book, I was honored. After reading a few chapters, the words began to speak to areas of my heart that had become hardened and prevented much needed healing. I soon realized that this message was a part of God's plan for the next chapter of my life.

Rita

Dawn's relentless pursuit of peace is a priceless treasure that she offers in this book. Her life stories of how she overcame traumas and how the God she loves walked her through the healing process is a gift that has the power to bring revelation and healing to your life, as it has mine. This book has given me hope, courage and the promise of peace. I intend to live out the steps I have learned in this book all my life.

April

*I became a servant of this gospel
by the gift of God's grace
given me through the working of His Power.*

Ephesians 3:7 (NIV)

I dedicate this book to my Lord and Savior Jesus Christ, who gave up His life for me. It was by His grace and mercy, and the power of His Spirit in me that He transformed my life into something worthy of giving away. This book is a record of my response to His great love! He loved me and came after me when I was broken and bound. He has walked me through the dark as I learned how to walk in the light of His amazing love and peace.

> *"Lord, You are my brightest smile, my highest thought, my joy beyond measure, and the source of my heart beating with the power of Your love and peace. I am forever Yours. I am so blessed to be Your daughter.*
>
> *Lord, I pray that You powerfully use this material in each reader's heart and life. I pray they know the warmth of Your amazing love! I pray they experience a deep relationship with You that carries, heals, equips, strengthens, and encourages them with peace every day. I pray You are seen brightly through each of us all the days of our lives!"*

Serving You and those You love
with all of my heart,

Dawn

A Note to My Children

Let this be written for a future generation, that a people not yet created may praise the Lord.

Psalm 102:18 (NIV)

I present this book to my children, their children, and the generations that are yet to be born. May you grab hold of the truths written throughout this book and be reminded of how to keep God's peace regardless of life's circumstances. Jesus is near, and you are loved by Him! As your Savior, He will never leave you! He will fill you and fulfill His plan for your life.

Rejoice in your calling. Trust Him and follow Him. Love Him and love one another deeply. Do God's next right thing and peace and joy will be your companions. Shine His light wherever you go. Enjoy your life. Live as the example of His love and you will become a blessing to many.

I pray that, *"The LORD bless you and keep you; the LORD make his face shine on you and be gracious to you; the LORD turn his face toward you and give you peace."* (Numbers 6:24–26 NIV)

With all of my love,

Dawn

You will keep in perfect peace those whose minds are steadfast, because they trust in You.

Isaiah 26:3 (NIV)

CONTENTS

A Note to My Children x
Introduction: My Life Prior to Peace xiii

Step 1 RECOGNIZE
Recognize the Obstacles

Chapter 1: The Foundation for Our Peace 3
Chapter 2: The Bullies That Rob 19
Chapter 3: The Impact of Our Obstacles 33

Step 2 RELEASE
Release the Barriers

Chapter 4: The Great Exchange 53
Chapter 5: Let It Go! 75
Chapter 6: Come as You Are 99

Step 3 REPROGRAM
Reprogram My Heart and Mind

Chapter 7: The Powerful Truth 119
Chapter 8: Overwrite the Lies 139
Chapter 9: Design Your Harvest 177

Step 4 RESPOND
Respond Faithfully

Chapter 10: Hold On. Hold On Tight 211
Chapter 11: Run Your Race 231
Chapter 12: Finish Well 247

Conclusion 279
Chart Your Course 280
Acknowledgments..*283*
Bonus Materials:...*286*
    Your 30-Day Challenge................................*286*
    Reprogramming the Lie Charts.........................*288*
    Reversing a Negative Harvest Chart...................*290*

Introduction:
My Life Prior to Peace

Now may the Lord of peace Himself grant you His peace at all times *and* in every way [that peace and spiritual well-being that comes to those who walk with Him, regardless of life's circumstances]. The Lord be with you all.

> 2 Thessalonians 3:16 (AMP)

Continuous Peace

WHAT IF I TOLD YOU THAT YOU CAN DESIGN A HARVEST OF PEACE? WHAT IF YOU FOUND OUT THAT YOU can learn how to uproot a disappointing, failing, or sparse harvest in your life and plant a plentiful harvest full of continuous peace? Would you be interested in finding out how?

Throughout this book we will learn how to design and cultivate a harvest of peace. Our fears, doubts, mistrust, and insecurities are like rocks, weeds, and debris that hinder good fruit from growing and thriving. This creates a sparse or negative harvest. Thank God, *our current harvest does not dictate our future harvest.*

> OUR CURRENT HARVEST DOES NOT DICTATE OUR FUTURE HARVEST.

When I first began this journey for peace, my harvest was a mess! In my childhood, many unhealthy seeds were planted. My alcoholic dad planted harsh, rude, unkind, and mean seeds that brought forth a *destructive harvest* of mistrust, anger, suspicion, and a lack of confidence. There were many seeds of loneliness and broken promises that were planted in my heart that affected every area of my life.

MY LIFE PRIOR TO PEACE

Allow me to share a snapshot of my life prior to having God's amazing peace. I was born to a gentle sixteen-year-old mom and an alcoholic twenty-year-old dad. Growing up with an alcoholic is tumultuous. The freedom to be myself was suffocated in the presence of a manipulative and violent father.

All creativity subsides and happiness hides when fear takes a front-row seat. Doubt and anxiety were the glasses that I wore to view the world. Suspicion, mistrust, and loneliness were my constant companions. As I grew, so did my anger, bitterness, and lack of caring.

Introduction

One of my earliest memories of the ongoing turbulence took place when I was five years old. It was a crisp fall day and the football game was about to begin. This was a weekly big event for my dad, and this week I was going to join in. I was excited because our home would be filled with lots of cheering and yelling at the players. My mom would add to the celebration by making us special snacks. That week she made buttered bread with hot pepper rings on it. It was one of my dad's favorites.

I remember pulling up to the coffee table next to my dad as we ate our hot pepper butter bread. I was full of joy to be a part of such an awaited event. I asked my dad what color our team's jerseys were so I would know who to root for. With that simple question, he snapped his head around and started to yell at me for irritating him.

I was stunned that he was yelling at me for just trying to understand the game. His abrupt anger caused me to slowly push away from the coffee table. I took a good, hard look at his face and I sadly remember thinking, *He is mean! I cannot trust him.* That was the day that the rock of mistrust was buried in my heart, and I determined that I could not trust my dad. I began to shut down in his presence. Soon I started to blend into the background. I stopped asking questions because I did not trust him with my heart any longer.

As a five-year-old, I had no idea that this event would begin to create a void of love and produce a stronghold of mistrust that would feed fear and loneliness. These types of wounds would later become *obstacles* that would affect my life for decades. They robbed me of truly living and became a barrier to God's peace.

When we are *not* able to trust those who are closest to us, we naturally have a hard time *trusting God and trusting others.*

Throughout the years, my dad's negative impact along with his broken promises continued to injure my heart. Those wounds created an ache for love and a desire to be known. Being wounded, empty, and numb in my teen years led me to choose my own destructive, sinful paths, which caused an even greater devastation to my already grieving heart. I did not know how to deal with my pain, so I tried to hide it. As the wounds entered my heart, I would place a boulder over the entrance, attempting to keep the pain from erupting and making its way to the surface.

But there was not a boulder big enough to cover the explosion of pain that was about to take place when I was nineteen and engaged to be married. That was the night that fear derailed my life and sorrow entangled me, attempting to consume my whole being. It was a warm summer night when I walked into a graduation party with my fiancé, and we left by ambulance with him clinging to life. He had been stabbed multiple times when a senseless fight broke out.

THAT NIGHT
I remember in the ambulance as they were trying to run an IV into his arm, he lay moaning and tried to resist their prodding and poking. From the front seat, I was able to remind him that they were there to help and that he needed to cooperate with them. He seemed to calm down just by hearing my voice.

The ambulance driver was relaying my fiancé's vital signs over the radio. After he finished, I asked, *"Is that good?"* He looked at me and hesitantly shook his head and softly said, *"No."* Hearing his response, my thoughts raced and my anxious heart pounded through my chest as I contemplated the severity of his condition.

As we continued to drive in the pitch-dark, I saw headlights appear from the other direction. Shockingly, both the ambulance and the other vehicle came to a complete stop in the middle of the road. The passenger from the other vehicle ran

Introduction

to the back of the ambulance, flung open the doors, and jumped in carrying a handheld cooler. As quickly as we stopped, we began to speed to the hospital once again.

Questions poured from within me, *"What just happened? Why did we pick up that man? Who is he and what was he carrying?"* I learned that the person who entered the ambulance was carrying a cooler full of bags of blood. My fiancé's wounds were so severe that he was losing blood at an alarming rate. They needed to begin a blood transfusion in the ambulance.

When we arrived at the ER, I flung open the door and ran to the back of the ambulance. As they wheeled him out on the stretcher, I could see the hospital staff anxiously waiting for him. Thank God they gave us a few seconds to say good-bye. Focusing only on one another, I remember our eyes met and he said, *"I love you!"* I pressed in and assured him of my love as we reached for one another. It was a tender moment amidst total chaos.

With urgency I was told by hospital staff, *"We need to get him inside!"* I watched as they wheeled him away, quickly turned the bend, and went out of sight.

Silently I stood, numb from all that was happening. I was still staring in the direction that they had taken him when I felt an arm gently wrap around my shoulder. Without words I was led into the emergency waiting room, where I paced and continued to pray. I watched as hospital workers ran with those small coolers to and from the ER room. In continuous prayer, I cried out to God asking that He heal him. During my frantic prayer, a sensation so strong comforted me. I felt like I knew that *his spirit had lifted* and that *he was on his way to heaven*. It was as if I could sense his departure. Somehow, I felt comforted.

It was then that I lost the desperate feeling that I had to pray. Emotionless, I just sat quietly. That was when I noticed, one by one, those coming from the ER who were once running were now walking with their heads hung low. I assumed that what I felt was true. He was gone. Still in shock, I sat in silence.

It was a while before the doctor and hospital staff came out to report that he did pass away. When their words confirmed his death, the reality that he was gone was more than my mind and heart could handle. Horrific pain gripped my heart. With no warning to myself or others, I released a loud cry: "*Noooo!*" My reaction shocked me and everyone in the room, but I had no control of it. I could not contain my pain. Abruptly I was told to stop crying and to listen to the doctors. They proceeded to say that he had died because his aorta had been cut near his heart, which was why he had lost so much blood.

DESPERATE FOR PEACE
His death was so senseless! It was unbelievable. He was here one moment and gone the next. My mind could not believe that I had lost him. Losing him shattered my heart, and the broken shards penetrated all aspects of my life.

The hours, days, and years of my life following his death were continually filled and overflowing with fear. When I say I needed God's peace, that is an understatement. In those early days, while I slept, I could forget the pain. But as my mind would slowly awaken, I would remember all that had taken place. Instantaneously, I could feel the sting of warm tears flowing down my face as my heart would remember that he was gone. It was hard to get out of bed. I had to push myself to do daily tasks.

As I would try to face my day, fear continued to entangle me, its grip reminding me of all the negative things that had happened. It was as if my already wounded heart and mind added this tragic loss to all the other losses, past pains, and sins in my life. It felt like the heaviest boulder was now upon me. That was when I hit the bottom of the pit I was in. The weight of the sorrow that I carried was so heavy. I knew I needed help. I knew I could not live like this, so I cried out to God.

GOD HEARD

Five weeks after I lost my fiancé, I visited a friend. Her mom was so sensitive to my pain. She knew how broken I was, and she lovingly began to share her faith with me. She told me about a loving Savior who would meet me where I was, forgive my sins, and fill me with His Spirit. With every word that she spoke, it was as if I was breathing for the first time. She then asked me if I wanted to accept Jesus as my Savior. With all of my heart, I agreed. I wanted to know Him as *my* Savior. As we prayed, an unspeakable joy rose up from within me. I knew I was changed. I did not just know *about* God; God's Spirit *now filled me*! I sprang to my feet and began to leap and jump for joy.

When my friend came downstairs and saw the difference in me, she exclaimed in an accusatory voice, *"What did you do to my friend?"*

Her mom laughed and said, *"I didn't do anything to your friend. God did this!"* She was right. God had filled my heart with joy. I walked into her home a broken mess, but God met me where I was, and I now knew He would be with me for the rest of my life.

That night I did *not* climb out of my pit. My God pulled me out! He came near to me and He heard my cry. He reached down into my miry pit, not concerned with how muddy I was. He pulled me out and forgave my many sins. He set my foot on a solid rock and put a new song in my mouth, one of praise to my God. I was filled with His Spirit. My change was evident to everyone. I could not contain my newfound joy. This was the beginning of my new Christian life.

Psalm 40:1–3 (AMP)

> I waited patiently *and* expectantly for the Lord; And He inclined to me and heard my cry. He brought me up out of a horrible pit [of tumult and of destruction], out of the miry clay, And He set my feet upon a rock, steadying my footsteps *and* establishing my path. He put a new song in my mouth, a song of praise to our God; Many will see and fear [with great reverence] And will trust confidently in the Lord.

Pretending to Be Whole

When I became a Christian, it was awesome, and it *did* change my life forever. I was comforted to know that God was with me. I understood that I was forgiven but *I still did not know how to be healed*. I did not know how to handle my past wounds and fears, so I continued to hide them. I was unaware of what else to do. *Pretending to be whole* while I was really broken produced no peace in my life. It only fed and fueled my fears and insecurities. They were permitted to grow wildly!

In the years that followed, I tried to live by faith, but I was blown off course by one fear after another. I felt stuck. I despised the fact that I was such a *weak* Christian. I knew I could be living a victorious life, but *I did not know how*. I went to church every Sunday. I loved God, but the truth was that fear ruled my life, not God.

I deeply desired a peace that I could live by, but my fearful way of living continually robbed me of my peace. I felt like a failure, unproductive, weak, and ashamed of how I was living. What-ifs—meaning "What if this happens or what if that happens?"—were obstacles stopping my forward progress. I felt far from God and far from His purposes. I was exhausted. I always felt like I was not good enough. I knew my answers were found in God, but I did not understand how to find them or apply them. *Can you identify with some of those same feelings?*

The following questions describe *how I felt prior* to having God's peace. *Underline* any of the questions that are true for you.

- Are you tired of allowing fear to run your life?
- Does the threat of "What if?" impact you as though it is a truth?
- Does the bully of fear try to change your direction?
- Are you exhausted from the indecisive battles over everyday decisions?
- Do you feel far from God?
- Do you feel far from His purposes in your life?
- Are you far from the peace that God has promised?
- Are you exhausted from trying to control situations?
- Do you feel overwhelmed, insignificant, or not good enough?
- Are you fed up with living a life that does not reflect the glory of God as it could or should?

If you answered yes to any of the preceding questions, then journey with me. I will walk you through the four steps that God continually uses to keep me in His amazing peace. We will learn how to live a life full of the peace that God intends for us. It may seem impossible right now, but stay the course and consider the alternative of living without the fullness of God's peace for another month, year, or decade!

FROM BROKEN TO PEACE
This book is a result of my desperation to have God's peace in my own life. For years, although I deeply desired peace, His peace was nowhere to be found. I had moments of happiness and I was happy with parts of my life, but peace—that inner calm that God promises—was missing. It is agonizing and exhausting to go through this life without His peaceful assurance.

God did not call us to live a life of failure, frustration, or fearful destruction. *He has provided a way for us to live a life full of peace, faith, and freedom.* He is faithful. If you have had a painful past, your heartache may cry out for you to stop this journey. Please press on. Our *pain is our clue* that a healing is needed. His peace is close.

Often we may even feel as if we are going through the motions of this fast-paced life, numb and without peace. We may desire peace but not understand how to receive His peace or keep it once we do have it. Now that I have experienced God's wonderful and comforting peace as a way of life, *I am compelled to share what I have learned with you.*

I have broken down the process of having God's continuous peace into four steps. I will systematically take you through the four steps of Recognize, Release, Reprogram, and Respond. I capitalize the *R*'s throughout the book. My hope is to make the words stand out and illuminate where we are in the process.

Living the Life of Peace
I faithfully utilize these four steps in *every* area of my life. God has used them to heal me and equip me to *keep* His peace. These truths have become my strong foundation, keeping me through the turbulent storms of life. I believe this process will help you to gain God's peace every day.

As we journey through these four steps, we will Recognize the *obstacles* that have kept us from living the life of peace God intended. We will Release the *barriers* that confine us. We will Reprogram with *truth* and learn to create a harvest of peace. We will be equipped with tools to Respond *faithfully* in all of life's circumstances. This way of living will cause us to overflow with His abundant fruit. I know if God can do this in my weed-ridden life, He can also help you to live a life full of His peace.

Introduction

Our past does not dictate our future harvest.

When implemented, these four steps can change the trajectory of our lives. They have changed mine! Throughout this book I will be sharing my life experiences and the amazing lessons that the Lord has taught me. Here are a few topics we will be covering in this exciting journey.

Step 1 RECOGNIZE
- What Peace Is and Where Peace Comes From
- The Power to Keep Our Peace
- The Bullies That Rob
- The Impact of Our Obstacles

Step 2 RELEASE
- The Great Exchange
- Remember Without Pain
- Come as You Are
- Release and Rely: My Mom's Story

Step 3 REPROGRAM
- The Condition of Our Cup
- Overwrite the Lies
- Design Your Harvest
- What We Feed Will Grow

Step 4 RESPOND
- Hold On. Hold On Tight.
- Run Your Race
- We Get To
- Finish Well

These steps will illuminate the way to live a life of peace, *no matter what the circumstances.* By transparently revealing my struggles and the truths that God has shown to me, my hope is to make each step come alive and be easily applied. When put into action, this process will promote transformation and help you to create a life filled with God's *continuous peace.* As you implement these steps, be willing to follow where God leads. It will be worth the effort. You will experience the peace that God intends for you.

What would change in your life if you had His continuous peace? How would your relationships, marriage, parenting, work, or dreams change if your life were transformed into a life filled with peace?

_____
_____

What are your hopes or expectations for this book?

_____
_____

JOIN ME

Throughout this amazing process, your relationship with God will deepen. I am thrilled with the transformation I have witnessed in those who have embraced the principles in this book. I have been blessed as they explain how rich their walk with God has become.

Some of them have been Christians for decades and are only now experiencing this awesome relationship with God. They have joyously explained their newfound depth with God, and how He meets them right where they are. They have shared how strong their peace has become. When an obstacle arises, they now have the tools to deal with it and keep their peace. I have had the privilege of watching the blessings of peace unfold in their lives and impact those around them.

This book will take you there. This material does lead us to Him, and *He will meet us right where we are.* Thank God He will not leave us where He finds us. He has a good plan, a plan for healing and peace that will flow out of a deep walk with Him.

Introduction

I am so excited about the journey you are about to begin. Know that my heart and my prayers are with you and have been with you for two decades. Over the years, when a specific fear would cause me to want to pull back, I would ask God to remind me of the *ones* who would *one day* be helped by my continuing to learn the way of peace. I found courage to face my own fears and go forward, knowing that this could help others someday. *You were always on my mind and in my heart.* I am so thankful that we finally get to journey together.

> YOU WERE ALWAYS ON MY MIND AND IN MY HEART.

It has been twenty-four years since I began this process. I can honestly say *I am so thankful that my younger self did not give up, give in, or abandon the process of knowing God's peace.* I would not be who I am today. My life has been changed *forever!*

Choose today to *live the life of peace that God intends for you.*

Let's begin to impact our future with His peace! As you read, I suggest that you use a notebook or journal to write down all that the Lord *will* show you. I pose questions throughout the book. They will help you to *capture your thoughts* in the moment and to receive the most impact from this study. God is with you! His peace is close.

Philippians 1:6 (NIV)

Being confident of this, that he who began a good work in you will carry it on to completion until the day of Christ Jesus.

4 Steps to Continuous Peace:

1. **RECOGNIZE the Obstacles That Rob**
2. RELEASE the Barriers That Confine
3. REPROGRAM My Heart & Mind with Truth
4. RESPOND Faithfully for a Continuous Life of Peace

Step 1 Recognize
RECOGNIZE THE OBSTACLES

Chapter 1
THE FOUNDATION FOR OUR PEACE

Peace is not for sale or everyone would buy it;
it is *a gift* from God.

WE HAVE BEEN GIVEN THE MOST AWESOME GIFT! God has provided *a way for us to live a life of peace*. This is not a fleeting peace but a peace that we can count on. Sadly, many of us do not know how to live this way. I was a Christian whose thoughts, words, and actions were the evidence that God's peace was *not* flourishing within me. I was coerced by fears, doubts, and the pains from my past, which continually robbed me of my peace. I longed for His peace. I desperately sought it. I would have bought it if I could, but since I could not purchase it, I had to *learn how* to *receive* it.

The principles that I have learned have been amazing. They have transformed my entire life. I now have a peace that supports me every day. When a situation arises and tries to rob my peace, which does happen, I remember these truths and I apply them. God's peace has carried me through my darkest seasons. Throughout this book, I will share my everyday life, including my difficult places and how God has led me to His peace in each situation. *I deeply desire to help you* live a life filled with His continuous peace.

I know what God has done for me *He will do for you!*

I will provide you with the four steps and the practical ways that God has used to cultivate peace in my own life. In this first step of Recognize, we will uncover *what peace is* and *what is robbing us of our peace.* This step is vital because *if* we do not Recognize the obstacles that are robbing us, we can continue to circle around the same worn-out path, frustrated and without His peace. I stayed on that well-worn path for years. I will help you Recognize and remove those obstacles. We *can* live the life of peace that God has intended for us.

Know that *I am cheering for you.* Peace can be your way of living! Let's begin to unwrap this awesome gift. In the first three chapters, we will learn to Recognize:

- What peace is and where peace comes from
- The power to keep God's peace
- The power of focus
- The bullies who rob our peace
- The impact of our obstacles
- How it physically feels to lose our peace

THE FOUNDATION FOR OUR PEACE
Peace is a gift—a gift from Jesus Christ. The Book of John reveals that Jesus did not want to leave us as orphans when He went home to heaven. He wanted to leave us with the most powerful gift to help us in this life. This gift is the *Holy Spirit in us.* His being in us implies that He will be with us no matter what we are going through or facing. He is our *Helper,* the One who gives us the ability to have God's peace.

John 14:16–17, 26–27 (NASB)

> I will ask the Father, and He will give you another Helper, that He may be with you forever; that is the Spirit of truth, whom the world cannot receive, because it does not see Him or know Him, but you know Him because He abides with you and will be in you.
> But the Helper, the Holy Spirit, whom the Father will send in My name, He will teach you all things, and

bring to your remembrance all that I said to you. Peace I leave with you; My peace I give to you; not as the world gives do I give to you. Do not let your heart be troubled, nor let it be fearful.

Let's unpack these amazing scriptures. I love that Jesus does not give as the world gives, but rather He supplies us with His peace. The world gives perishable things such as money and belongings. These possessions may make us temporarily happy, but they *cannot* produce God's peace.

God has lovingly given us a Helper. This Helper is the Holy Spirit. He is the One who will be with us FOREVER. We receive the Holy Spirit when we *believe in* the Lord Jesus and accept Him as our Savior. By our *faith* in Jesus, we are *filled* with His Spirit, who gives us the capacity to have God's peace. By His Spirit we are transformed, renewed, and set apart for His purposes.

THE POWER TO HAVE HIS PEACE
God gives us the power within to help us navigate this life. He equips us with His powerful Holy Spirit so that our hearts will not be troubled. His power *within* us can keep us from being afraid! We will continue to explore this further, but for right now let's Recognize that we will never walk alone. It is comforting to know He is always with us, no matter what we face. What an awesome gift!

Without the Holy Spirit in us, we cannot have God's peace.

It is by His Spirit living in us that we can have God's peace. As God's Spirit bears His fruit within our lives, *His fruit will become evident.* What is the fruit of the Spirit?

Galatians 5:22–23a (NASB)
> The fruit of the Spirit is love, joy, peace, patience, kindness, goodness, faithfulness, gentleness and self-control.

The first time I experienced the fruit of the Spirit was the day I told you about in the *Introduction*. It was five weeks after my fiancé was murdered. I walked into my friend's house heavy-laden with fear and sorrow. Her compassionate mom shared the truths of God with me. At one point she said, *"There is an emptiness in each of us. Many explain it as a God-shaped void. But when you ask the Holy Spirit to fill you, He will fill that empty place within you."* She continued to explain that I might not realize an emptiness existed. That was when I assured her that *I knew that I was empty.*

She continued to share her faith with me, and for the first time, I prayed and asked Jesus to forgive all my sins and become my Savior. During that prayer I asked to be filled with the Holy Spirit. That was when joy erupted from within me. In that moment, I had a joy so strong that I began leaping and jumping up and down in her kitchen.

A true transformation had taken place. Even though my circumstances had not changed, I was changed. I will forever be grateful. I know many who have been filled *without* such a strong response. Each experience with God is unique. All I know is that I walked into her house a broken mess. God filled me, and I left with joy. I still had to work through the pain of losing my fiancé. It took many years to be healed and full of God's peace, but it all started on that wonderful day.

> The Spirit of God is a gift that keeps on giving.

By His Spirit we have been equipped to hear God, be led by Him, and bear His wonderful fruit in our lives. He is our Helper and *the source of our peace.*

WHAT IS PEACE?
What is your definition of peace?

_____

Ask yourself: Have you had times of happiness, momentary joy, or feeling blessed but can't say that you have experienced God's peace? Would God's peace take you by surprise? Have you felt His peace only to have it disappear once again?

> ***Peace*** can be defined as wholeness, harmony, reconciliation, unity, serenity, calm, quiet, rest, stillness, tranquility, composure, levelheadedness, or peace of mind.
>
> ***The opposite of peace*** can mean panic, uproar, chaos, confusion, turmoil, commotion, unrest, instability, agitation, anxiety, worry, nervousness, tension, or distress.

Which aspect of peace do you desire the most?

_____

_____

Does any aspect of *the opposite of* peace affect you?

_____

_____

For me, having God's peace makes me feel *complete in Him, lacking nothing and being at rest.* Even though our circumstances may be scary or hard, God has made available His peace to help us in every situation. His peace consists of quietness of mind and an inner calmness. God's peace can calm our unrest, anxiety, nervousness, and distress through His Holy Spirit. He will empower us with His peace, which will impact our everyday lives.

Shallow and Not Flourishing

> If our relationship with God is only surface-deep, then we will hinder the peace of God from flourishing.

Many times we can be desperate for His peace, desiring that inner harmony and tranquility, but if our relationship with God is only surface-deep, then we will hinder the peace of God from flourishing. Peace is not found in a religion that we follow. Our peace comes from our relationship with Almighty God, which is developed more deeply day by day.

I had a shallow relationship with God for the first nine years of my Christian life. I kept God contained, causing peace to be just a word and not a heavenly rest within me. I knew little about how to live as a Christian. I fumbled fearfully through this life trying to hide my wounds, fears, and indecisiveness. I attempted to look like I had it all together, but it was an empty, failing, and exhausting facade.

Our relationships stay surface-deep until we share our heart with one another. It can be scary to share our wounded hearts with anyone, including God. My past wounds caused me to build fortified walls that enclosed sections of my heart. I knew God wanted to make my heart whole, but that unknown process was frightening. I had to *choose* whether I would keep God at arm's length and stay as I was or if I would allow Him to enter every boarded-up room.

The Day I Gave God Full Access

I knew I had to give God full access to my heart in order for Him to heal me. I did not *feel* ready, but I knew that I finally wanted God's will for me more than I wanted my own will. I needed His freedom more than I desired to keep my heart tightly sealed. I was desperate for His peace because I was continually allowing fear to rule my life!

Even though I loved God and I prayed often, I still felt *vulnerable* inviting God into my messy heart. Being desperate to be changed, I finally put down my guard and let Him into every boarded-up room. I sobbed while praying a prayer like this:

> "You know I am so afraid to give You access to my whole heart, but Lord, I know You want more for me than the way I am living. I lay down my *past*, every wounded place, and all that is in my heart. I give You full access to it all. I give You my *present* day, and every day. I give up my right to hide. I do not want to dictate my way. I even reluctantly release my *future* to You. I am afraid of what You may require of me. But I want You to fulfill the plans You have for me, more than I want to control my life. Prepare me for all that You want me to do." I ended my prayer, conveying clearly, "You have to do this work because I cannot!"

That day, my loving God met me where I was. I had known Jesus as my Savior for nine years, but that day I made Him my Lord, Lord of all! He was the One I wanted to lead me.

SURPRISED BY PEACE
He was faithful! After I surrendered my wounded heart to Him, step by step and week by week God began helping me to heal some of those injured places. It was then that I began to have this really good feeling that would not go away. I did not know what it was, so I said to my pastor, "*I have this really good feeling and it is not going away.*"

He looked at me, tilted his head, and said with a smile, *"That is God's peace, Dawn."*

Amazed, I quickly responded, *"You mean I can live this way?"* With a joyful laugh and a gleam of delight in his eyes, he went on to assure me that I could live *every day* with this incredible peace.

I was amazed that after I entrusted my aching heart to God, He began the cleansing process, and peace sprang up. By allowing God into those painful places, He was able to teach me how to replace my pain with His peace. He also helped me to Recognize that my daily *fears were obstacles* that continually robbed me of my peace.

> God's peace had come like a warm, comforting light
> as He restored those cold, painful, and dark places.

OUR STARTING PLACE

Are you at the place in your walk with God where you are *willing to entrust your heart to Him*? It is the starting point for our peace. If you are not willing, what could be keeping you from entrusting your heart to Him? Could it be fear, shame, distrust of God, or fear of what might happen? Those were some of the *obstacles* that kept me from all that God had for me. Let's not allow anything to keep us from a deep relationship with God. If we are far from Him, *we will be far* from the peace that He has in store for us.

My desire is to meet you where you are. I want to help you take the next right step in living the life of peace God intended. Let's allow today to be our starting place. Perhaps you have not entrusted your heart to Him fully or you may feel like, *Here I am again*. (I have felt like that many times.) Wherever you are, *if this prayer applies, please pray it with me:*

Father, today I want to make sure that You have access to my heart. I have tried to do things on my own. I have tried to fill my life with things or relationships that I thought would bring me peace, but they do not. I have tried to control or keep order as an attempt to feel peaceful, but it is just a mirage.

I Recognize that I want Your peace and I know that it is found in a personal relationship with You. Please forgive my sins that have separated me from You. Thank You for sending Jesus, who died paying the penalty for all my sins. He bridged the gap so that I can have a relationship with You. By faith, I choose to receive Jesus as my Savior. Please fill me with Your Holy Spirit, equipping me to live for You. I desire the fruit of the Spirit to be evident in my life. I want to be free, healed, and full of Your peace. Be my Lord. Complete the good work You began in me. In Jesus' Name, I pray. Amen.

Once God has our heart, our journey to peace begins. This is an exciting journey! If today was the first time that, by faith in Jesus, you asked God to forgive your sins and fill you with His Holy Spirit, write down this date. _____Today Jesus became your Savior and you began your relationship with Him, or perhaps today was the day that you gave God full access to your heart. No matter where you are in your journey with Him, He is our Wonderful Counselor, Mighty God, Everlasting Father, and our Prince of Peace. (Isaiah 9:6b NIV)

Ephesians 2:8,13–14a (NASB)

> For by grace you have been saved, through faith; and that not of yourselves, *it is* the gift of God ... But now in Christ Jesus you who formerly were far off have been brought near by the blood of Christ. For He Himself is our peace.

2 Corinthians 5:17 (AMP)

> Therefore if anyone is in Christ [that is, grafted in, joined to Him by faith in Him as Savior], *he is* a new creature [reborn and renewed by the Holy Spirit]; the old things [the previous moral and spiritual condition] have passed away. Behold, new things have come [because spiritual awakening brings a new life].

We who were far off have been brought near. We have been made new *in* Christ. Our sins have been forgiven. Our new life has begun. God has equipped us with His Holy Spirit to help us fulfill the plans that He has for us. Our God is with us now and He will be with us forever. He will never leave you nor forsake you. (Deuteronomy 31:8 NIV)

What a *complete gift* we have been given by believing in Jesus as our Lord. He has become our peace. Let's dive deeper into our knowledge of Him. Our relationship with Him grows as our knowledge of Him deepens.

KNOW WHO HE IS

Our peace will grow exponentially by knowing Him. It is a gift to know who He is. The word *know* is better explained as to *know by experience*. I have come to know God as the Bible has revealed Him, which has helped me to grow in my personal relationship with Him. But by taking my Bible knowledge and living it out as true, I now *know* Him by *experiencing* Him throughout my life.

> OUR PEACE IS STRENGTHENED BY KNOWING GOD THROUGH OUR PERSONAL EXPERIENCES.

For example, you may know from the Bible that He is our Provider.

However, when you trust God to provide specifically *what you need*, and He does, you now know Him *as your* Provider. It is so powerful to know Him personally! *Our peace is strengthened by knowing God through our personal experiences.*

If I were to ask you to write down descriptive words about who He is, what would you write? Take a few moments and consider who He is and then write it down:

He is:

_____
_____
_____

Here are only a few reminders of who *He is*: Faithful, Strong, Loving, Mighty, Compassionate, Merciful, Unchanging, All-Knowing, Understanding, Able, Sovereign, Just, Powerful, Protector, Teacher, Maker, Wise King, Provider, Savior, Friend, Cornerstone, Rewarder, Healer, Leader, Refuge, Rock, Helper, Shepherd, Constant Companion, Encourager, and Creator of you and me.

How blessed we are to know who He is! Let's pray and thank Him for *who He is*.

"Thank You, Lord, that You are _____
_____
*and You are my*_____."

Know Who You Are in Him
Another great gift that brings us peace is to know *who we are in* Christ! We were created uniquely by the One who made heaven and earth.

Psalm 139:13–16 (NIV)

> For you created my inmost being; you knit me together in my mother's womb. I praise you because I am fearfully and wonderfully made; your works are wonderful, I know that full well. My frame was not hidden from you when I was made in the secret place, when I was woven together in the depths of the earth. Your eyes saw my unformed body; all the days ordained for me were written in your book before one of them came to be.

God created you wonderfully with specific gifts, passions, and desires to accomplish the best in you! He also made you to view and process life in your own unique way. Often *we dismiss how God has created us*. We try to hide the fact that we are sensitive or bold and even strong-willed. Others may have tried to discourage our personality, but our God created us perfectly.

There is only one you. Even identical twins have their own unique set of fingerprints, hopes, desires, and personalities. Do not try to hide who you are. Embrace it. By doing so you will embrace the One who created you uniquely.

If I were to ask you to write down descriptive words about *who you are*, how would you describe yourself? What if I asked what the Bible says about *who you are in Christ*? Take a few moments to consider those two questions and then write down descriptive words that describe who you are and who you are in Him:

I am:

_____
_____
_____

Sadly, many of us have a hard time pointing out the "good" within us. We may have believed negative lies about ourselves for so long that it is a challenge to see the good in ourselves, but it is evident. Here are a few truths to consider. *Underline* those that are true for you. *Add* those truths to your *I am* statement.

In Him, I am . . . Loved, Saved, Redeemed, Beautiful, Forgiven, Protected, Set Free, Filled, Fruitful, Wise, Kind, Enough, Safe, Covered, Never Alone, Unique, Gifted, Called, Anointed, Faith-filled, Courageous, Patient, Joyful, Faithful, Heard, Seen, Helped, Cherished, a Light, a New Creation, a Worshiper, and a Dearly Loved Child of God. I am blessed!

That is who we are, no matter *how we feel.*

Here are some additional *I am* statements from others who have applied the principles in this book. I am . . . His Child, Creative, Smart, Compassionate, Loving, Helpful, Caring, Strong-Willed, Focused, Fun, Real, Diligent, Free to Be Me, Free for All Eternity, Artistic, Creative, Complete, Wanting Nothing, Full, Loyal, Sensitive, Observant, Accepting of Others, Encouraging, Determined, Musical, Responsible, a Hard Worker, a Counselor, and a Good Listener. I am His!

One ended with the truth that *"I am . . . in need of You, Lord!"*

How do you feel after reading those truths?

_____

By being uniquely you, others will see a *facet of God through you.* Let's thank Him.

*"Thank You, Lord, that I am*_____
_____
_____."

It is so wonderful to know who He is and who we are in Him. These truths will *safeguard our peace*. Let's embrace these truths by believing them. It is helpful to write down what we want to remember. We can make note cards of *who He is* and *who we are in Him*, then strategically place these truths throughout our home or car. This will make it easier to memorize, believe, and incorporate into our daily lives. *Our peace will be strengthened as our relationship with God continues to grow.*

THE POWER TO KEEP GOD'S PEACE

> A WEAK RELATIONSHIP WITH GOD IS AN *OBSTACLE* TO OUR PEACE.

A weak relationship with God is an *obstacle* to our peace. Our God wants a deep relationship with each of us. But when we *do not believe* who He is or we *doubt* who we are in Him, this leads to a shallow relationship with God in which peace does *not* grow.

In our pursuit of peace, we must Recognize the relationship *we are able to have* with our Lord. Let's be convinced of *who we are in Christ*! That way we will not leave room for the enemy to minimize our relationship with God, nor allow him to rob us of God's peace.

God has *equipped* us with the *power* to keep our peace, but how? It is by His Spirit in us that we are *capable* of holding on to His peace. Yes, it is by His mighty strength that lives in us that we have the ability to live in God's peace continually. It is amazing that the same powerful Holy Spirit who lives in us *is the same mighty strength that raised Jesus Christ from the dead.* (Ephesians 1:19–20)

Let's recall our beginning scripture in John 14:27: "*My peace I give to you; . . . Do not let your heart be troubled, nor let it be fearful.*" Jesus first taught that peace comes from Him. He then directed, "Do not let" because He has provided a way through His powerful Holy Spirit, which is in us, to *be able* to keep our heart from being troubled. "Do not let" reveals that we *must* watch what our heart believes in, because that will either strengthen or rob our peace. What we believe matters.

PEACE IS A HEART ISSUE
Having peace is directly connected to what is in our heart. "Let" demonstrates that *we have a choice in what we believe.* If we are *thinking too little of God* or we do *not believe* His truths, this will block the Spirit's fruit from growing in our lives.

Ask yourself: *What am I believing?*

- Am I believing the best about God and keeping my peace?
- Do I doubt who I am in Him, causing myself to be tossed by doubts and fears?
- Am I filling up with the concerns of this life and letting fears or frustrations influence and rule my heart?

Is there something that your heart is believing that is robbing your peace?

_____
_____

He is trustworthy.

He created us uniquely.

He equipped us thoroughly.

We can enjoy Him personally.

In Christ we have been given all that we need to have His peace! He encourages us that we can keep our peace as a way of life. He warns us *not* to allow our hearts to be troubled.

We will continue to Recognize *what* is robbing our peace, and we will learn *how* to Release those barriers. This is a journey you do not want to miss. We will learn *how* to keep God's continuous peace, no matter the circumstances that arise. I will share many personal examples to help you grasp each concept as we journey through these four steps. We will begin by learning *how we forfeit our peace*.

Chapter 2
The Bullies That Rob

We Can Forfeit Our Peace
Once I experienced God's consistent peace, I quickly realized that I could also *forfeit* my peace. This realization sent me on a mission to find out *why* and *how* I could lose my peace so easily. I found that *I was choosing to give it away*. I was choosing to forfeit my peace!

How ridiculous it is that I would willingly give away this amazing peace that I longed for. It felt like a mystery that I could lose my peace so quickly. It seemed so sneaky. I did not even Recognize that the exchange had taken place until my peace was gone.

Here is one exchange that took place about twenty years ago. As I was making dinner, I suddenly lost my peace. Filled with fear, I turned off the burners on my stove, ran to my couch, knelt down, and began to cry out to God. *"God, I lost my peace! Where did it go? Why did I lose my peace?"* I waited.

God revealed to me that *it was a thought that I believed*.

Inquisitively, I asked, *"A thought! What thought?"*

Then I remembered the thought. *Something bad could happen to your kids.*

I gasped and said, "Yes, God, that was the thought, but the problem is that I believe it! I have run with it! I feel as though it has already happened!"

Just to recap, I had peace while I was cooking dinner. I received a sneaky fearful thought that something bad *could* happen to my kids. I *focused* on that thought. I *believed* that thought. I *ran* with that thought *as though it were real*.

That fearful thought entered my heart and then entangled itself with my past losses, pains, and doubts. By continuing to feed that negative thought, it quickly flooded my heart with fear and anxiety, which made it feel as though it had already happened. I was now gripped by fear! I was consumed with the fearful possibilities, even though nothing had taken place. Can you identify with that scenario?

Have you ever had a fearful thought grip you as if it were real?

Have you run with a lie as if it were a truth? It's as easy as that! It only takes one negative thought *that we believe* to forfeit our peace. In those early years, I continually fed my negative thoughts, which caused them to grow. They became obstacles to my peace. By *focusing* on the negatives, I naturally *let go* of God's amazing peace and *grabbed hold* of *fear* and *anxiety* once again.

THE POWER OF FOCUS

The first time I taught the principles in this book to a group, I wanted to have a visual example of what took place within me. So I created two pillows. The first pillow had the word *peace* written on one side and the word *faith* written on the other side. *Faith* and *peace* were on either side of the same pillow. The second pillow had the word *fear* on one side and *doubt* on the other side. *Fear* and *doubt* were on either side of the second pillow.

Picture me holding the pillow of *peace* close to my heart. This exposes the word on the opposite side, which is the word *faith* that everyone else sees. This is a good visual because when we are going through hard times and we *choose* to hold on to the peace God so lavishly gives to us, others will see our faith.

This is what happened as I demonstrated one of my real-life issues with my group. I held the peace side of the pillow close to my heart as I began to share that my husband had suddenly lost his job. I squeezed the pillow tighter, demonstrating how we have had to hold on to God's peace during the tough circumstances. One of the women pointed to the pillow and said, *"What we see is your faith."* referring to the word that was visible. That is exactly what happens in our lives when we hold on to our peace. Others will see our faith by how we are living.

WE HAVE A CHOICE
I had a choice of what I would focus on during that extended season. I could have focused on fear; that would have been easy to do. Fear and doubt taunted me to focus on all that had suddenly changed since my husband had lost his job. Fear wanted me to *forfeit* my peace by focusing on the negative circumstances. It would have been like grabbing hold of the second pillow of fear and doubt. *If* I would have allowed fear in, I would have been doubting God's faithfulness. *If* I doubted His faithfulness, I would have lost my peace and been filled with fear.

Pressed by fear yet desiring to hold on to my peace, I went to God and shared that I was struggling. I told Him I was having a hard time believing the best in this situation. I realized that I had to *choose* what I was going to focus on. I asked God for the faith to trust Him. It was then that my heart was prompted to think, *What did David do when his soul was downcast?* I remembered that David told himself to *place his hope in God.* I quickly looked up the scripture.

Psalm 42:5 (NIV)

> Why, my soul, are you downcast? Why so disturbed within me? Put your hope in God, for I will yet praise him, my Savior and my God.

David was going through a very hard time when he told himself to put his hope in God and to praise Him. The circumstances in His life had not changed, yet he made God his focus and was determined to hope in and praise Him through the hard season.

Just like David, I had to choose. Would I focus on the *faithfulness* of my God or would I choose to focus on the *circumstances* of my life? By faith, I chose to focus on my God! I put my hope in Him. I trusted in *His will* for my family. I believed He would lead us in the way we should go. I opted to trust Him with our every step along the way. As I entrusted Him with all that concerned me, it was then that my peace became an *anchor*. Peace and praise immediately illuminated my heart!

Isaiah 26:3 (NIV)

> You will keep in perfect peace those whose minds are steadfast, because they trust in you.

PRAISE HIM IN THE DARK
In every season we can choose to focus on Him. We can place our hope and expectation on Him. By trusting God in the dark and choosing to hold on to His amazing peace, we get a front-row seat to watch Him work. That is how we can praise Him in the dark places. We get to follow the light that God is shining right before our feet. Focusing on God's faithfulness, we can continue to take our next obedient step, no matter how big or how small it is. By faith, step by step, we will go forward.

> Faith does not have to see every step,
> but faith takes the next step that is illuminated.

It can be hard to walk by faith, but *as we focus on God's faithfulness*, He graciously gives us His amazing peace. In our everyday lives we can choose to focus on God's ability to keep us, and thereby remain in His peace. We can also choose to focus on the negatives that *can* happen or *did* happen, causing us to forfeit our peace. We choose what we will focus on.

MAKE GOD YOUR FOCUS
Here is an everyday example of how I learned *once again* to keep my focus on God. I was recently driving to attend a friend's church. Running late, I became irritated as I got behind a motorcyclist who was really enjoying the scenery. He slowed to look at the horses on the right. He seemed to be drawn to all of the surroundings. I was listening to worship music, but I was becoming more and more upset at his slow pace. I knew my impatience could easily cause me to forfeit my peace.

> WE CHOOSE WHAT WE WILL FOCUS ON.

I noticed that my irritation turned to frustration as he was making me later than I already was. I wanted to yell, *"Let's go!"*

All the while, I kept feeling this nudge within me, saying, *"Are you really frustrated with a man who is enjoying His life and enjoying My creation?"* I knew I was in the wrong. I knew if I had left on time, I would not have been in a hurry, so I settled down and *focused* on worshiping. I felt prompted to entrust my timing into God's hands. I determined to enjoy the ride.

I prayed, *"Lord, You are able to bless the time that I arrive, and You are able to bless this entire experience, so I entrust it all to You! I am going to praise You instead of wasting my energy on negative things. You will be my focus!"*

Praise Him is what I did. I praised Him loudly in my car with my focus upon Him and His timing. All frustration subsided, and praise, peace, and joy rose up and led the way. That day I decided I needed to be quicker to trust Him and to Respond in Praise.

I know that my spirit *will be full* of what *I am feeding* it.

- *If I feed* frustration by focusing on the negatives, then I will be full of irritation and anger.
- *If I Release* myself and all that concerns me into His hands, and fuel up with the praises of God, I will be full of His Spirit of peace, joy and rest.

I became more determined than ever to retrain my emotions and my responses to stay focused on Him and praise Him more quickly!

When we choose to entrust ourselves or our situations to Him, we will have His peace. Many can witness our faith as we trust Him. We are blessed to be guided by His peace during the frustrations of our everyday lives and throughout our difficult, fearful circumstances. His peace is real, and it can be the reality that we live by!

> **WE CAN LAY DOWN OUR FEAR AND DOUBT AT ANY TIME BY CHOOSING TO HOLD ON TO OUR FAITH.**

Let's remember the pillows, which remind us that we can lay down our fear and doubt at any time by choosing to hold on to our faith. This may seem challenging at first, but it will produce His continuous peace in our lives.

Is there a difficult situation in your life right now, where you need to adjust your focus? Are you focusing on the faithfulness of God and keeping your peace, or are you focusing on the negative circumstances and forfeiting your peace? Explain.

_____

_____

Which pillow do you hold most often, the *faith & peace* pillow or the *fear & doubt* pillow? Why?

_____

_____

What we focus on will lead to the path that we will take.

If you are not where you want to be, pray and ask God to help you focus on His love and faithfulness. This life is tough, and we will face many hardships and trials. *How we Respond to those issues can be the difference between keeping our peace or forfeiting it.* The choice is ours, and the Bible instructs us what to do.

WE NEED TO RESIST
1Peter 5:8–11 (NIV) *(I added in questions.)*

> Be alert and of sober mind. *(Why?)* Your enemy the devil prowls around like a roaring lion looking for someone to devour. Resist Him, *(How?)* standing firm in the faith, because you know that the family of believers throughout the world is undergoing the same kind of sufferings.
>
> And the God of all grace, who called you to His eternal glory in Christ, after you have suffered a little while, will himself restore you and make you strong, firm and steadfast. To him be the power for ever and ever. Amen.

The Bible teaches us to Recognize that our enemy, the devil, is looking for someone to devour. He is *like* a lion that roars loudly trying to get us to focus on him and to *focus* on his *intimidations*. He may be loud like a lion, but he is *not* a lion. He is looking for someone to devour. But *if we do not give in to* his temptations, we cannot be devoured by him. Our enemy uses these tactics as obstacles trying to stop our forward progress with God and others.

> **The word *intimidation*** means pressure, bullying, fear, terrorization, coercion, extortion, and threats.

We are instructed to *resist* him. How? By *standing firm* in the *faith*. Remember, his intimidations are not against you alone. He roars at all of us in Christ. We must resist him by standing firm in our faith. This scripture reminds us that *when* we go through tough times and have suffered, the God of all grace will Himself restore us and make us strong, firm, and steadfast.

I had to hold on to that truth before I ever felt strong in the Lord. I vividly remember those early days when I was struggling to hold on to my peace. The enemy's lies were so convincing. I knew that if I wanted to keep my peace, I could not believe his lies or give in to his bullying. Even though my faith was weak and I was barely standing firm, I chose to remember that *one day God Himself* would *restore me, making me strong, firm, and steadfast*. I held on to that truth until it became *my* truth.

> **EVERY TIME THAT I HAVE RESISTED THE ENEMY, MY FAITH GREW.**

I am thankful that Peter tells us, "Be alert and of sober mind" to *resist* the enemy when he comes roaring at us. It is not *if* he will roar at us, it is *when* he comes roaring, trying to take our peace. He spews his lies and tries to entangle us with his tactics. Every time that I have resisted the enemy *by holding on to my faith and not giving in to his intimidations,* my faith grew. As I chose to stand firm in my faith, God restored me, making me stronger and more steadfast. Through this process, I have learned to become more aware of the enemy's attempts to bully me.

> **What is a bully?** A *bully* is a tough aggressor with the intentions to intimidate, terrorize, persecute, torment, frighten, oppress, or harass.

Can you identify with being bullied by the enemy? The truth is we have all been bullied by him. I believe he bullies us on many fronts. He attacks our worth, our impact, our passions, our relationships, our purpose, our ways, and our faith. We need to be alert and aware of the many strategies used by our enemy to bully us, so that we can be quick to deal with them.

RECOGNIZE THE BULLIES OF OUR PEACE
Have you been bullied by any of the following? *Underline* the tactics that you Recognize in your life.

- Fear
- Negative thoughts
- Low self-esteem
- Your past, present, or future
- What-ifs
- Frustrations
- Disappointments
- Humiliation
- Shame
- Guilt
- Doubts
- Anger
- Lies about yourself, others, and even lies about God

These bullies rob us of the peace God intended for us!

Continuous Peace

I was bullied by all of those tactics. Fear, negative thoughts, and low self-esteem became ingrained within me. Frustrations, disappointments, shame, and guilt tightly gripped my heart. I was held captive by my painful and sinful past. Doubt-filled thoughts undermined my way. My indecision invited fear to lead me down a darkened, unsteady path.

When I would attempt to go forward, doubts in the form of *what-ifs* derailed most of my decisions. For example, I often thought:

- *What if this* negative thing happens?
- *What if that* occurs?
- *What if* I do not make the *right* decision?

I was a Christian yet weak in my faith. I chose to believe and fill up with many lies—lies about myself, others, and even lies about God. Unknowingly, I allowed these tactics and lies to become obstacles that continually robbed me of the relationships that God intended. Because I willingly gave in to these tactics, God's peace was far from me. We need to Recognize our bullies so that we can stop them.

What do our bullies do? They push us around and make us second-guess *who we are* and *what we are able to do.* These lies become *obstacles* in our relationships, including our relationship with God. For example, as you are about to take a positive step, a bully may try to discourage you by saying, "*You are not able to do that! Who do you think you are?*" We must *resist* those lies or they will become the truths that we live by.

Fill in the blank: (be honest)

Our bullies call us names, such as,
"You are_____."

Bullies are full of negative words and condemnation, which prompt undesirable emotions within us. They *distract* us from what we are supposed to be doing and try to *consume* our thinking so that we stop our forward progress.

Does any of this sound familiar?

These bullies can affect every area of our lives. They will influence, rob, or try to destroy our relationships, including our relationship with God. We need to know the bullies' tactics and the lies that are used against us. Even the bully of frustration can attempt to overtake or ruin our day. Cunningly it can use one disappointment to *entangle our thoughts* all day long.

RECOGNIZE THE LIES
Here are some of the lies that the bullies shout at us. *Underline* those that apply to you. *Star* the ones that are most used.

- You are not good enough!
- You are not capable.
- You are stupid. Don't even open your mouth. You can't help anyone.
- Your life will never change.
- Things will never get better.
- You messed your life up so badly that there is no coming back.
- Do you really think God will help you *this* time?
- God is mad at you for what you thought or did.
- No one really likes you. They don't care what you have to say.
- You are alone.
- You need to protect yourself because no one is out for your good.
- You will fail. You are a failure.
- You are not gifted. You are ordinary.
- You will embarrass yourself.

- You cannot trust anyone.
- You need to be in control.
- What if this or that happens?
- Something bad is going to happen to you, to those you love, or to the things you love.
- You cannot change.
- You are too fat, too thin, too loud, too quiet, or too _____.

Just writing those statements hurts my heart because I know many of those lies have been spewed over you, and you may even *believe* them. I believed *all* of those lies at one time or another. They bullied me and robbed my life of the good that God had for me. By believing those lies, I stayed stuck! I was stuck in negative patterns of thinking, speaking, and believing.

These lies can cause great destruction in our lives. We can allow them to *define who we are*, which will lead us down a path that is far from God's heart and His purposes for us.

Looking at the list of lies, write out the main lie(s) that you are told.

_____
_____

How do these lies make you feel?

_____
_____

Almost every faithful step that we are about to take is met with obstacles of doubt or fear. They attempt to stop us or obstruct our growth with God and others.

Bullies try to make us change our direction by what they spew at us. Think about the child who is bullied at school. They usually walk the main street to their home, but because of the bully's threats, fear causes them to redirect their route.

The fearful path is usually way off course from God's purposes.

RECOGNIZE THE BULLIES' PURPOSE
Have bullies tried to redirect your course? *Underline* the tactics that are true for you.

The Bullies' purpose is to:

1. Magnify flaws
2. Cause division
3. Speak lies or distort truth
4. Create false truths and try to convince you they are real
5. Minimize your purpose
6. Weaken or destroy your confidence
7. Stall or malign your way
8. Redirect your path

Which of those points are most used to create havoc in your life?
_____
_____

Today we have begun to Recognize the obstacles to our peace. *We will take our life back!*

Chapter 3
THE IMPACT OF OUR OBSTACLES

I ENDED CHAPTER TWO WITH THE LIES THAT WE are told and the lies that we believe. These lies can become obstacles in our lives, robbing our peace. As I mentioned in the *Introduction*, growing up with an alcoholic father was the *beginning of my obstacles*.

- My dad's negative behaviors, hurtful words, and careless actions were all negative seeds sown into my young heart.
- Once planted, those detrimental seeds grew into many destructive weeds that entangled my life.
- Those negative weeds affected me and influenced the decisions that I continually made.
- My thinking was consumed with lies and entwined in a negative way of processing life.

For years, each obstacle and destructive lie had a way of entangling me, which kept me bound. They made me feel hollow, worthless, and without purpose. This led me to an empty, sinful path of my own, trying to fill up with the love my heart was longing for. I struggled with feeling like I was not enough. Fear and anxiety ensnared my every step. Doubt's unrest made me second-guess my decisions.

Rejection dismissed my value and left me empty and lonely. My sin and shame covered me like a cloak, suffocating me further. Deep grief and loss weighed heavily upon me. Those painful places caused me to hide my heart from God and others. I struggled to trust. This caused me to have a weak relationship with God for years!

VULNERABLE AREAS
Our *painful past* and our *current pain* cause us *to be vulnerable* to the enemy's lies. If we believe those lies, they will shape *how we think about God, ourselves, and others. If these lies are not dealt with, they will feed destructive weeds and become cumbersome obstacles. These obstacles and the lies that we believe will obstruct our forward progress. They will keep us far from the truths of who we are in Christ, which will hinder God's plan for peace in our lives.*

When I started my quest to learn how to have God's peace, I began to Recognize the obstacles that were robbing me of the peace I so desperately desired. In future steps, we will continue to deal with these weeds and overwrite the lies. But *our first step is to Recognize them.* I have combined the obstacles into seven main areas that I perceive have the greatest impact. You may have other areas affected, but I believe these seven resonate the most.

RECOGNIZE THE OBSTACLES THAT IMPACT
1. Not Able/Not Enough
2. Fear/Anxiety
3. Doubt
4. Rejection
5. Sin/Shame
6. Sadness/Grief
7. A Weak Relationship with God

The following descriptions for each obstacle will help us to Recognize where we are most vulnerable to the lies of the enemy. We must become quick at Recognizing *what is robbing* us of our peace. It is vital that we Recognize what we allow ourselves to think on, and what lies we believe. As you read through each obstacle and their lies, you will notice that the lies can be written as "You" as an accusation or as "I" like a self-condemnation. They can be interchanged.

Underline any part of the obstacle's *description* or *lies* that are true for you.

1. Not Able/Not Enough:
When things do not go right, we quickly blame ourselves. We feel that we are not able or not enough, which can lead to insecurity, lack of confidence, timidity, or fear of stepping out to try something new. We perceive others as better, smarter, or more capable than ourselves. Perfection can become our goal, causing us to continually fall short.

LIES: You are not able to do that! You will fail! You are a failure. Everyone is better than you. Stop trying—you will embarrass yourself or you will make things worse. Others can do this much better. I am never enough. I cannot do enough. I am not smart enough—just not enough.

2. Fear/Anxiety:
Fear and anxiety can greatly affect our minds and bodies. They can affect our ability to make decisions. Fears can make us indecisive, causing us to avoid a situation, feel paralyzed, and/or be unable to progress. We attempt to control situations or others in our life. Fear pushes us to demand or manipulate our own way. When things are perceived as bad, they become magnified and feel overwhelming.

LIES: You will *never* get rid of these fears. You *must* take control of this issue. Stay safe! What if this or that happens? Do not try something new. You will embarrass yourself. This bad *feeling* is a warning that something bad is about to happen. I can't decide what to do, so I will do nothing.

3. Doubt:

Doubt makes us question everything and everyone's motives. We doubt others and ourselves, and we may even doubt God's love, power, strength, and His heart toward us. Jealousy and comparison arise when we doubt our own worth. Doubt prevents anything from being perceived as solid, unchanging, or secure. Doubt's skepticism causes us to hesitate before receiving anything good. Our doubt and unbelief trigger a general *lack* of positive expectation.

LIES: Does God *really* love you? God is not out for your good. You can't count on anyone! What did they mean by that? (suspicion) Things will *never* get better. *What if* this is not the *right* decision? I can't even trust myself. No one is out for my good. Will this *really* work out?

4. Rejection:

Past rejection can cause us to be easily wounded. We feel left out and excluded. We can feel unfairly judged, unknown, unaccepted, empty, and jealous. We may feel as if we must prove ourselves. We tend to be on the lookout for the next negative incident, negative word spoken, or disappointment to occur. We suspect that pain looms around every corner. We can feel insignificant, unimportant, unconnected, or irrelevant, which produces loneliness. We tend to try to please others to get their approval.

LIES: No one really wants to be in a relationship with you. No one will help you. You will be alone. You cannot trust anyone. You are the cause of this mess. I am on my own. No one likes me. I do not fit in. They will see through my attempts to make them accept me. No one is going to listen. I need to protect myself. I will not succeed. No one will care even if I do succeed.

5. Sin/Shame:

Sin and shame can cause us to feel guilty and unworthy. We can be hard on ourselves and sometimes hard on others. We may point out their flaws to make ourselves feel better. Past wounds, mistakes, and unhealed personal sin can be carried as a weight, causing us to feel far from God and others. Shame can be worn as a heavy dark cloak that attempts to hide our sins and keep out God's healing light.

LIES: You really messed up. God can never forgive you! You are not worthy to be a part of anything good. No one can know the *real* you. I will never change. I'll never really be loved. I can never be forgiven and healed. If others knew my past, they would reject me.

6. Sadness/Grief:
Sadness and grief can be caused by losses of many kinds, such as the loss of loved ones, dreams, health, positions, and possessions. Sadness and grief can also be caused by unfairness, tragedy, or a heavy burden that we carry.

LIES: God doesn't care if you are hurting. You will never feel better. Your circumstances will never change or improve. A more painful loss is right around the corner. Don't be a baby! Get over it. I can't let anyone know I am sad; I must hold it in. No one wants to see me cry. I must pretend to be happy.

7. A Weak Relationship with God:
When a negative issue arises, we run to a person for help, not God. He is the last one we seek for advice. Trusting in God is hard for us to do. We don't want to stop what we are doing to fully surrender our heart and life to Him. We don't make changes to our lives in order to make Him a priority. Life is too busy to read the Bible. If we pray, we pray on the run.

LIES: You cannot trust God with your whole heart. If you say yes to Him, He may ask you to do more than you are willing or able. Judging from your past situations, He has *not* been a good Father. I don't *need* God. I can handle my own life. I can figure things out myself. At least I go to church on Sunday. That is *enough* time for God right now.

Is there an area(s) that resonated with you?
_____

Which are the main lies that you are told?
_____
_____

Is there something you can add?
_____

How do the bully's lies make you feel?
_____
_____

RECOGNIZE THE AREAS THAT ARE AFFECTED
Underline the areas that are affected by these lies. Then *star* the main area.

Personal life	Relationship with God
Marriage	Family Relationships
Parenting	Friendships
Work	Participation in Events or Activities
Goals/Dreams	Relationship with others

By believing the bully's lies, how has your life been affected?
_____
_____

Write any thoughts or feelings that this section has provoked.
_____
_____

Here's the problem:

> *We believe the bully's lies
> instead of believing God's truth.*

That was my life; I was a Spirit-filled, fearful Christian. That is an oxymoron because Christians can *live by faith* and *have His peace*, which is the fruit of the Spirit. I have found so many of us who do not know how to live this way.

Why Am I a Weak Christian?

I had been a Christian for many years, and I was so *frustrated* with the way I was living my life. I remember the night that my two worlds of fear and faith collided. I was in the car with my husband and we were on our way to dinner. As we drove through the darkness, my inner turmoil got the best of me.

Abruptly, I blurted out these words in frustration. *"Why am I so weak as a Christian? As a non-Christian, I was tough and bold. I did not allow fear to push me around! But now as a Christian, I feel so weak and beat up by fear. Why? Why am I so weak as a Christian?"*

The car became silent except for the continued hum of the tires. No answer was given. My wise husband was in deep thought. Quickly, we arrived at the restaurant, which was unexpectedly closed, so we circled back. At the same point in the road, I repeated, *"Why am I such a weak Christian?"* Before my husband could speak, I blurted out, *"Why? Because I don't pray enough!"*

He looked at me and softly said, *"No... because you are not walking by faith."* That answer still brings tears to my eyes. I knew that he had just given me my answer. I did not know what it fully meant, but I finally knew *why*

> **I WAS ALLOWING FEARS AND LIES TO DERAIL MY FAITH.**

I had no peace. It was because I was not walking by faith. I was allowing fears and lies to derail my faith.

Do you remember the peace and fear pillows that I spoke about in chapter two? One pillow had *faith* written on one side and *peace* written on the other side of the same pillow. On the other pillow was written *fear* and *doubt*. At that time in my life, my fear pillow was worn-out, because I tightly held on to my fear. I lived by fear. My faith and peace pillow was nowhere to be found. I desired to live by faith, but *I did not know how*. Over time, I learned how to cling to my faith and resist the fears that continued to taunt me.

Jesus tells us in John 10:10 (NIV)

> The thief comes only to steal, kill, and destroy; I have come that they may have life, and have it to the full.

Do you Recognize how the obstacles of not enough, fear, doubt, rejection, shame, sadness, and a weak relationship with God *steal* our peace, *kill* our testimony of faith, and *destroy* our relationship with God and others? We need to Recognize the bully's tactics, but we must also be fully aware of the power of Jesus, which brings us life and life to the fullest.

WE CHOOSE WHAT WE WILL BELIEVE
The great news is that we can choose what we will believe. Yes! We choose if we will believe the bully's lies or if we will believe God's truths.

Say out loud, *"I choose who and what I will believe."*

Do you believe that? Do you realize that we do *get to choose* who and what we will believe?

For example:

- If our hearts become afraid of something and we *choose* to give in to the *fear*, then we will forfeit our peace.
- Likewise, if something begins to trouble our hearts and we do *not* give in to it but rather *choose* to place our *faith* in God, then our peace will continue to flourish.

We are *not* a victim of fear. We choose if we will believe fear's lies or if we will believe God and His truths. The same Holy Spirit that produces peace in our lives also produces *self-control.* (Galatians 5:22–23) With the Spirit in us, we can overcome the enemy. We can resist him and his taunts. But we must Recognize the enemy's tactics so that we do not fall for them time and time again.

Make this your truth: "I, _____, am not a victim to fear! I am equipped with the Holy Spirit, and by faith, I *choose* to trust Jesus with every aspect of my life."

BE ON GUARD AND STAND FIRM

Let's continue to look at other tactics that will keep us from God's peace. It is good to know that when the bully attacks us, he usually piles on added assaults to try to pull us down further.

We need to be watchful when we are *disappointed* or *tired* because negative thoughts can cause an avalanche of emotions to overwhelm us further. This is quite common. We need to Recognize this tactic.

For example:

- When we get discouraged, tired, lonely, hurt, or overwhelmed, that is when we are to *expect* to be hit by additional negative thoughts and feelings.
- We also need to be aware of the sneak attacks that come just after a victory. I think those attacks shock us the most because while we were celebrating a success, our

radar was not up to catch the bully's attack. Bullies like to pounce on any opportunity.

We need to be on guard against these types of attacks. *The Bible instructs us what to do.*

1 Corinthians 16:13-14 (NIV)

> Be on your guard; stand firm in the faith; be courageous; be strong. Do everything in love.

I have been meditating on this scripture. It is so powerful. We are given commanding words. Three times we are told to *be*. We are told to *be* courageous and *be* strong, but first we are told to *be on our guard*. I believe we are to be on guard against the schemes of the enemy and the obstacles that will trip us up. Our answer as to *how* to be on guard is given. We are to *stand firm*. But how do we stand firm? We stand firm in our faith. When our faith is in Almighty God, we can be courageous and be strong knowing that our strength comes from Him. We can then do all things in love.

2 Corinthians 1:21 (NIV)

> Now it is God who makes both us and you stand firm in Christ. He anointed us.

We can stand up courageously! It is *by His Spirit* that we can stand firm in our faith. It is God who strengthens us. That is why He can instruct us to stand firm, be courageous, and be strong. If we were not able, God would *not* instruct us to act. But He knows that by His Spirit, we can be strong and choose to do the next right thing in the power that He provides. Choose to believe God's truths and determine to *resist* the obstacles and lies.

I shared this scripture in chapter one, but I like how the Amplified Bible instructs us in John 14:27, *"Do not let your heart be troubled, nor let it be afraid. [Let My perfect peace calm you in every circumstance and give you courage and strength for every challenge.]"*

In His perfect peace He gives us courage in the face of fear. Yes, we can choose to stand firm in our faith *even while we are afraid*. Walking by faith while we are afraid will silence the enemy. I believe that our bullies attempt to hinder our walk with God because they are concerned that we may stand up and make a difference. They are worried that we may trust God and truly change.

> WE CAN CHOOSE TO STAND FIRM IN OUR FAITH EVEN WHILE WE ARE AFRAID.

THE BULLIES' IMPACT
Obstacles are a ploy of the enemy to *keep us from God* and all that He has called us to do. They are used to prevent us from fulfilling God's purposes and remaining in God's peace.

Underline those that apply and *star* the ones most used.

Bullies try to *impact* our lives by keeping us:

- Too busy and overwhelmed
- Angry and disconnected
- Unforgiving and wounded
- Prideful and distant
- Scared and marginalized
- Doing good things but missing God's best
- Being a people pleaser
- Isolated and not being fully known
- Unproductive in our calling

The list can go on and on. Which of those bullet points are the ploys that the enemy uses the most to impact your life?

WE GIVE THE BULLIES POWER

Let's Recognize that bullies have no power to rob our peace unless we yield it to them. *Mark* which ones apply to you.

We give the bullies power when we:

- Entertain or believe their threats
- Run in fear
- Avoid decisions
- Stop moving forward
- Get discouraged, overwhelmed, or paralyzed
- Lose our confidence and second-guess our decisions
- Shut down
- Stop believing God's truths

Can you add anything to that list?

_____

We give the bullies power when *their lies become* our truth.

As soon as the bully has been given power, we lose our peace. The bully does not gain power as soon as he speaks the initial lie. He gains his power the *moment* that we *believe* the lie. That is when we *forfeit* our peace.

Do you Recognize how believing the lies *as if they are true* forfeits your peace and perhaps hinders your forward progress? When we believe the lies, we can immediately see how it affects us. These lies may stop us in our tracks. They may make us feel like running, avoiding the situation, or cause us to get overwhelmed and shut down. Perhaps it is not until we lay down at night that the negative thoughts affect us the most, *robbing us* of our restful sleep. *These are some of the clues* that reveal that we have forfeited our peace.

The Impact Of Our Obstacles

What are the signs that you have lost your peace?
Check the ones that apply to you.

- Does a panic come over you?
- Do you feel your heart begin to race?
- Do you feel a painful physical tension in your head, neck, or body?
- Do you break out in a sweat with possible pains in your stomach?
- Do anxious thoughts cause a sinking or uneasy feeling?
- Do you lose your train of thought and feel frustrated, short-tempered, or angry?
- Do you lose your confidence?
- Do you feel like running, hiding, or avoiding the situation?
- Do you feel lost or out of control?
- Do you attempt to control your environment?
- Do you become guarded?
- Do you attempt to build a wall of self-protection?
- Do you feel lonely?
- Do you feel defeated?
- Do you feel preoccupied or distracted?

Can you identify with any of those symptoms? Can you add any symptoms to this list?

When I lose my peace, I feel like ...

_____

Can you recall a time when you lost your peace? What were the circumstances? How did you feel and how did you react?

_____
_____

It is vitally important that we can identify and Recognize how we feel when we lose our peace, because this is the *signal* that *we are being robbed.* When we Recognize that we are losing our peace, we need to stand up in our faith, believing God's Spirit is in us, equipping us to hold on to our peace. Once we have peace, *we need to be diligent to guard it.*

Romans 15:13 (NIV)

> May the God of hope fill you with all joy and peace as you trust in Him, so that you may overflow with hope by the power of the Holy Spirit.

Let's Wrap Up Step One!

As we review this foundational first Step, we Recognized: what peace is and where it comes from, the power we have been given to keep God's peace, who He is, who we are in Christ, the power of focus, the bullies that rob our peace, and the obstacles that impact us the most. It is vital that we become excellent at Recognizing what has robbed our peace. We need to Recognize the first signs that we feel in our body when we are forfeiting our peace, *so that we can stop the bully in its tracks.*

I suggest that you go back through Step 1 (chapters 1–3) and write down in a journal, a notebook, or on index cards the *scriptures* that you want to remember. The Word of God is so powerful.

John 8:32 (NIV): Then you will know the truth, and the truth will set you free.

By Recognizing these foundational truths, we will safeguard our peace. Ask God to help you to Recognize what you need to remember and apply from this first step. The following questions are a review. Please take the time to answer these questions. Your answers will help you in future steps.

I feel God has revealed

_____

I need to focus on

_____

My relationship with God has been impacted by

_____

I have listed some of the obstacles to our peace below. *Underline* the *obstacles* that are true for you. *Star* the *main obstacles* that you want to deal with first.

1. Not knowing God as Savior or Lord
2. A weak relationship with God
3. A weak understanding of who He is
4. Not knowing or believing who I am in Him
5. Not entrusting my heart to God fully
6. Believing lies about myself, others, or God
7. Feeding negative thoughts
8. Not resisting the intimidations of the enemy
9. Allowing myself to be bullied
10. Embracing the lies that I am not able or not enough
11. Giving into fear and anxiety
12. Yielding to doubt
13. Reacting out of past rejections
14. Holding on to shame and past sins
15. Not healing my sadness and grief
16. Giving in to schemes or pitfalls of the enemy that trip me up

The most destructive lies I believe are

_____

_____

I Recognize the bully's purpose is to

_____

_____

The signs I have when I lose my peace are

_____

_____

I have been helped the most by knowing

_____

_____

Let's Wrap Up Step One!

Notes I want to remember

_____
_____
_____

You can then share what you have Recognized with God in Prayer. **He cares for you,** so share your heart with Him.

Let Him know:

- Lord, I Recognize ...
- This is how that makes me feel ...
- This is how it has impacted my life ...
- Please help me to ...

You could consider sharing your takeaways with a friend. I have found much healing when I have shared my vulnerable places with my husband or a trusted friend. It can be helpful to join a friend to do this type of study. I believe we can grow deeper when we process the material with one another.

THIS WEEK: As your week progresses, *write down the lies* that you Recognize. You can use the following space or write them in your notebook or journal. *Writing down the lies makes them tangible* so that you will be able to deal with them properly. Do not get overwhelmed by the amount of lies you Recognize. They will be overwritten as we take our next steps. I look forward to the freedom that you will discover in step two as we Release the barriers that confine us.

The Lies I Recognized this week

_____
_____
_____

4 Steps to Continuous Peace:

1. RECOGNIZE the Obstacles That Rob
2. **RELEASE the Barriers That Confine**
3. REPROGRAM My Heart & Mind with Truth
4. RESPOND Faithfully for a Continuous Life of Peace

Step 2 Release
Release the Barriers

Chapter 4
THE GREAT EXCHANGE

A FEW YEARS AGO, WHILE AT A WOMEN'S CONFERence, a blank sheet of lined paper lay on the table in front of me. Finishing our morning session, the leader announced that we could proceed to lunch. As the words left her mouth, she quickly remembered the blank sheet of paper and abruptly said, "Wait! First, I need you to write a letter to your dad."

Without thinking, these words rushed from my mouth. *"What?!! Write a letter to my dad? You've got to be kidding me!"* Immediately, the women around me snapped their heads to see who blurted out that statement.

The blank paper stared at me and I stared back as I thought about my dad, who had passed away six months prior. I knew I had dealt with so much of the pain. I thought I had forgiven everything. I thought to myself, *I have no issue with him.*

In obedience I picked up my pen, but I was not prepared for the torrent of emotion that was going to pour out of me like a flood. Heavy and harsh words immediately crashed out of my heart and angrily erupted from my pen. It was as if I could not hold back the rage within.

"I hate you!" My eyes widened as I questioned my heart. *"Did I just write I hate you?"* The words became stronger like angry waters about to break through a dam.

"I hate you for how you treated my mom! I hate you for how you treated my stepmom! I hate you for how you treated my sisters. I hate you for how you treated your mom, your sisters, your old girlfriends, and other precious people. These lovely and gentle women were treated with disrespect, vulgar language, and/or physical abuse. I hate you for destroying so many women's lives. I hate you!"

Tears flooded my eyes and stained my paper. I was shocked by the amount of anger and hatred I had toward him. I had worked with God through the years to process the many painful issues related to my dad. I guess I did not Recognize the deep sorrow I felt for those he had hurt, and the *hatred that sorrow had produced* in my heart toward him.

In my childhood, my young mom diligently protected us from him. She hid the physical and mental abuse that he heaped on her. One night, however, my brother and I were awakened by a huge crash! We ran to the top of the steps as we watched my father grab hold of our mom. My brother and I screamed for him to stop. My mother immediately tried to protect us by telling us to go back to bed. I will never forget my little four- or five-year-old brother screaming at the top of his lungs, *"Don't you touch my mom!"*

What a terrible scene. That night was my mom's turning point. She did not want her children to witness that type of violence. It was not long until my mom and dad separated, and she began to raise us on her own. Unfortunately, I continued to watch as my dad carried these vicious, vile, and manipulative actions into every relationship he had for decades. My deep hatred came from witnessing his life affecting everyone around him, like a destructive tornado devastating everything in its way.

The letter I wrote about my dad was a form of *Release*. I was amazed that as I willingly opened my heart and allowed the raw emotions to pour out, I became aware of what was really within me. By *not* hindering those emotions, I Released the sorrow, hate, and anger. That letter began an incredible time of healing. *It was a cleansing I did not even know I needed.* But once those emotions were Released, the truth became clear that I needed to be healed. In the weeks and months that followed, I knew that I was experiencing a deeper healing. I had found a new freedom. Release works!

RELEASE WORKS
In this second step, we will Release the barriers that are holding us back from God's peace. As a young Christian, I did not know how to Release those old wounds, so I continually carried them. Those wounded places became a root of fear and anxiety that ensnared my heart and mind. Unknowingly, I allowed those wounded places to remain, which made it hard for me to process life accurately. My past pain influenced my every step and made it hard to make forward progress. Being stuck in my pain was a barrier to God's peace.

I am so glad that God knew what I *needed* to Release. He was faithful to illuminate what was hidden. He was just as faithful to help me Release it to Him. *I did not have to go digging* for what needed to be Released; God revealed it. He helps us to Recognize and Release those *barriers* that *confine* us.

Recognize is our step one and *Release* is our step two. They go hand in hand. As we Recognize the wounds or obstacles that have become barriers to our peace, by faith we can Release them to God. Issue by issue they will be replaced with God's healing and His powerful peace.

We will walk through many ways of Releasing in order to let go of what is holding us back from *the life of peace God intended.* In this chapter, we begin with the truth of knowing that *the Lord is near* to us. He *wants* us to bring Him our anxiety so that He can provide a peace so strong that it will guard our hearts and our minds. This is truly one of God's greatest gifts.

THE ANCHOR TO OUR CONFIDENCE
Philippians 4:5–7 (NASB)

> Let your gentle *spirit* be known to all men. The Lord is near. Be anxious for nothing, but in everything by prayer and supplication with thanksgiving let your requests be known to God. And the peace of God, which surpasses all comprehension, will guard your hearts and your minds in Christ Jesus.

What is the reason we are to *be anxious for* NOthing? Our answer is given in the four words prior to "Be anxious for nothing."

_____ _____ _____ _____ .

Yes. *The anchor to our confidence* is the fact that *the Lord is near*. He is the reason that we are not to be anxious about anything! He is near us. He does *not* tell us *not* to be anxious.

> He teaches us HOW to be anxious for NOthing!

How are we to be anxious for *nothing*?

1. By being *confident* that He is near to us!
2. By prayer we are to *Release* all our:
   - concerns
   - fears
   - worries
   - anxieties
   - wounds
   - shame
   - lies
   - doubts
   - guilt

> *What a great exchange—our mess* for His peace!

I love the Amplified version of the Philippians 4 scripture.

Philippians 4:5b–7 (AMP)

> The Lord is near. Do not be anxious *or* worried about anything, but in everything [every circumstance and situation] by prayer and petition with thanksgiving, continue to make your [specific] requests known to God. And the peace of God [that peace which reassures the heart, that peace] which transcends all understanding, [that peace which] stands guard over your hearts and your minds in Christ Jesus [is yours].

RELEASE REAL LIFE ISSUES
We are to Release our real-life issues that cause us anxiety. He tells us not to worry about anything. But in everything, every circumstance and situation, we are to take it *all* to Him in prayer! *He already knows everything about us.* We can come to Him *as we are.* He loves us. He wants us to bring Him our heart, fears, dreams, and broken places. We are to tell Him what we need. God desires a close relationship with each of us.

I have had so many people tell me that *they do not want to bother God with their problems.* That type of thinking is absurd, and it will keep us *from* a *close relationship* with Him. He assures us that He is already near to us. He is waiting for all our anxieties to be given to Him. He does not want us living with worry or unease. He wants us to experience a life that is so full of His peace that it protects our hearts and guards our minds from being tormented by fear. Fear and anxiety put a wedge between us and our faithful Father.

We can confidently and with thanksgiving continue to make our requests known to Him.

We may pray:

> Lord, I do not want to worry about this issue. Instead I am going to bring it to You in prayer. Lord, I Release _____. I trust You with this issue and its outcome. I am so thankful for what You have already done in my life. I am also thankful that I get to bring my current and past unresolved anxieties, worries, and cares to You. I am relieved to know that You are always near to me. Lord, guard my heart with Your amazing peace as I trust in You. Amen.

When we Release our anxiety to Him, we can be thankful because we are assured that He is the One who can effect change in our lives. He is close to us. He will guard and calm our hearts and minds. But how? *God guards our hearts and minds by giving us His peace.*

> **GOD'S PEACE IS A CALMING SHIELD, ASSURING US THAT EVERYTHING IS GOING TO BE OKAY.**

The key to having His peace is trusting Him with our issues or situations. Have you ever had peace in a situation that in the natural you know you should not have peace? His peace guards us from fears, anxiety, and unrest. God's peace is a calming shield, *assuring* us that everything is going to be okay. We can have peace knowing that no matter how things work out, God is near. He is with us no matter what we face.

THE CIRCLE OF FEAR

In our everyday lives we can have situations or occurrences that can cause us to worry about today. If we allow those fearful anxieties to penetrate our heart, we can start to worry about tomorrow, and even worry about what the future holds.

This is *the circle of fear*. It starts with worrying about *today's* problems, and it turns into fearful anxiety about *tomorrow*. Many people, including me, have been stuck in this type of ongoing *fearful habit*.

Jesus tells us in Matthew 6:34 (AMPC)

> So do not worry *or* be anxious about tomorrow, for tomorrow will have worries *and* anxieties of its own. Sufficient for each day is its own trouble.

We are *not* shielded from distress. We live in a fallen world. This life is tough! When something troubles us, *we have a choice*. Will we allow worry and fear to direct our steps around and around the issue, or will we run to God and Release it to Him? Yes, we *can* Release our daily cares, worries, anxieties, and problems to God in prayer.

Who Will We Run To?
An important part of *Release is to Recognize who we will run to in our time of need.*

When a situation presents itself, we are to recall the truth that the Lord is near to us. This is the beginning of our peace. If we forget that our loving Lord *is* near, we will be prone to worry. *Worry is the fruit of not trusting God.* Do not let your heart be anxious, because *Almighty* God is with you. Trust in Him. Be anxious for nothing! He created all, and He created you. He will carry you through with security and rest.

> **Worry is the fruit of not trusting God.**

Trusting God is the fertile soil that is used to make the *fruit of peace grow.*

Psalm 91:1-2 (AMP)

> He who dwells in the shelter of the Most High will remain secure *and* rest in the shadow of the Almighty [whose power no enemy can withstand]. I will say of the LORD, "He is my refuge and my fortress, My God, in whom I trust [with great confidence, and on whom I rely]!"

This scripture is a gift! We are told that we can dwell, which means we can live and stay in the shelter of the Most High. When we dwell with God, we will remain *secure* and be *able to rest* in His presence. What a great assurance we have in Him! Confidently we can depend on Him as our refuge and our fortress. He will keep us safe. We can know by experience that *He is my God, in whom I trust [with great confidence, and on whom I rely].* When an anxiety or issue arises, will we allow Him to be our strong fortress?

He is close. We can share our heart with Him. We can start by letting Him know *what* we are afraid of or *what* is causing us to be anxious. This may take some thought because understanding *why* we are anxious is not always easily known.

A good first step of Release *is to* *write down what is causing you to doubt, worry, or have anxiety.* Perhaps there is an ongoing habit of negative thinking, or something new that is causing you anxiety today. It could be dread or shame over a past pain, or an unknown, unseen answer to a current situation. It could be a fear about the future. Maybe it is a health concern or a fear that something bad could happen. It may be a rocky relationship, unhappy job, a painful loss, or lack of having enough. Perhaps it is a consistent frustration, doubt, loneliness, or place of anger. It could be a dissatisfaction with your relationship with God.

Write down your specific issue or anxiety:

_____

_____

Now take that very specific issue, fear, worry, concern, anger, or frustration to God in prayer. Tell God exactly how you feel. *He can handle it.* He welcomes you to share your heart with Him.

Let your anxiety be known to God!

Prayer. Your prayer may sound something like this:

> Lord, in this situation I am overwhelmed. It is even hard to know how to pray, but I Release this entire thought to You. Lord, only You know the way that this situation can work itself out. I pray You provide everyone and everything needed to bring it to a good completion. I pray that You will lead, guide, give wisdom, prwotection, and everything else that is needed to bring about Your will. Lord, I need You and I desire Your help. I want Your will and Your way to be done in this situation.
>
> I even add:
>
> Lord, You know that I am fearful that this or that may happen. I am afraid that something bad is going to come of this, so I choose to Release my heart and those who I love and what I care about into Your loving arms. I ask that You lift all sadness, worry, doubt, and concern regarding this issue. Heal my heart. Be Lord over this situation and give me Your peace. Thank you for loving me. In Jesus' name, Amen.

"I Release _____ into Your mighty and capable hands."

We must Release our daily concerns to God as they arise.

Going Through a Hard Season

A friend of mine was going through an extremely hard season. Her work environment completely changed when a new manager was hired. This caused a lot of frustrations as this one new person turned a peaceful, joyful, and productive office into a place of chaos. My friend was dealing with one painful situation after another. It was hard to believe that one new person could create so much turmoil and pain. My friend did everything that she knew to do. She was kind, helpful, and extra-friendly but to no avail. The negative situations continued. They were beginning to affect her whole life. She was losing hope that things would ever get better.

Desperate to see a change, she became serious about entrusting this difficult situation to God. She determined to fight this battle on her knees. That day she set up a prayer space under her steps, which were on the bottom level of her home, where she could be alone with God. She created a prayer poster board where she wrote her concerns on sticky notes and then added them to the board. She prayed about each concern. She Released her real-life painful issues to God. Those posted notes *directed her focus* during prayer. Daily she came to God to pray about those specific issues. She added new sticky notes when needed.

In that season, she became quick to Recognize the issues that continued to cling to her. She became aware of ways that she was trying to control the situation by things that she would say or do. When she Recognized it, she would remind herself that *God was in control.* She then was able to Release it all to Him once again. She did this for a few months. God heard her concerns. He answered her prayers. His answers were beyond what she could have even imagined.

In this process He taught her so much about herself. She learned how to *run to* God and Release *all* her concerns to Him. He healed her heart. He provided a better job that she now loves.

What amazes her the most is seeing how *God grew her faith exponentially* during this difficult season of trials.

Are you aware of areas that need continual prayer? If so, record them here.

_____

_____

Consider writing your concerns on sticky notes as a reminder to pray. We get to Release what troubles us to God. He cares for what we entrust to Him. Perhaps as God answers your prayers, you could transfer your sticky notes to an "Answered Prayer" board. It would be a great reminder and a place to praise Him for all that He has done!

OPEN HANDS OR CLOSED FISTS

Do we have open hands or closed fists? During this process of Release, there have been times when God knew I had a closed fist over a certain area. I have sensed Him tapping my hands and saying, *"Will you entrust this to Me?"* Many times I did not even realize that I had a closed fist over anything.

Closed fists. There have been times in my life when I have had to Release that which was tightly closed in my fists. I have had my children, their safety, or their well-being clutched in my hands. I remember how hard it was for me to completely trust God with my children. I remember sitting at a red light as He was convicting my heart to place my children into His hands. *I just clenched tighter.*

That's when He directed my eyes to the sky. There was a cloud that looked like two massive manly hands open with the palm side up, as if waiting to hold something of value. That's when God clearly spoke to my heart. He said, *"Look at your hands and then look at the example of my hands in the sky. Today, I want you to choose whose hands you want to protect your children."*

I literally cried, as I knew that I had to open my hands and entrust my children into God's loving, mighty hands. At that moment, I knew that in His hands was where they were supposed to be! That day, God put everything into perspective. My little hands were trying to lovingly protect my children, but my hands were only in one place at a time and extremely limited. His hands could hold my children, protect them, and by His Spirit, He could lead them in the way they should go.

God has mercy on us as we *try* to control the things in our lives. He helps us to understand that when fear strikes, we may attempt to control, but *our control is an illusion.* Control becomes a barrier to God's peace. When we are afraid we can choose to trust God.

There can be many things that we have tightly gripped in our hands. Ask God if you need to *open your hands* and *Release control* of any of these areas. *Check* the ones that apply to you.

- Our spouse or future spouse
- Our children or desire for children
- Our home or desire for a new home
- Our ability to keep order or be in control
- Our ministry, purpose, or significance
- Our jobs or financial future
- Our health or safety
- Our past sins, shame, or guilt
- Our relationships
- Our will (wanting what I want when I want it)
- Our pride (*I have to* do it)
- Our attitudes (the right to have *this* attitude)
- Our hopes, dreams, or broken dreams
- Our need to be perfect or perfectly liked
- Our high expectations

Open hands are what God is calling us to. When we *entrust all that is dear to us* into His mighty hands, this makes *Him Lord* of our lives.

Are there areas that your hands or fists are closed over? Are there places where you have *not* Released total control to God? If so, write them down.

_____

_____

A main question we may ask ourselves is: *Why am I able to give God control of some areas but not all areas of my life?*

I think we all have had areas or issues where we were afraid to Release control to God. I believe our desire to control is rooted in fear. We may be *hesitant* to Release what is dear to us because we are afraid of *what may happen*. The *fear of loss* may grip us. It is scary to trust God with what we deeply care about. We may be tentative to fully open our hands and relinquish total control.

We need faith to truly trust God with what we love. Fear wants us to hold on to our grip. Our faith helps us to trust Almighty God with *those* we love and with *what* we care about. Our faith reminds us that *He is faithful*.

God is faithful no matter how I feel.

I had to choose to believe that God would be faithful with what I entrusted to Him, even if I did not see the way through. He was *not* my good-luck charm that I trusted in. He was my Lord. I had to resolve to believe that Jesus would be faithful even if the worst thing in my mind did happen. The reality is that bad things can happen in this life, but *will I trust Him all along the way?*

THE ICY HILL
Many years ago, I would give in to great anxiety that I later Recognized was stemming from a *fear of loss*. God used many situations to help *untangle* its grip on me. This was one such event.

One evening I noticed that our neighborhood was starting to become covered in snow. I texted our twenty-year-old son and I told him that he might want to come home before the roads got bad. He was having fun at a friend's house and told me he would be home in a little while. Still not home, I was praying for him as I fell asleep. I awoke to my cell phone ringing and our son telling me that he was stuck on a snow-covered hill. He happened to be stopped behind an ambulance and they were both *attempting* to inch onto the shoulder due to the icy roadway. There were oncoming cars that were slowly cresting the hill and sliding as they came toward their vehicles.

We hung up the phone and I immediately began to pray. I hurried to my living room, sat on the couch, and watched for him to return home. Knowing that he was still stuck on that icy hill, I waited. That is when anxiety gripped my heart. My fear snowballed from the *reality* that he might be stuck for a while to the *possibility* that he would get into an accident. This thinking continued until, without warning, the *fear of loss produced thoughts telling me* that he might die. My heart sank as my mind sprinted to the worst outcome. As only fear can do, it made me feel *as though it had already happened*. Anxiety filled my entire body as I fearfully waited for my son to return home.

In that moment I felt God speak to my anxious heart and clearly ask, *"Would I not still be God?"* The thought took my breath away. I knew He was asking me, *"Will I still be God if your son dies tonight?"* I gathered myself to consider the thought.

In the darkness of the night, I sat and pondered, would God still be my God and Lord as He is right now if my son were to die on that icy hill? Would I trust Him? Would I walk with Him as

I do now? The real question was: Is Jesus truly Lord of my life no matter what happens?

I contemplated who He is to me. My answer became obvious: *"You are my God, in whom I trust. Yes. You would still be Lord."* Then by faith, I went a step further. I pictured myself giving the eulogy for my son. I envisioned what my Response would be if the worst thing would have happened. I knew the heartache of losing my son would have forced its way into every fiber of my being. Yet I could see myself praising God for what a wonderful son He had entrusted to me for the last twenty years. I could imagine thanking God for this precious son who had brought so much joy into all our lives. I also knew I would have the amazing hope that it was not a final good-bye, but it would have been, *"Until I see you again."*

FACING MY FEAR OF LOSS

As I faced my fear of loss, I knew that no matter what will happen in this life, Jesus will still be my Lord. He will uphold me. He will get me through. I knew His faithfulness from past experiences, but I needed to be reminded in this present situation that He was able to keep my son and myself. I had to keep my perspective that my son is His child whom He has entrusted to me. Ultimately, he is God's son. *God loves him more* than I ever could.

The root of my anxiety was the fear of loss. In that moment of *acknowledging Jesus as my Lord, fear lost its grip on me.* As the anxiety and fear were lifted, I immediately began to praise God for all that He had done. I especially praised Him for the renewed confidence of knowing my son will be cared for by God now and in all eternity.

The truth is that nothing else would have restored my peace like confronting my fear head-on. *My peace was restored when I lifted God up as Lord of all.* Anxiety had to loosen its grip on me as I realized that my Lord Jesus Christ is bigger than my fear of loss. In that moment, I was able to cast all my anxiety upon Him because I knew that He cared for me. He faithfully sustained me with His peace.

1 Peter 5:7 (NIV)

> Cast all your anxiety on him because he cares for you.

After a little while, I saw headlights piercing through the darkness. Joy filled me as I realized that it was my son making his way up our snow-covered hill. He slowly pulled into our driveway safe and sound. I immediately thanked God for His mercy and loving kindness that He had shown toward us that night.

As a side note, my husband slept through the whole thing because he had not given in to fear like I had. He naturally trusts God. But because of my past and the hard things I've gone through, I continually need to *choose to trust* God. As I Release my anxiety to Him, He gives me His peace. What a wonderful exchange! *My relationship with God deepens with each exchange.*

Later that night I lay awake in bed contemplating all that had taken place. I thanked God for His mercy and loving care of my son. I was amazed at how quickly my peace had returned once I *entrusted my son into His hands.* Once again, I learned that in His hands are where my children need to be. A smile covered my face as I realized that God had chosen to place my son behind an ambulance. I felt like God was showing me that He was with him *all* the way.

Throughout this journey for peace, God has *always* been faithful! That does not mean life was easy. No! He was faithful every day and throughout the hardest of times, and He continues to be.

> True trust is followed by walking in a way that reflects that *God is good* and *He is faithful*.

Romans 8:28 (NIV)

> We know that in all things God works for the good of those who love him, who have been called according to his purpose.

He cares for us as He works on the details of our lives. Above all things He desires *a relationship of love* with us. As we trust Him with what is dear to us, we have entrusted our heart to Him. We are walking closely with Him. I often say, *"Lord, I love You and I trust You with my heart and all that I care about. My life is in Your hands."*

When we choose to trust Him with all that concerns us, it does not mean that we give up our responsibility in those areas. No, we Release them, and then we are to faithfully fulfill the call to love and care about what has been entrusted to us. In doing so we have let go of our desires to control people, situations, or circumstances.

Hard to Release

I met with a friend recently. She had a heavy heart due to a long string of events that continued to occur week after week. She realized that some things in her life were a lot harder to Release than others. Her precious dog had been recently hospitalized, and she Recognized that *she was carrying the weight* of her dog and his illness instead of Releasing him to God. My friend and I prayed. We started our prayer by thanking God for blessing her with this companion. We then Released his health, care, and life into God's hands.

Do you know what happened? *She felt lighter* when we were done praying. As she was leaving, she said to me, *"We have to tell others how to do this. Release really works!"* By the way, she and her dog are doing very well.

We feel lighter when we Release our situation, outcome, and emotions to God. By doing so we are making Him Lord over our hearts, lives, and all that we care about. He is faithful. He can carry us through every circumstance, no matter how big or how small. Do you Recognize areas or issues that are more difficult to Release? Do you tend to carry the weight of those situations instead of Releasing them to God?

> WE FEEL LIGHTER WHEN WE RELEASE OUR SITUATION, OUTCOME, AND EMOTIONS TO GOD.

THINK BACK TO STEP ONE
What were the obstacles, fears, anxieties, disappointments, lies, or areas of control from step one (chapters 1–3) that you want to Release to God?

List the issues you Recognized from *this chapter* or *from step one* that need to be Released:

1. _____
2. _____
3. _____

Knowing that we are working with God and He is near, we can immediately pray and Release all our anxieties to Him. This can be the way that we live! Let's Release the preceding issues one by one to God in prayer. We can ask Him to Release the weight of the lies, fears, or disappointments and replace them with a confident heart that trusts Him for the outcome.

You could write a simple prayer of Release or pray the following prayer, which is similar to the one my friend and I prayed concerning her beloved pet. Take what you have Recognized and Release those barriers to God.

_____
_____

Prayer of Release
Your prayer may start like this:

> Lord, First I want to thank You for __(insert name or the positive in the situation)__. You know how I feel about_____. I ask for You to _____ but ultimately, I Release _____ into Your Mighty hands. I ask that Your will be done. I Release control and ask that You completely work out all the details. Give me a heart of wisdom to know if and how to proceed. I Release my emotions to You. I Release worry in exchange for trusting You in this situation. Sustain me with Your peace. I trust You with the outcome, and with all of my life.
>
> Thank You for the truth found in Philippians 4:5-7. I know You are near and that I am to be anxious for nothing. But in everything by prayer and supplication with thanksgiving, I am to let my requests be known to You. And Your peace, which surpasses all comprehension will guard my heart and my mind in Christ Jesus. Thank You Lord.

It is very appropriate for us to thank Him for what He has done and what He is still to do. Perhaps *take a few moments to praise Him* for *who* He is and *all* that He does, beyond what we ask of Him. He is worthy of all our praise!

Reoccurring Fears
After we have Released what is dear to us, and the fearful or negative thoughts *reoccur*, we must tell ourselves that we have trusted God with this issue. I confidently remind God, *"I am still trusting You with this situation."* I ask Him to, *"Show me if there is anything You want me to do."* I then follow through by trusting in Jesus as I continue to do the next right thing! If we find ourselves wavering with unbelief, it helps to remember that He is

near. We can ask Him to help us with any unbelief. Here is an example of a father who was asking Jesus for help.

In Mark 9:22b-24 (NASB)

> "But if You can do anything, take pity on us and help us!" And Jesus said to him, "'If You can?' All things are possible to him who believes." Immediately the boy's father cried out and said, "I do believe; help my unbelief."

Our God meets us right where we are! Do we doubt His abilities by saying, *"If You can"?* Unbelief will stop us from fully Releasing our concerns to Him. This is when we cry out to Jesus, *"I do believe; help my unbelief."*

We do not need to have it all figured out. We only need to trust the One who does. We do not have to wrestle with issues. We can choose to trust Him, asking Him to help us. He will lead us by faith as we *trust His will* above our own will. If we demand our will and our way over our heavenly Father's will for our lives, we will *not* remain in His peace. *A key to Release is letting go of our will and desiring God's will to be done!*

Your Will Be Done!
Our prayer can be, *"Lord, today I have Released my heart and concerns to You. I ask that Your will be done in every situation and throughout the entirety of my life. I will trust You."*

We can trust Him to exchange our pain, fear, and anxiety for His peace—a *peace* that *safeguards* our hearts and minds. What an awesome exchange! We can be confident knowing that God is completing the good work He began in us. He is faithful. *He will not leave us where we started.* He will complete the work He has begun.

Philippians 1:6 (NIV)

> Being confident of this, that he who began a good work in you will carry it on to completion until the day of Christ Jesus.

This is the great exchange we get to have with our Lord. We bring Him our cares and concerns, and He gives us His peace!

Chapter 5
LET IT GO!

RELEASING PAST WOUNDS
IF WE DO NOT UNDERSTAND HOW TO RELEASE OUR broken mess to God, we can feel *weighed down.* I will share how we can exchange our mess for His peace!

THE BACKPACK
God gave me an amazing analogy many years ago of what it looks like *when we do not* Release our wounds to Him. As we go through this life, we tend to accumulate past wounds. If these wounds are not dealt with for whatever reason, it is as if we store them or accumulate these wounds in a "backpack."

This analogy showed me that many of us carry a backpack everywhere we go. Its size and weight depend upon how many wounds are stored within. Because of its close proximity, we are able to open it at any time and retrieve the old wound in order to share it, talk about it, or relive it. These wounds that we retrieve are old, festering wounds that have not been healed. *It is not a scar that would reveal a healing and point to the Healer.*

No—our backpack carries old wounds that have not been healed. It is very common that over time we can accumulate wounds, fears, and negative ways of thinking.

I saw this in the life of a sweet and gentle friend. During past studies, I noticed that she would bring up the same past wounds and issues. She would retrieve the upsetting event, we would discuss it, and then we would move on. But she did not seem to move on. These issues would resurface again with no evidence of healing.

After one such incident, I took my concern to God and I pleaded that He would show me what was going on and why these issues were not getting resolved in her life. I fervently prayed, and in the morning, God gave me a picture of what was happening.

It was *as if* my friend was wearing a backpack full of past wounds, issues, and disappointments. Often while participating in our studies, the discussions would *trigger* one of those painful areas. She would open the backpack, pull out that old wounded memory, and we would discuss it. After our discussion, she would say with good intentions, "*I know I need to forgive. So I forgive.*" She would then place the old memory back into the backpack, thinking she had resolved it, only to retrieve it once again in another study or discussion.

God showed me that although she was saying "*I know I need to forgive,*" she never really did forgive. Sometimes she would even point to her head and say, *"I know I need to forgive."* However, she was only forgiving with her mind. She was not going to God and Releasing the offense to Him so that He could deal with the pain and bring healing to her.

INVITE HIM INTO YOUR WOUNDED HEART

When we begin to work with God, we are inviting Him into our wounded hearts. The backpack was a picture of an external way of confining the memories. As we Release those painful places, people, and memories to Him, He will remove the backpack and begin healing our heart.

We do not receive healing through our mind only. We must give Him access to our heart. I remember those early years as a Christian. I had certain sections of my heart boarded up with a bold sign that read, *Keep Out!* My standard was "Do not enter!" and that included both God and myself.

The walled-off sections of my heart included my own sinful places that I did not want to acknowledge or deal with. Those sinful and painful roots allowed fear, loneliness, and shame to grow. My lack of knowing *how* to Release my pain kept my painful past barricaded in with no hope of healing.

Do you have painful areas in your heart that are walled off with no hope of healing? This is not how God intended for us to live.

Healing is a process and *forgiveness is a choice.*
This includes forgiving ourselves.

FORGIVE YOURSELF
Some of those boarded-up areas were places where *I had to learn to forgive myself.* I had to Release myself and my painful, sinful past to God. Yes, I have had to ask God to Release me from the pain of my own guilt, shame, and regret.

If you do not let your past die, it won't let you live.

What do I mean by letting your past die? Our past pain can feel so alive within us. Our guilt can consume our thoughts. Our progress can be thwarted by our disdain of ourselves due to our past actions. We can hold ourselves in contempt, hating the very things that we have done *yet not letting them go.*

We can block our own healing. I believe many times we do not seek healing because first, it is too painful to admit our actions, and second, we hold our sins against ourselves. Our biggest obstacle may be that we don't believe or accept God's desire or ability to completely forgive us. Sometimes we feel as if we should be suffering, because of what we have done. We become the judge, jury, and warden over our own lives. When we are constantly embracing the wounds from our painful past, we remain chained to those pains and we will not walk in the freedom that God has prepared for us.

In my life, I had asked God to forgive me multiple times, but I was still confined because I was not Releasing my shame, guilt, and regret of my past sin to Him. It was as if those sins that had once imprisoned me still had the power to keep me locked up. Even though the blood that Jesus shed for me unlocked my prison door, my shame caused me to remain seated on the floor of an unlocked cell.

My healing took place when I went beyond asking Him to forgive me and I actually allowed Him into those painfully deep places in my heart. As I faced those ugly truths, He met me with His unconditional loving embrace, which filled me with His peace. I entrusted my painful past to Almighty God, and *He set me free*. Walking as a *forgiven* child of God allowed me to finally live the life that He desired for me. Applying God's forgiveness to my heart was key for me to forgive myself. It was then that I was able to feel valued, accepted, and loved.

The very things that I held against myself, and the extremely painful places in my heart, became the areas in which He blessed me the most. *It was in those profoundly wounded places that I found His love ran the deepest.*

> Letting God into the truth of my life
> allowed Him to write **His story**
> of love, forgiveness, and acceptance
> over my past painful **history**.

DO YOU BELIEVE THAT YOU ARE FORGIVEN?
Romans 4:7 (NIV)

> Blessed are those whose transgressions are forgiven, whose sins are covered.

Romans 5:8 (NIV)

> But God demonstrates his own love for us in this: While we were still sinners, Christ died for us.

1 John 2:12 (AMP)

> I am writing to you, little children (believers, dear ones), because your sins have been forgiven for His name's sake [you have been pardoned and released from spiritual debt through His name because you have confessed His name, believing in Him as Savior].

Luke 5:20 (NIV)

> When Jesus saw their faith, he said, "Friend, your sins are forgiven."

When Jesus *saw their faith*, He called them *friend*, and He assured them that their sins were forgiven. Have you embraced the truth that your sins *are* forgiven? Our Lord loves us so much that even while we were still sinners, *He died for us*. When we accepted Jesus as our Savior, one aspect of our relationship with Him is that He saved us from the penalty of our sin. We have been covered by His blood! How amazing is the *depth* of His love for us!

> HE SAVED US FROM THE PENALTY OF OUR SIN.

We were once guilty of our sin, but Jesus has covered all our sins and has given us a complete pardon! *Pardoned* is a strong legal term that means *forgiven, absolved, exonerated, acquitted, released, let go,* and *not condemned*. In a courtroom if a defendant is acquitted or exonerated, they are completely vindicated, *cleared of all charges*.

I hope with all of my heart that you have Released your sin to God and accepted Jesus' forgiveness. His complete pardon is a full Release. Our God has Released us! *We are set free, liberated, made new, set apart, and unconditionally loved by God!*

Are you living free from your past sin?

Perhaps the question is, *will you forgive yourself?*

If you need to forgive yourself, please take a moment and talk to God about those areas. *He is your friend.* Release it all to Him. He desires *to heal you*! If you want, you can pray a prayer like this.

Prayer:

> Lord, this is a scary step for me. I am afraid to open my heart up completely to You. I am afraid of the pain that is within, *but* I want to be healed. I entrust my healing to You. I want to be free. I have sinned. I carry the weight of this sin in the form of guilt and shame. I choose to Release it all to You today. I Release _____ to You. I know that the blood of Jesus has covered all of my sins and that I have been set free! Now I ask that You help me to live in the freedom You have provided. I want to be free of all that holds me back from You and from Your best.

This step of Release gave me my life back. It was through Release that I was able to work with God. He brought healing to my broken and sinful heart.

I treasure the love I found in His redemption.

Release Others
Many times we struggle in this life because we have not forgiven others. Others have hurt us and the pain they caused *is*

real and can be *lasting*. Entangled within the pain *can be* unforgiveness, bitterness, anger, frustration, resentment, cynicism, hatred, and contempt. We can also experience embarrassment, sadness, doubt, rejection, fear, and shame. This often hinders our relationship with God because our past pain makes it hard to trust Him. All of this is a heavy weight to carry. *We were not created to carry this weight.* Jesus wants to deliver us from all of our troubles. He is gentle. When we cry out to Him, *He hears us*. He wants us to find rest for our souls.

Matthew 11:29-30 (NIV)

> Take my yoke upon you and learn from me, for I am gentle and humble in heart, and you will find rest for your souls. For my yoke is easy and my burden is light."

Psalm 34:17 (NIV)

> The righteous cry out, and the LORD hears them; he delivers them from all their troubles.

Is your heart heavy because of those who have caused you harm? Are there individuals who you may need to Release? Consider Releasing them into God's mighty hands. This does *not* mean that we give them a pass, or that what they did wasn't wrong. It only means that we have *entrusted our heart* to our caring Father and we are Releasing those who have harmed us into His hands. God is the *only* One who can *justly judge*. Paul is a great example of this.

2 Timothy 4:14-15 (NASB)

> Alexander the coppersmith did me much harm; the Lord will repay him according to his deeds. Be on guard against him yourself, for he vigorously opposed our teaching.

Paul released Alexander, the one who had harmed him, into the Lord's hands. He knew the Lord would repay him according to what he had done. He did not hold on to the pain, allowing resentment, bitterness, and anger to grow. *He did not ignore it.* He Released it to the Lord, who would handle it.

We are not meant to carry the weight of unforgiveness, hatred, and painful memories. Jesus is calling us to come, bring Him our pain, and receive His healing and peace in return.

In the *Introduction* I shared about the night my fiancé was murdered. In the months and years that followed his death, I had to be careful not to allow the excruciating pain of losing him to become entangled with a heavy weight of unforgiveness. Those in the world tell us to blame, point fingers, and not to forgive. I knew I had a choice.

I desired an overall peace that was worth more to me than holding onto any unforgiveness.

By the grace of God, I chose to forgive. Layer by layer, I Released all my pain to God, and He healed my heart. Over time the healing became so deep that I was able to pray for the man who caused his death. I prayed that God would transform his heart and life.

Through this healing process, I can now remember my fiancé's death without pain. That is a miracle. God does amazing things in us and through us when we entrust our pain to Him.

> **GOD DOES AMAZING THINGS IN US AND THROUGH US WHEN WE ENTRUST OUR PAIN TO HIM.**

Can you trust Jesus by Releasing those who have harmed you into His hands?

When you Release others, it is *not* equivalent to them being innocent.

No. Releasing them into God's capable hands *sets you free*. Let your faithful Father deal with them and the consequences of their actions.

Most times, this step of Release is just between you and the Father. The other person does *not* even need to know what you are doing. Release is used to set *your* heart free.

If there are those who you need to Release, let this be the beginning of your healing. You can start with a prayer of Release.

Prayer:

> God, I cannot imagine letting go of this offense. It feels impossible to Release it, but I know *all things* are possible with You. Lord, I want to be free! I want to entrust my wounded heart to You. I do believe that You will complete the good work You have begun in me. I trust You to completely heal me. So, by faith, I take hold of Your hand and I choose to Release this offense to You. I choose to Release, (insert name or situation) _____ to You. What happened was not right! I trust You to care for my heart and my life. I entrust the entirety of this difficult situation to You. Do what You know is best. I Release it all to You! In the powerful Name of Jesus, set me free! Amen.

Take a deep breath. When we Release our pain, *our healing has begun*. Release brings with it healing because Release removes the negative issue from within us and entrusts it to God. By Releasing the situation, we make room for God to work. He will complete our healing and guard our hearts and minds with His wonderful peace.

BOUNDARIES

To Release also does not imply that we must be in a relationship with the one who harmed us. Sometimes it is wise and necessary *not* to continue in the relationship. We may need to set up boundaries with that person. Some boundaries are unspoken but you completely understand the secure boundary that you have set for yourself.

Boundaries can be very important. I found this to be true with my dad. Just as Paul cautioned his companions to *be on guard against Alexander because he had caused him much harm*, I also had to be on guard and set up boundaries with my own father.

After the sorrowful season of losing my fiancé, I began to pray for a godly husband. God brought an amazing Christian man into my life. Shortly after we were married, my dad called my home while I was out. He was extremely rude to my husband. I knew I would not allow my dad to negatively affect my husband, so I called my father and set up a boundary.

I told him that the way that he had spoken to my husband was unacceptable. I continued to explain that if he were drinking, he was *not* to call me. From then on, if he called and he had been drinking, I would calmly say, "*Dad, I can tell that you are drinking, so I will talk to you later. I love you. Bye.*" Then I would hang up the phone. It was hard at times, but I knew that nothing good would come out of us talking when he was drinking.

> **BOUNDARIES CAN KEEP US FROM FURTHER HEARTACHE.**

That boundary kept my family and me from much turmoil. I watched as others were reluctant to set up a boundary with him, and sadly his drunken mental abuse continued in their lives.

Boundaries such as these can keep us from further heartache. They can create the space we need to Release our past hurts to God. Our God is faithful. He will carry us. He will carry the weight of our load as we Release it to Him. In the process of being healed, He will set us free and give us His peace.

WAYS TO RELEASE
I have found some helpful ways to Release our wounded places.

> **Write a letter to the person** but do NOT send it. I opened chapter four with a heart-wrenching letter to my dad. Just the process of Releasing the hatred was a healing. Others have written a letter and then imagined reading it to the person who had wounded them. Then they destroy the letter.
>
> **Use a phone/device to write a memo** but do NOT send it. Pour out all of your anger, frustrations, and disappointments, and then delete it. Since it is *not* being sent, you can be painfully honest in what you write, and it can be a full Release. Then you can *let it go* by deleting the memo.

This works amazingly! A friend of mine was healed from a huge disappointment and wound. She used her phone for one month, and as the negative emotions continued to surface, she got them out by typing them in a memo. By writing it out, she could Recognize *what* the root of the wound was. There were a few times she called, and we discussed the painful root that was being exposed. We ended each conversation with a prayer of Release. Her pain subsided with each deleted memo.

I was witnessing new freedom and healing in her every time she Released her pain. Her healing became very apparent when she began to pray fervently for the person who had caused the wounds. Her heart had changed by her Releasing the wounding offense. It was awesome. She was set free.

When we write out our wounded emotions, those words become tangible. Instead of the emotions just swirling in our heart and mind, we can *see* them for what they are. By writing down our invisible thoughts, they become words on a page that we can discern as *concrete* wounds and frustrations. This helps us to Recognize the root of the pain and then Release it all to God in prayer. After we Release the pain, we can let it go by shredding the letter or deleting the memo.

Release can be done with:

- You and God
- You and a friend, family member, or spouse
- You and a counselor
- You and a specific group or grief group
- You and a Bible study that addresses your painful issue

God has many ways to Release us. Did you Recognize that "You" is the common denominator in each of those points? *Avoiding* the issue *will not* Release its pain. We choose how and when we will Release these painful places to God.

RELEASE WHEN GRIEVING
Let it out! Grieving deep sorrow needs to be Released. We mourn losses of many kinds. We can mourn the loss of how we thought our life would be, loss of tangible things, loss of a marriage or a significant relationship. We can experience deep sorrow over the death of loved ones. We can be sorrowful because of unfulfilled or forfeited dreams. We can grieve the loss of our childhood.

The grief I felt after my mom, who was my best friend, went to heaven was crushing. It was as if the sorrow became a powerful vacuum that sucked the joy and happiness from within. I felt as if I were going through the motions of life, trying to be present, but empty. Then the pressure of grief would build like a geyser without me Recognizing it. God was always faithful to Release the mounting pressure. Many times the pent-up grief would sneak up on me, and when I was by myself, the tears would flow freely. Most times there was no warning that the pressure needed to be Released, but afterward I would feel so much better.

In those times, I could Release a few tears or have a torrential downpour that would last a few minutes. Every single time the Release was a gift from God. He relieved the pressure of sorrow that had been building. I would always thank God after the wonderful Release.

> **RELEASE IS A GIFT FROM GOD.**

In that season there were two places where Release occurred the most. First, while I cleaned my bedroom without having other distractions, I could transparently share my feelings with God. My bedroom held many special reminders of my mom. Often I would pick up a card she had written to me. Reading her handwritten words would overwhelm me, but it was as if I needed the comfort of hearing her words once again. She even had a lipstick kiss on one of the envelopes. There were times I would put my lips to the envelope *as if to kiss her back.*

Other times, my life would be so hectic that it wasn't until I got into my van and drove that my mind would slow down and my heart would remember that she was gone. Tears would quietly fall.

When we Release these losses, the waves of emotion will come with the grief, but do not be afraid. Know that *God is opening a way* for you to Release the emotions that are within. Don't hold it back. He will heal our hearts and renew our spirits *as we let go* of the pain that is causing the pressure.

This incredible principle of Release creates *a lighter way to live.* As we get into the habit of Recognizing and Releasing issues to God, this keeps our hearts clean, clear, and full of God's peace. Imagine, God leans in to care for us as we Release our wounds to Him.

Psalm 147:3 (NIV)

> He heals the brokenhearted and binds up their wounds.

Taking the time to do the hard work of Release is worth every effort we will make. Ask God to help you in the process of Release so that you can take your next right step. This is a process, so take it one step or issue at a time. Remember that He heals the brokenhearted and He will bind up their wounds. He is with you. He will help you.

As a difficult issue or specific memory arises and needs to be Released from your backpack or heart, write it down. Next to each issue, decide the way you want to Release it.

Choose the method of Release: Praying to God, writing a letter or memo, (do not send it), talking and praying with another, discussing it with a counselor, doing a specific Bible study, joining an appropriate group, letting it out, or using another helpful approach.

_____
_____
_____

Psalm 51:10 (AMP)

> Create in me a clean heart, O God, and renew a right *and* steadfast spirit within me.

CLEANING OUR ROOM

I got fed up with the *past emotional pain* and past memories *dictating my present day*. Imagine we have one room that we have been given. This one room can be kept how we want. Let's say that over time many things have happened in that room to create disarray. Others have come in and left a mess. This is your room. You choose how you want to keep it.

- Do you shove everything under the bed so that you can walk through the room?
- Do you open the closet and throw everything in it, and vow that the door will never get opened?
- Do you pretend the mess does not exist?

I have had a real physical room that I called a "catch-all" room, meaning I threw everything in that room because I did not want to deal with those things. But the day came when I chose to open the door and assess the damage. I was overwhelmed. A few times I shut the door and thought, *I am not dealing with this mess today!*

Finally, I decided that I wanted more from that room than just a mess. The room was not being used as it could have been. It had the potential of being a beautiful room, but it would take me cleaning the mess before its beauty would shine and could be enjoyed as it ought to be.

Can you identify with having a mess that needs to be cleaned up so that the room can be used to its full potential? How about the rooms in your heart being cleaned so that you can grow to your full potential?

The rooms of our heart can be just as overwhelming. When we look in, we may want to slam the door closed and pretend we did not see the mess within. We may want to sweep old wounds under the carpet so we don't have to deal with them. We may want to shove our pain in the closet and slam the door. That *seems* easier.

As I have shared this lesson on cleaning our room, many have identified with having emotional rooms that they try to hide.

The rooms of rejection, rooms of not enough, or rooms where they feel unheard. These emotional rooms can replay a negative situation or store negative emotions, including sadness, shame, embarrassment, fear, anger, and resentment.

I lived this way for years as I pretended to be a Christian that had it all together. Yet I had rooms in my heart of emotional pain. My cleaning process did not begin *until* I opened the door of my heart and invited God in by saying, *"Okay, God, I give You full access. You are the One who will lead me through this mess."*

When I had the courage to finally clean my *physical* "catch-all" room, I

- Stepped into the room
- Assessed the mess
- Got overwhelmed

Then I asked God to

- "Show me what this area should look like."
- "Show me one thing I can do right now."
- "Okay, what next?"

God was faithful to show me what to tackle in my physical room, and He was just as *faithful* to lead me step by step through my messy heart.

- First, I had to Recognize the *emotional issue* that I had *not* dealt with, which was still hindering me.
- Next, I had to Release it into His loving arms.
- Then I joined God for the strength and wisdom to process it so that I could be healed.

Many times we do not fully know that we have these negative emotional areas in our heart. A clue for us is when we overreact to a "normal" situation. Have you ever asked yourself, *"Why did*

I overreact in that situation or to that comment? Why did their action, look, tone, or statement hurt so deeply?" When a situation penetrates much deeper than it should have, it usually points to a *trigger*. Under the trigger, you will most likely find a hidden or unresolved wound.

TRIGGERS

I know triggers are hard to understand. Years ago, when I heard my boys in another room wrestling, just hearing the noises of them rolling around would trigger a deep-seeded terrible emotion. Fear, anxiety, and a rush of adrenaline would surge through my body. I would immediately begin to shake. I would run into the room only to see them having a good time. I would say, *"Please stop that wrestling!"* They would tell me that they were having fun and they were fine.

My immediate reaction was to stop what was causing the deep anxiety from rising to the surface. I wanted to silence the trigger. But I have learned if I can Recognize that something was triggered and then try to find its root, I will begin to heal.

FINDING THE ROOT

That night I pulled my husband aside and I spoke about the horrible emotions I had felt when I heard our sons wrestling. I knew he did not have any negative reactions to them wrestling, and I wondered why I did. During our conversation I recalled another time in my life when I felt those emotions. That is where I found the root and my answer.

I have shared earlier about hating the way my dad treated the women in his life. As a young girl, when I would stay at his apartment, he would fistfight with his girlfriend in the bedroom behind closed doors. I would hear the thuds and the awful sounds of fighting. I screamed. I cried. I pleaded through the door. But there was nothing I could do to stop their fighting.

> My overreaction was proof that I needed a healing.

It was then that those sounds were planted so deeply within me. Those memories were infused with the anxiety, fear, and the flood of adrenaline that I experienced as they fought. We can carry past pain that has been shoved back, never fully dealt with, and forgotten until there is a trigger. My overreaction to their wrestling was proof that I needed a healing.

Triggers are like pouring salt into an old wound. When the issue arises, it usually comes equipped with the full emotion that we felt at the time of the initial pain. It can feel scary, but after we Recognize the wound, we now have something tangible to talk to God about.

Are there issues that you overreact to? Do you Recognize any triggers that are trying to *illuminate* an area that needs to be Released and healed? If so, expound on them.

_____
_____
_____

PROCESSING THE WOUND
Processing with God or another can start like this:

- This is how I felt when . . .
- These are the emotions I was feeling . . . I still feel . . .
- These are the fears I had . . . I still have . . .
- When they did that, I felt like . . .
- Lord, please help me to Release these painful places to you.

I told God exactly how I felt. We should not hold back our true feelings from God. He can handle it! He knows how we feel anyways. When we share our vulnerable, broken places, those truths will begin to Release the root of our wound. As I told God exactly how I felt, those truthful conversations were the beginning of Releasing my negative emotions *so* that I could be healed.

CAST YOUR CARES
We all have some mess in our backpacks, messy rooms, or hearts. But what are we going to do about it? Leave it, hide it, ignore it, or deal with it as it arises? The choice is ours, but we do not have to go it alone. God desires to come alongside us and teach us to cast all our cares upon Him because He cares for us! He will never leave us alone. He watches over us very carefully.

1 Peter 5:7 (AMP)

> Casting all your cares [all your anxieties, all your worries, and all your concerns, once and for all] on Him, for He cares about you [with deepest affection, and watches over you very carefully].

Many times I *tried* to care for myself and my own pain, but that proved to be *fruitless*. It was when I entrusted all my cares to Him that God gave me the grace, mercy, and love that empowered me to let them go. He heals. He forgives. God wants you to cast, throw, rid yourself of your burdens because He cares for you!

HE TRANSFORMS OUR MESS
God transformed my mess into the message
I am sharing with you!

He will redeem our lives and miraculously make us *more like Him*. He can turn those dark places into lights that shine for Him.

John 8:12 (NASB) Jesus Is the Light of the World

> Then Jesus again spoke to them, saying, "I am the Light of the world; he who follows Me will not walk in the darkness, but will have the Light of life."

Psalm 29:11 (NASB)

> The LORD will give strength to His people; the LORD will bless His people with peace.

Our strength and peace come from the LORD. As we entrust Him with all of our heart, He will give us the strength to let go of our painful dark places that have been hidden for so long. Jesus will heal us and fill us with *His light of life*, which includes His *peace*.

REVISITING AN AREA
Do not be afraid of revisiting an area that may have another facet or layer that needs to be addressed and healed. Some deeper wounds may have a few different phases of healing. Just like with the wounds from my dad, I had many layers that had to be healed over the years. Often I would say, "*Lord, here I am again.*" Jesus faithfully met me where I was every time. Our Lord will Release and heal us a little deeper with each aspect of the wound that He is restoring.

When we revisit a specific wound that God has brought to our attention, we:

- *Recognize* the issue
- *Release* all of it
- *Repent* if necessary
- *Choose to forgive* others and ourselves
- *Let go* of our shame, embarrassment, jealousy, bitterness, disappointment, or pain

Which of those points are the hardest for you? Why?

_____
_____

Do you need to ask God for the strength to take this step of Release? If so, take a moment and *ask Him* for help. *"Lord, help me to _____."*

Don't Dwell
In our healing journey, we must *be careful not to dwell* on a specific part. Overly dwelling on one point or a disappointment can keep us stuck. We can easily *magnify* one detail, making that our focus. We can stay fixated, dwelling on that one issue. If we do not see our healing quickly occur, we can become hard on ourselves. We need to trust God and His timing with the healing process. His healing may come layer by layer.

As we allow Him into our heart to *Release the offense* that had been done *against* us or done *by* us, He will bring healing. When healing occurs, our heart is transformed, and then we can remember the offense without pain. Often it feels like a miracle!

Remembering Without Pain
Are there places in your past that you would like to remember without pain?

After I Released my wounded and sinful places to God, I was able to remember them *without* pain. I shared this principle of Releasing the old wound with my friends who were also stuck with painful memories. They were eager to find healing.

Sometimes healing comes without us realizing. For instance, while I was at a Bible study with some of these friends, one of them was asked to share some of the tougher parts of her childhood. I watched as she sat, thought, and even searched, but what she said amazed us all.

She went on to explain, *"I know that my life was hard growing up, and that some really bad things happened, but I have given it all to God and I guess He has healed me so much I don't remember it like I once did."* She and I smiled at one another, as we knew we had witnessed a work of God.

During our healing process, we may not Recognize that the healing has taken place. It may not be until later that we recall the incident or the issue, and we realize the pain that was once prevalent is now gone. It has been replaced with God's healing and peace. It is just like a scar that gives proof that there was a wound that needed healing. The scar does not hurt. It is only proof that a healing has occurred. *The scar now points to our amazing Healer.*

> THE SCAR NOW POINTS TO OUR AMAZING HEALER.

In these seasons of healing, imagine God drawing near to you, holding you close, and caring deeply and tenderly for you. He has a heart of compassion and love for each of us. This is so important to remember as we go through our healing process.

I have had to *reprogram my mind* to see my loving God as being close and smiling down on me. When I imagine Him smiling at me, it reminds me of His accepting nature, loving Spirit, and gentle heart that always desires to draw us in, especially when we are hurting. *Take a moment and imagine* God smiling on you and drawing near to you.

How does that make you feel?

THE HEALING PROCESS
We have a choice. I had a choice. You have a choice. It is amazing the difference *in us* when we Release our heart into His loving care! Some issues we can Release and gain immediate peace! With other wounds, *the action of Release will begin the healing process*. It is okay. He knows just what we need in each healing. He is faithful to complete the good work that He has begun in us. This is the beginning of our journey for *lifelong peace*.

He is faithful! His name is Jehovah-Rapha, *The Lord that Heals*.

We are in good hands! When our healing occurs, it will bring with it so much peace and joy that it will *redecorate* our heart. *Faith* will *remove* those boarded-up places. *Peace* will *illuminate* our heart with the warmest of lights. *Joy* will *decorate* with beautiful colors. His *comfort* will *provide* welcoming furnishings, and His *love* will *make itself at home*!

Think about that for a moment. Do you need:

- *Faith* to remove those boarded-up areas?
- The warmth of *peace* to illuminate your heart and life?
- *Joy* to lift every step you take?
- *His comfort* to cover you?
- And *His love* to be at home within you always?

I did, and I still do.

LOOKING BACK
Can you look back and Recognize an area that has been healed, and you can now remember it without pain? *His healing is amazing!*

Are there other places in your past that you would like to remember without pain? If so, list them.

It is *in* His strength, not ours, that we are set free. Look to Him. Ask Him to provide all you need. Your prayer can begin something like this:

> Lord, I see this reoccurring issue. Please help me Release it all to You. I want to remember it without pain. I am tired of its impact in my life. You are my Healer! I trust You with my healing. I desire this area to be illuminated and redecorated by You.

_____
_____
_____

Chapter 6
COME AS YOU ARE

GOD CHOSE TO ENTRUST ME TO A SIXTEEN-YEAR-OLD mom and an alcoholic dad. He knew the gifts and strengths that I would need to fulfill His plan for my life. He also knew that the hardships in my life would produce compassion and a passion for the hurting. For instance, when I was in first or second grade, I saw a boy in my class who looked sad. Being young I knew I could not help him, so I walked up to my teacher's desk and said, *"Mrs. ____, Johnny looks sad."* Annoyed with me, she told me *to go sit down*! Sadly, I do not think she spoke to him.

This is one of my earliest memories of feeling *compassion* and *wanting to help the one who was hurting.* Our painful past can produce in us compassion and kindness that we would not otherwise have.

COMPASSION OUT OF PAIN
As an adult, I have experienced God's compassion. He restored my heart and gave me a desire to share with others the same compassion that I was given.

2 Corinthians 1:3–4 (NIV)

> Praise be to the God and Father of our Lord Jesus Christ, the Father of compassion and the God of all comfort, who comforts us in all our troubles, so that we can comfort those in any trouble with the comfort we ourselves receive from God.

My God knew the heart of compassion that He would ignite within me because of the *compassion*, *love*, and *mercy* that He used to *comfort* me. He knew that my broken life would be mended by Him. He also knew that out of my pain, I would be able to reach many more than I could have ever reached without the pain that I had endured.

THE POWER OF THE SCAR
As I mentioned before, our scars point to our Healer. Our scars do not hurt. The pain is gone. We carry the *evidence* revealing that we have been healed. *I have found that the very scars I carry can become hope for another who is wounded.* They hope in the fact that *if* God has healed me, He *will* heal them. That is the power of the scar. It points to our Healer.

> HIS SCARS REMAIN TO BRING US HOPE.

Jesus is the best example of how scars can bring hope to others. Jesus bears the scars that He received when He was nailed to the cross for *all* of our sins. His scars remain to bring us hope that *we are loved, our sins have been forgiven, and we have been set free*. The power of His scars remains as a testimony of His love for all time.

God can cause our scars to work for good. Let's remember in Romans 8:28 (NASB) it states, *"And we know that God causes all things to work together for good to those who love God, to those who are called according to His purpose."*

Even in our pain, God works for the good of those who love Him. He has compassion on us, and He equips us to give away that same compassion and mercy to others. It is so powerful! God takes our areas that have been *healed* and allows us to share *what He has done* in our lives. This helps those who are wounded to find their own healing.

THE UGLY SIDE OF PAIN
Our pain can also cause us to act in ways that are very unbecoming.

When we are wounded, especially with ongoing wounds or wounds that have *not* been dealt with, those wounds sit and fester. We may not have understood what to do with our pain, so we may have done nothing. When I was younger, I had no idea that my wounds could be dealt with in a positive way, so I held them within me. At times, my inner pain changed me for the worse. I became harsh, hard, rude, and even mean. The pain I had within me was creating so much havoc that when it pushed its way to the surface, it spewed out in hurtful ways. You have probably heard that *hurt people, hurt people*. It is so true.

Our past wounds, disappointments, disillusionments, rejections, sins, and shame can cause us to act in ways that are not in line with *who we were created to be*. These can cause us to be unforgiving, rebellious, insecure, jealous, mean, harsh, rude, insensitive, irrational, sarcastic, suspicious, vindictive, doubtful, sinful, and hard to love. We can even reject a good thing in fear that it may turn into another wound. Our undealt with pain can sabotage us, causing us to see life as mainly negative. These are additional weights that we can carry.

After I became a Christian, I began to remember the hurtful things that I had done. I really mourned over how I had acted at times. I asked God to forgive me, and I prayed for God's blessing on those I had hurt. What can hurt people do when they hurt other people? *They can repent.*

REPENT AND BE FILLED
***Repentance* is** having regret, sorrow, or remorse for our thoughts, words, or deeds.

***Repentance* can include** *acknowledging* our negative way, *Releasing* it to God, *expressing* our sorrow for what we have done, *amending* our actions, and *correcting* our course.

When we repent, we turn away from our sin, forsaking our wrong ways, and turn back toward God, trusting Him to change our heart.

Did anything about repentance stand out to you?

_____

Repentance *restores* relationships.

I love that *repent* means *to correct our course.* When I have Recognized a negative way that I have spoken, thought, acted, or lived, I had to decide whether to remain on the negative path *or* to change my mind about my sin. Repentance is having a *godly sorrow* that redirects our course *back toward God.* By faith we can honor Him with our repentant heart, words, actions, and ways. Repentance *restores* the relationship between us and God.

We may need to repent for times that we have not trusted God with the circumstances in our life. Hebrews 11:6 (NIV) tells us that, *"Without faith it is impossible to please God."* Many times we may have allowed fear to run our lives. Fear redirects our course away from faith, not letting God lead us in the way He wants us to go.

Repenting can also be the catalyst to restore our relationship with others. Now, when I hurt another I will, with a sincere heart, say, *"I am sorry for how I acted. Please forgive me."* I then ask God to *change my heart to make me more loving like Him.* We can be more like God, because His Spirit is in us, empowering us to stay the course that He has laid before us.

Let me ask you a few questions.

- Do you have regret for something you have done or spoken?
- Have you injured another?
- Do you feel far from God?
- Do you need to change your course?

What are the areas where you want to repent and entrust your heart to Him?

_____
_____

Repent and then be filled. We can ask God to fill us again. Even though we had been filled with the Holy Spirit when we trusted Jesus as our Savior, *we can be filled many times* thereafter. Let's pray and ask God to fill, enable, and empower us with His love, peace, faith, freedom, wisdom, perseverance, and courage. We can ask Him to fill us and multiply His fruit in our lives!

COME AS YOU ARE
Ephesians 3:12 (NIV)

> In him and through faith in him we may approach
> God with freedom and confidence.

When we Release our anxieties to God, we are to come as we are, knowing we are loved!
Say aloud:

> GOD ACCEPTS ME AS I AM.
> GOD ACCEPTS ME WHERE I AM.
> GOD ACCEPTS ME.

But HE LOVES ME TOO MUCH TO LEAVE ME HERE!

How did it feel to say those statements?

___

Are you able to *believe* those statements for *yourself*? If not, why not?

___

___

I am shocked by how many people struggle with feeling they cannot come to God as they are. Many times, we have believed the *lies* that we must get ourselves cleaned up and our lives figured out before we can come to Him. This is a lie that is intended to keep us from a relationship with God.

The truth is He wants us to come to Him *as we are.*

God wants a deep, real relationship with each of us. A deep relationship requires us to *be real* and learn to rely on Him!

RELEASE AND RELY
We *Release to Him* and then *we rely on Him*. In this last section on Release, we will assess whom we rely on in this life. We will decide what or whom we will rely on.

- Will we rely on God and His love to care for us?
- Will we rely on our own abilities?
- Will we rely on others for the help we need?
- Will we rely on our position, possessions, or our financial accounts?

These are heart decisions. The reality is that what is *most valued* in our heart is what we will rely on. During those times in our lives when things suddenly change and there is a shaking of all that we thought was secure, what do we rely on?

In the past, I have relied on:

_____
_____

Did you know that God wants us to *rely* on the *love* that He has for us?

1 John 4:15 (NIV)

> If anyone acknowledges that Christ is the son of God, God lives in them and they in God. And so, we know and rely on the love God has for us. God is love.

The question is, *"Do we really rely on God's love?"*

When we trust in God's love, we will rely on Him, depend on Him, and count on His faithfulness. We can rest in His love, which will give us a confident assurance that will shield us from doubting His goodness.

Where are you in this process? It is *normal* to go back and forth from trust to doubt, as we grow into a mature faith.

1. Do you rest in Him to keep you?
2. Do you confidently rely on God without doubt?
3. Is it hard to Release things into His hands?
4. Do you tend to take back what you entrusted to Him because you do not fully trust Him?
5. Do you struggle with knowing or accepting how loved you are?
6. Do you want to know and experience more of His love?

Of the preceding statements, which one(s) describes you best? Why?

_____
_____

RELY ON ME
You probably have seen a demonstration to show whether we are relying on someone or not. It starts with one person standing behind another and seemingly holding them up. The person being held leans back on the one holding her. However, when the one who is the holder takes a step away and the person leaning does not fall, that shows that the one leaning only *looked* as if she was confidently relying on the other person, but she was really *relying on her own strength*.

That is how it can be with us and God. We can say, "*Yes, of course, I know and rely on God's love.*" But the reality is that if we run with our fears, doubts, and anxieties, that is the *opposite* of relying on the love of God. It is easy to do. I think we all have done this.

As I was learning to rely on God, He would prompt my heart to trust Him. This changed my mindset because when a difficult issue would arise, I would normally want to immediately call a friend to pour out my problem. Other times fear would cause me to either want to hide or frantically try to figure it out by myself. God would convict my heart that I was not relying on Him nor was I relying on His love for me.

Knowing that God really loves each one of us personally
is something *we must believe* if we are going to lean on Him.

DO YOU LOVE ME?
Many years ago I struggled knowing if God really loved me. I had to be honest with God, so I told Him, "*I do not know that You love me.*" I continued, "*I believe that You love everyone else, but I need to know that You love me.*" By expressing the truth of not fully feeling loved by God, my eyes were opened, and I began to see Him show His love for me in the strangest of ways.

Amazingly at my local grocery store, God began to show me that He loved me. It began when I suggested that an elderly woman proceed ahead of me. Then with the brightest look upon her face, she said to me, *"No, honey, you go first."* I remember feeling so loved by this stranger. It was not the way that I would feel if someone just allowed me in front of them. It was richer, deeper, and it warmed my heart.

I asked God, *"Lord, why did she act so kindly toward me?"*

He responded, *"I am showing you that I love you."* I felt loved. That happened a few more times, and every time, God was continually showing me His love.

Other times, I was shown great favor, as others would go out of their way for me. Again God showed me that He was having random strangers show me favor. As I experienced His love, favor, and kindness, great healing was taking place in my heart. I began to rely on Him as never before. We need *to know* that we are loved by God!

My Mom's Example of Relying on God's Love

I was able to witness the best example of someone relying on God and relying on His love for her. My mom was fifty-five years old when she had an MRI of her brain to see if her breast cancer had spread. Realizing that she could receive a bad report, she pulled her coworkers aside and said, *"Hear me and hear me well. No matter what happens tomorrow, I will be victorious! If my doctor tells me that I will die, I am victorious because I will live with my Savior forever. And if He allows me more time with my children and grandchildren, I will be victorious! I just want you to know that no matter what I am told tomorrow, either way, I will be victorious!"*

> **NO MATTER WHAT I AM TOLD TOMORROW, EITHER WAY, I WILL BE VICTORIOUS!**

Wow! What amazing faith. Her faith was *not* always this strong. She now trusted that she was loved, and she knew that her God would be faithful no matter what she faced! My mom became an amazing example of Releasing her cares to God and resting in Him during her time of need.

The following day I accompanied her to her doctor appointment. The young doctor sat wringing his hands as he told my mom that she only had a few months to live. We both sat in disbelief. We discussed her quitting her job and immediately moving in with my family. Of course, tears were already beginning to flow from my eyes. My mom was my absolute best friend and the best nana a kid could hope for.

As we left the doctor's office, we were silent. Approaching the bottom of the steps, she turned to me and said, "*I know that the doctor told me that I do not have long to live ... but I have peace.*"

Astonished I looked into her eyes and said, "*Mom, I do too!*"

She said, "*Let's pray for Grandma to have this peace also.*" God was merciful. Thankfully amid her deep heartache, my grandma also received His peace that surpassed all understanding!

That day on the way home, as my mom contemplated all that the doctor had told her, she said, "*Dawn, I could have died in a car accident and never gotten to say good-bye.*" She became overwhelmed and said, "*Stop the car!*" Shocked at her request, I came to a stop. She threw her arms into the air and exclaimed passionately,

"*Thank ... You ... Jesus ... for Your mercy ... and Your peace!*"

I looked at her in amazement, thinking, *Mercy? Didn't you hear the doctor say you are dying?* My mom was overjoyed that God mercifully gave her *time to say good-bye* to her family and friends. She was thankful because *she knew* she was loved. Even on the hardest of days, she could see how God was providing for her. He provided time for her to say good-bye.

Through the seven weeks that my mom was with us, she taught me more about life, faith, and dying than through all my other years combined. Every day, we all were sustained by God's amazing peace. In the face of death, she continued to stay faith-filled.

We had been praying and believing that God could heal her. I remember one night I thought to myself, *We have had so much peace, I am not praying powerfully for her like I should.* So I went into her room and told her how I felt. I then asked if I could pray for her. As I prayed, I guess I began to strongly plead with God to heal her completely, because I did not want to lose her.

As I continued to pray, she looked at me and said sternly, *"Dawn, don't you ever . . . pray your will for me! Only pray God's will for me!"* The air left my lungs and tears fell from my eyes as I knew she was content with *whatever* His will was.

My heart hurt knowing I would lose her. Yet I was blessed by how she was faithfully relying on Her God for His best. *Her faith in Him was a bright light of hope shining for all of us to see.*

> HER FAITH IN HIM WAS A BRIGHT LIGHT OF HOPE SHINING FOR ALL OF US TO SEE.

One warm summer day my grandmother, my mom, and I were outside cherishing our time together as the heat of the sun warmed our faces. My mom's heart was full as she sat on my swing and admired the birds in flight, the flowers blooming, and her grandkids, who were running and playing in the yard. She truly loved having her family so close. She was taking it all in.

Then unexpectedly she sat back, her face lit up, and with a huge smile she exclaimed confidently, *"I am the happiest that I've ever been!"*

My grandmother could not believe her ears. Later she said to me, *"I wanted to say to her, 'Don't you know you are dying?'"* Grandma was bewildered by Mom's *deep joy* in the midst of dying. But at the same time, seeing my mom as the happiest she had ever been comforted us all. We realized that Jesus was so close to her. His same peace and strength covered us.

My mom remained continually filled with God's joy and peace. I found out why as I cleaned out her house. On a little sticky note she had written:

> *When you don't see His hand,*
> *Trust His heart. Re: God*

When you don't see His hand, trust His heart, regarding God. She could not see God's hand in her cancer. She decided to *trust His heart for her* no matter what she faced in this life. She knew she was loved! *She had Released herself, her life, and her future into God's mighty hands.*

SHE RELIED ON HIM AND HE SUSTAINED HER
The night before my mom went to heaven, some of her friends from church came to visit her. Before they left, I asked if we could pray together. All agreed. During the prayer I prayed *that God would not let my mom suffer.* As my mom heard those words coming from my mouth, she was shocked that I would pray such a prayer. She abruptly turned her head toward me, and with *obvious irritation* she said, *"He won't!"* We immediately broke into a roar of laughter. We were all amazed at her great faith.

Her faith was so strong that she was indignant that I would even think for a second that He would let her suffer. The following night as she lay with her eyes closed now for hours, all at once she opened wide her eyes and gasped in delight as if to see the best sight ever. *I knew at that moment my mom had just seen Jesus.* With that she let go of three little breaths, and she was gone. *She was now with her faithful Lord.* In His presence, she was being held and comforted by His mighty love.

> SHE OPENED WIDE HER EYES AND GASPED IN DELIGHT AS IF TO SEE THE BEST SIGHT EVER.

Sometimes it takes seeing someone else who has had God's peace in the midst of great turmoil to let us know that God's scriptures are not just good words on a page. They are the truth! They are our truth! They are the truth that we can live by!

As I shared in chapter four Psalm 91:1-2 AMP tells us that we can *dwell in the shelter of the Most High.* We will *remain secure and rest in the Almighty [whose power no enemy can withstand].* We can *say of the LORD, "He is my refuge and my fortress, My God, in whom I trust [with great confidence, and on whom I rely]!"*

> My mom was blessed with God's peace because she trusted in Him.

She Released all of her fears to Him. She confidently relied on Him and rested in His love. I am so thankful to God for giving us His sustaining peace throughout that most difficult time.

I will forever cherish my mom's example of faithfully holding on to God no matter what she faced.

How did my mom's story impact you?

___

Is there something that you want to take away or remember from her faith-filled story?

_____
_____

If you desire to know and rely more on the love of God, let Him know. If you are not certain of the amazing love God has for you, then pray:

> Lord, I want to be certain of Your love for me. Please show me the love You have for me personally. Help me to walk closely with You! I want to rely on You and rely on Your love. Sustain me with Your peace. Thank You!

We are in a growing relationship with Christ. We are taking new steps forward and trusting Him with more and more of our heart. Every time we Release an issue, concern, wound, or fear to Him, He will fill us with *more* of His *peace*. We will find Him *faithful* as we journey with Him!

We may not be where we want to be,
but THANK GOD we are not where we used to be!

Let's Wrap Up Step Two!

As we review our second step, we have Recognized that *the Lord is near*. As we *Release the barriers that are confining us*, He will fill us with His wonderful peace. His peace will guard our hearts and our minds.

What is the main point that you want to impact your thinking or life? *Talk to God* about it. *Write down* what He is showing you. *Ask Him to help you* proceed forward in power and in faith.

_____
_____

What scriptures do you want to write down and memorize? God's Word is so powerful!

_____
_____

I feel God has revealed

_____

I need to focus on

_____

My relationship with God has been impacted by

_____

The main issues that I want to Release are

_____

The most destructive weight I carry is

_____

Continuous Peace

I Release myself from or forgive myself for

_____

I choose to forgive _____ and I trust God to heal me from the negative impact they have had in my life.

In the process of "Cleaning my Room" I want to focus on

_____
_____

I want to remember _____ without pain.

I want to repent for my actions and/or attitudes

_____

I want to rely on God for

_____

Notes to Remember:

_____
_____
_____

I hope that it is your prayer to be filled with *more* of Him, as you *rely* on His love to keep you in all your ways. He cares for you! As your week progresses, *continue to Release* what God reveals.

As issues arise the following prompts can be helpful.

- Lord, I want to Release ...
- This is how that makes me feel ...
- This is how it has impacted my life ...
- Please help me to ...

Let's Wrap Up Step Two!

Finish this chapter with a prayer of what you desire.

_____
_____
_____

Remember that the Lord is near to you and He will walk with you step by step. After we Release the barriers that confine us, we will be ready to *plant a fruitful harvest of peace*. I am looking forward to the new harvest we will be planting in step three!

1 Corinthians 2:9 NIV

> However, as it is written: "What no eye has seen, what no ear has heard, and what no human mind has conceived"— the things God has prepared for those who love him—

4 Steps to Continuous Peace:

1. RECOGNIZE the Obstacles That Rob
2. RELEASE the Barriers That Confine
3. **REPROGRAM My Heart & Mind with Truth**
4. RESPOND Faithfully for a Continuous Life of Peace

Step 3 Reprogram
REPROGRAM MY HEART AND MIND

Chapter 7
THE POWERFUL TRUTH

BRING YOUR CUP

HAVE YOU EVER BEEN SO FRUSTRATED IN YOUR walk with God that you cry out,

> *"How long . . . O Lord . . . will I be like this!?!"*

That is where I was as a young Christian woman. I grew up in a non-Christian home. Starting a family of my own, I was *desperate* to be changed. But my change felt as slow as molasses.

It was during a time of reading the Bible that I got so frustrated with myself and my progress with God that I stood up and cried out, *"How long, O Lord? How long will I be like this?"* Abruptly I walked to the kitchen sink with my cup of coffee in hand, and I turned on the water. That's when I felt God gently speak to my heart, saying,

> *"Place your cup of coffee under the running water."*

As I placed my cup of coffee under the water, the pure, clean water poured into my cup. I watched the good go in and the dark come out. Although the clear water was pushing out the dark coffee, I really saw no change within the cup. Again I cried out in frustration, *"Nothing is happening!"* That is how I felt in my own life. I was putting the Word of God in, but nothing was happening. *I was not changing.*

I felt God prompt my heart, "*Watch and see.*" So I waited as the good, clean water pushed out the dark water. After what seemed like a very long time, I could see the coffee water was getting lighter and then lighter still, until it ran crystal-clear.

Lovingly God spoke to my heart, "*This is what I am doing in your life. Keep coming to Me daily and bring Me your cup. I will fill it, cleanse it, and I will overflow your cup with good things.*"

Although I was not where I wanted to be in my walk with God, that day I realized God was cleaning the inside of my cup. I knew it would take some time because my cup was full of dark water.

Day by day God wants us to bring Him our cup. He wants to fill us, cleanse us, heal us, and bless us. God's Word is like the crystal-clear water that He uses to transform us. Just like the dark coffee water changed over time, so will our lives be transformed by the renewing of our mind through the Word of God. He is faithful, and He will do it, but we must bring Him our cup to fill and to overflow.

Over the years our cups (our heart and our life) can become full of hurts, pains, regrets, shame, selfishness, sins, and even fears of the past, present, and future. We live with cups full of darkness when God has called us to live pure lives filled with His power and His presence. Bringing our cup to God may make us feel vulnerable and weak, but the truth is when we surrender our cup to Him, He will set us free. As we daily come to be filled by Him, He will free us from all that holds us back from His best.

It has been many years since I first cried out to be changed by God, and I have cried out many times since. As I continually set time aside to be in His Word, wanting to know Him better, He has completely changed my life. I am not the same person I was all those years ago. I have found an intimate Savior who always meets me where I am. He has healed me and has taken those dark places and filled them with good things, such as love, joy, and purpose. His *continual presence* has given me a new *confidence* in my God and a *peace* that has carried me through some of my darkest days. I have given Him my cup and He has given me *a gift beyond measure*!

Are you frustrated with your progress with God?

Are you willing to give Him your cup?

Will you ask Him to fill it and even overflow it?

He calls us to come and bring Him our cup no matter what the condition of the contents. When we Recognize the darkness within our cup, our first response may be, *"I can't come to God like this. I have to clean myself up first!"* This mind-set will become an obstacle that keeps us far from God. Often we try to clean the outside of the cup, attempting to look like a "good Christian." I lived like that for nine long years. That way of living left me empty and without God's peace. God has called us to keep coming to Him as we are. By staying close to God, being in His Word, and trusting Him with our heart, we will be *transformed*!

A surrendered life . . . is a life that He will fill and overflow!

HE REPLACES THE DARKNESS

I was able to share the analogy of *Bring Your Cup* with a group of women. I brought a white coffee cup as an illustration. I wanted to show visibly the darkness that had been in my own heart, so within the cup I wrote in black permanent marker the following words: *pain, sorrow, mistrust, insecurity, lack of love, loneliness, paralyzing fears, sin, shame, regret, let down, fooled again, rude, controlling, jealous, broken promises, crushing losses, and shattered dreams*. The permanent marker was an example, showing the permanence of those pains that can remain unless they are healed.

What I found was that as I tried to remove those written dark words from the cup, it was difficult. Suddenly I had the idea to use a Magic Eraser. When I added water to the Magic Eraser, the permanent marker was removed easily from the cup.

This became a great example of how it can be in our own lives when we work with God, the One who created us and knows us intimately. We can bring Him our messy cups, which represent our wounded lives. His powerful Holy Spirit that is at work within us will overwrite and heal those painful places. He will rework our lives into something beautiful. God's Spirit (Magic Eraser) is in us, and when we add God's powerful Word (water) to our past wounds, He will cleanse us, heal us, and overflow our lives with good things!

We are in good hands when we give Him our cup. He gently holds us, knowing exactly how to remove those darkened places. God diligently does His part, but *we also have a part* to play in our own healing. During my healing, I was going to God, *reading* His Word, and *praying* for Him to help me through my painful mess. *I was choosing to work with God* as He revealed new areas that needed to be cleansed and healed.

My recognition of my need for healing became so frequent that when a negative way of thinking or living was brought to my attention, instead of becoming defensive, I began to ask, "*Okay, Lord, what are You trying to show me, teach me, or remove from within me?*" I then worked with Him so that He could heal me.

> HE REPROGRAMS OUR HEART WITH HIS TRUTHS.

Beautifully, He replaces the darkness within our heart with the light of His truths. He Reprograms our heart with truths such as these: *"You are seen, known, loved, redeemed, whole, cared for, precious, forgiven, complete, righteous, free, justified, led, strong, blessed, protected, child of God, and light to the world."*

HE WILL LEAD US
The Holy Spirit will be our *navigator* as we meet with God through His Word. The light of truth will begin to Reprogram our mind with His love and His perspectives.

- The Word will reveal the truths about our God.
- His Word will illuminate truths that will realign our thinking.
- His Spirit will prompt us how to apply His truth to our daily lives.
- We will mess up!
- We will miss His leading.
- But He will lovingly instruct us in the way we should go. (He is out for our good!)
- As we remain in Him, He will lead us.

WE CHOOSE THE RELATIONSHIP WE WANT WITH OUR LORD!
It is true that we choose the relationship we want with our God. We can Recognize the negatives within us but resist working with God to remove them, or we can come to Him as we are and allow Him full access to cleanse us. Let's be encouraged that God sees us and He beckons us to come closer to Him. He desires that we grow in His love, His ways, and His truth.

From my heart to yours:

> **Search for the heart of God** . . . for He loves you!
> **Always love and trust Him** . . . for He watches over and cares for you!
> **Rely on Him and His wisdom** . . . for He will lead you!
> **Pray and communicate with Him** . . . for He wants an intimate relationship with you!

WE ARE ALL A WORK IN PROGRESS!
We are a masterpiece being fully developed by our Creator. If we will allow Him, He will teach us, develop us, and equip us for every good work. We are transformed when we are in His Word and when His Word is in us. His truth can become the truth that we live by. Don't take my word for it; let's look to the Word of God.

2 Timothy 3:16–17 (NIV)

> All Scripture is God-breathed and is useful for teaching, rebuking, correcting and training in righteousness, so that the servant of God may be thoroughly equipped for every good work.

The absolute best way to Reprogram our mind is by reading our Bible regularly. God uses His Word to train us in what is right. He will use the Word to convict our heart and teach us in the way we should go. We will be equipped thoroughly by knowing and applying the Word of God.

Truth + known in heart + lived out = transformed

It is not enough to just know God's truth. We must believe it in our heart as our truth. When *His truth becomes the truth that we live by*—that is when our lives will be transformed.

HIS WORD WILL ACCOMPLISH WHAT HE DESIRES
Isaiah 55:10–12a (NASB)

> For as the rain and the snow come down from heaven, And do not return there without watering the earth And making it bear and sprout, And furnishing seed to the sower and bread to the eater; So will My word be which goes forth from My mouth; It will not return to Me empty, Without accomplishing what

I desire, And without succeeding *in the matter* for which I sent it. "For you will go out with joy and be led forth with peace;"

Being in the Word is like daily planting truth as a seed or as many seeds. *God's Word accomplishes His will.* It will not return to Him empty without bringing about what He desires. When we choose to water those seeds by doing what the Word says, this will produce a good harvest, full of the fruit of His Spirit. His fruit, which includes His joy and peace, will bless our own lives and become the fruit that we can share with others.

> *The Spirit of God through the Word of God is His #1 way to help us in this life.*

The Word of God is an awesome tool for living! Our minds are renewed daily by the truth found in the Bible. When His truth is known and lived out, it will transform our lives and create the harvest we desire! Every *faithful* step in our journey will produce good fruit. The sum of that fruit will create a harvest that is a gift that keeps on giving! *Our harvest changes as our thinking and actions are transformed.* I know this from personal experience, and I am delighted as I continually watch others' lives be transformed by beginning this journey into God's Word.

HE ILLUMINATES OUR WAY
Psalm 119:105 (NIV)

> Your word is a lamp for my feet and a light on my path.

The light of God's Word guides us in the right direction. The Word shines on our path, revealing God's way. His Word helps us to know Him better so we can walk closely with Him. By knowing the Word, it will make clear life's pitfalls so we can avoid them. The Bible is our instructional manual to help us navigate this life successfully. God's Word does illuminate the very next step that we are to take. It also lights the path just before us so that we can walk steadily and without stumbling.

However, I understand the Word of God can be overwhelming. We are all learning and growing. We may *question where to start* and *what to do*. We may also struggle when we don't understand what we are reading. I have personally wrestled in those same ways. I am going to share the different stages that I went through as I matured in my faith in hopes that I encourage you to jump in wherever you are.

I Struggled Reading the Bible

> Our transformation will occur day by day and throughout the years.

Maturing through the Word is *not* easy. It is not quick. No, our transformation will occur day by day and throughout the years. The summer that I began my life in Christ, I tried to read my Bible, but I could not understand the simplest terms. Reading the Bible felt like I was reading a foreign language. I avoided reading it because I did not understand it. Without spiritual truths, I was constantly *leaning on my own understanding*, which was a fruitless way of living. Thankfully, I became aware of Bible teachers on the radio. I had not known this amazing spiritual guidance existed. Those teachings fed me when *I did not know how* to feed myself. After listening to them, I realized that I was like a dry desert plant that had found a well of living water.

I remember that same summer I was listening to a wonderful Bible teacher while I drove home. I recognized a friend who was walking, and I asked if he wanted a ride. He quickly accepted and jumped into my car. As I pulled out, I was drawn back to the poignant point that the teacher on the radio was making. Moved by what he taught, I tapped the friend on his arm, and with excitement in my voice, I exclaimed, *"Wow! Isn't that amazing?"* He just looked at me and laughed awkwardly. Once again, I pointed out the powerful truth that we were being taught. With that, my friend said, *"At the stop sign, let me out. It would be less painful to walk."* Although it makes me laugh now, at that time, I was astonished that he was not interested at all in these amazing truths.

READING ON MY OWN
When I began to date my husband, I still had very little biblical understanding. After we were married, my husband and I would read a portion of the Bible together. We would discuss it, which made it easier for me to understand since he knew more than I did.

Shortly after that, I wanted to read the Bible on my own, so I started by reading a woman's devotional Bible. This Bible was filled with devotionals that women wrote about portions of the Word. Their teachings filled me, and for a while I read only those devotionals, which helped me begin to grow. But just like a young baby becomes dissatisfied with milk alone, and craves solid food, I became spiritually hungry. I desired to *know* about the scriptures that compelled these women to write such rich material.

As I began to read the portion of scripture that the devotionals were referencing, this caused me to become even more hungry. I found myself desiring to read before and after the scripture to discover the context myself. I was being drawn into the Word. Over the years, my appetite really expanded and I explored study Bibles. Using a study Bible was like having a teacher sitting with me. That was when the Bible began to come alive! I was being taught by the Lord. It became an exciting journey day by day.

HARD TO LIVE OUT
Although I was reading the Word and beginning to understand some of it, I still had a hard time living it out. I found myself knowing some truths but frustrated that *I was barely able to allow those truths to determine my steps.* I grew tired of the one-step-forward-and-two-steps-back lifestyle.

I believe I was frustrated because I was not being consistent in my time with God. I remember one day I got up to seek Him after missing a day in the Word, and nonchalantly I asked God, *"What did I miss yesterday?"* I recall Him reminding me that the manna, "food," that He had for me yesterday was gone. Only the manna, "food," He had for me today was available. My heart was saddened to know that I had missed what He would have taught me yesterday. I had missed it because I had chosen to sleep in. I remember thinking I needed to start valuing my time with God!

I knew my wounded, selfish, and fearful heart was keeping me from God's best. I had to surrender it all. I became determined to stop living the exhausting life run by my fears and selfish desires. I chose to trade it in for *a life that reflected* Jesus as my Lord.

THE DAY THAT CHANGED MY LIFE
When I started pursuing the life of peace that God intended, I was reading my Bible at lunchtime. That worked for a while, but then I was sensing that God wanted me to get up before everyone else to read my Bible. The problem was that I loved my morning sleep too much. Honestly, even though I loved the Lord, I desired to sleep in more than I desired to read the Word. Sadly, my relationship with the Lord reflected my first love, which was sleep.

One day, a young friend I was mentoring came to visit. As we were reading a portion of the Bible, she became amazed with what we read in Nehemiah 9:3 (NASB).

> While they stood in their place, they read from the book of the law of the LORD their God for a fourth of the day; and for *another* fourth they confessed and worshiped the LORD their God.

This rocked her world because she said, "*I am not consistent enough to do anything every day, let alone set aside half of my day in reading the word and then confessing and worshiping God.*" As if a lightbulb illuminated in her mind, she exclaimed, "*I think we need to do this! We need to read our Bible, worship, pray, and confess our sins. We need to set aside time every morning to spend with God!*"

I, being the good teacher, said, "*If you feel God is calling you to this, then you do it.*"

She said, "*No! We both need to be consistent in reading our Bible, confessing our sins, and worshiping God.*" At that point, I became the student, and she was my teacher.

I did not want to commit, but by the grace of God, I reluctantly agreed. I declared, "*Okay, we will set aside one hour every morning to spend with God. We will read the Bible for half an hour, worship for fifteen minutes, then for the next fifteen minutes we will pray and confess our sins.*"

I then decided we should call one another when we finished each morning. She agreed, and we decided to do this for one full month. It was a thirty-day challenge that changed my life!

My 30-Day Challenge

Every morning I woke up early and sought God. As I awakened, I began to talk to Him. I thanked Him for who He is and all that He has done. I quickly prayed for those who came to my mind. I asked for guidance for my day. I then got up and read my Bible. I would write down what I was learning. Next, I put on worship music and I worshiped God. I focused my attention on Him and Him alone. That was a huge turning point in my relationship with the Lord. Prior to this I had never worshiped God at home, although I had Christian music playing all the time.

Worship was such a sweet time in His presence. It always amazed me that while I was focusing on God during my worship, He would speak so gently to my Spirit and make the biggest impact. It was during worship that God would give me answers, illuminate an awesome truth, or reveal my sin.

I remember a time during worship when He pointed out a place within me that needed repentance. My heart was soft due to my worship of Him, and my tears began to fall. Being sorrowful for my sin, I began to confess it to God.

My prayer sounded like this: *"Lord, You have exposed a negative attitude within me. Please forgive me. I am sorry for giving into subtle but harsh thoughts and speaking in an unloving way. I want to be full of You, Your Spirit, and Your love. Help me, Lord. Change my heart. Convict me of wrong thinking and any negative words before I speak them, so that I can turn and choose love. Thank You, Lord, for Your rich forgiveness!"*

Matthew 5:4 (AMP)

> Blessed [forgiven, refreshed by God's grace] are those who mourn [over their sins and repent], for they will be comforted [when the burden of sin is lifted].

If God illuminates something within us, it is to bring to light what needs to be Released. We may be convicted of a negative way of thinking, speaking, or living. Conviction is always used by God to illuminate the negative and have us replace it with His positive way of living.

That month changed my life for good. Continuing to spend time in God's Word, worshiping Him, praying, and confessing my sin did more for me in my walk with God than anything else I had ever done.

My friend and I had disciplined ourselves to get up earlier. It had not been easy, but we wanted to have our time with God uninterrupted by our children or phones. It was well worth the sacrifice of our sleep, because while others were sleeping, we were communing with God. This is when we *learned* to *worship the God we loved*. I have never been the same!

Hebrews 12:11 (NASB)

> All discipline for the moment seems not to be joyful, but sorrowful; yet to those who have been trained by it, afterwards it yields the peaceful fruit of righteousness.

FRUITFUL YEARS

As we know, all discipline does not seem to be joyful, but for those who are *trained* by it, it will yield the peaceful fruit of righteousness. It is hard to prioritize time to know God better, but it has huge dividends. We will reap the peaceful fruit of righteousness when we are right with God, when we are living according to God's standard and not our own.

- Every time we are in God's Word, we are planting good seeds in the soil of our *softening* hearts.
- When we apply God's Word to the way we live, it creates an abundant harvest that will impact our entire lives.

Being in the Word daily changes us. The Word will influence how we perceive and treat others. Then one day we will notice that *we handled a situation differently* than we would have in the past. Our new way of living will bless us and impact others for good. This creates an abundant life. The blessings we will receive from reading the Word daily are cumulative and can become so dense that we will not fully see their impact until we get to heaven.

When Reading

It is easy to get sidetracked while reading the Word. Thoughts of responsibilities can infiltrate our mind and try to hijack our time with God. When this has happened to me, I would write down what needed to be done and then rein in my thoughts and refocus on where I left off reading. Often I realized that the greatest truth was sitting right in front of me, waiting for me to grab hold of it and make it my own. I would have missed it if I had stayed distracted.

> **Each day in the Word is uniquely different.**

Each day in the Word is uniquely different. It is *not* important how much we read but *what we receive.* I read until I receive. When I have an "aha" moment, many times I will write it in my journal or notebook. It is nothing fancy or in-depth. I usually write the scripture that jumped out to me. Amazingly, once I begin to write, it becomes even more alive. I receive more out of the scripture by writing it than I ever did by just reading it. Next I follow up by thinking about what I was shown. I write out how it has impacted my heart. I date it and then talk to God about it.

Sometimes I have a newfound understanding about God, and it creates an amazement. I allow my awe of Him to wash over my heart and mind throughout the day. Other times I am convicted by the Word. I write down what I am convicted of and repent for my sin. Desiring to turn back toward God, I confess my need for more of His presence in my life. I purposely mull over the convicting scripture, reminding my heart of the truth I was shown.

Writing things down also leaves a trail for where we have been. I often go back to reread a prayer that I had written or a scripture that had impacted my heart. Rereading them blesses me again. God's Word is so powerful. It is a gift that keeps on giving.

PRACTICE MARGIN
Before I begin my time in the Word, I usually ask God to:

- lead me to the truth He wants me to receive.
- give me wisdom and understanding to apply what I learn.

I also may start by asking God:

- *"Lord, is there anything You want to say to me today?"*
- I patiently wait and listen. This takes practicing margin.

Margin is creating enough time to sit still and be quiet before Him, knowing that He is God. It helps us to breathe and relax as we focus on Him alone. Margin allows us to think on His truth or to *be still* before our God. I have found that when I pause for a few moments and give Him room, God will respond. He may *speak to my heart*, illuminate a *truth*, give me an *answer*, or provide an *encouragement*. He may even put a *dream* in my Spirit. It is so sweet to sit in His *presence*.

This margin helps us to enjoy the relationship *we get to* have with our Lord. Even in prayer I have learned to wait on God. Instead of *only* praying what I know to pray, I now go to God and ask, *"Lord, is there something You want me to pray about today?"* Then I wait to see if He puts anything specific on my heart. Margin helps us to more thoroughly enjoy the intimate relationship we get to have with our Lord. It still amazes me that we are so blessed to have an open-door communication with Almighty God.

I have been a Christian for more than thirty years. I am so thankful for all the times that God has been patient with me as I found my way with Him. He has taught me to be *willing and obedient* to follow Him. I am grateful for His conviction and encouragement to dive deeper and know Him better. I cannot imagine my life without His transformational power. I would *not* be who I am today if I had not been in my Word daily! If I had *not* sought God over the years, *I would have regret for a life half-lived.*

> **IF I HAD NOT SOUGHT GOD OVER THE YEARS, I WOULD HAVE REGRET FOR A LIFE HALF-LIVED.**

THE DEPTH OF OUR RELATIONSHIP

We choose the depth of the relationship we want with our God. He desires that we experience a close and personal relationship with Him. This step of Reprogramming our heart and mind becomes deeply rooted when we map out *our decision to follow Jesus* and we *choose* to make Him a *priority* in our lives.

When it comes to Reprogramming your heart and mind:
Is there something that stands in the way of Reprogramming with God's Word daily? (Desiring sleep, lack of focus or lack of desire, media, others, or other priorities?)

_____

How important is reading your Bible? I am *not* asking how important it *should* be, but how important *is it to you*? Be honest with yourself, 1–10 _____ If it is not important, it will not be a priority. It helps to Recognize the *battle is in our heart* with a *lack of desire*.

Consider your routine. Remember I was all over the board during my journey. Be honest. Your answers will reveal your starting point.

Why do you want to know God better through His Word?
_____

Do you have a daily routine? Do you hit and miss? Are you not reading at all?
_____

What are some of the ways you seek God?
_____

How often do you write down any insight from your time with God or journal what you are learning?

Never_____ Sometimes_____ Always _____

Describe what your time with God looked like at its best.
_____
_____

Will your mind be renewed by what you are doing right now?
_____

What would you like to change?
_____

> Let's keep fixing our eyes on Jesus the **Author** and **Finisher** of our faith…
> (Hebrews 12:2a NASB)

LET'S COME UP HIGHER!
I am going to present a challenge that has the potential of Reprogramming your heart and mind. It can transform your life. *This can be your turning point*, your chance to come up higher with your loving God and be filled with His *peace*!

As I have shared the 30-Day Challenge with my groups, it has provided *the biggest transformation* in their lives. Please consider taking this challenge. God desires to meet with you! Remember how the cup was changed over time by the clean water. So can our lives be changed by the Word of God. Decide to meet with God. Get to know Him better. He will overflow your life with good things!

YOUR 30-DAY CHALLENGE
Underline what your next step will be.

- Read your Word consistently.
- Write down the scripture that impacts you the most.
- Write any insight that you receive or a prayer to Reprogram your mind.
- Worship the Lord.
- Pray and confess your sins.
- Be still. Listen for God's small, still voice.
- Apply what you are learning from God's Word into your everyday life.
- Tell a friend. Ask to be kept accountable. Encourage each other to grow.

When I took my 30-Day Challenge, it was the beginning of blessing. I never went back to hit and miss reading. I daily desired to get to know my Lord better. I would not be *who* I am or *where* I am without the time that I have *dedicated to grow in the Word*!

CHART YOUR COURSE
Many times, we need to reroute our course. I *prayerfully* rethink and tweak my course usually three times a year; January as the new year begins, June as summer starts, September when school resumes. Then I *willingly* and obediently follow my course for that short season.

Visualize and write what your time in God's Word would look like. Where would you sit? What would you need: a Bible, devotional, notebook, pens, highlighters, a blanket, a basket or container to keep it all together? (Coffee/tea/water?)

_____

_____

Take a minute and personalize your time with God.

Devise a plan: set your daily goal—*not a law* that you are under but *a goal that you desire!*

- When to read? Morning before your day begins, lunchtime, or at night?
- Where to read? Select a place in your home, deck, bus, etc. (a place with few distractions).
- What to read? Choose a book in the Bible, a Bible study, or a devotional.
- What journal or notebook will you use to capture your thoughts?
- When will you start? Mark down the date and time.
- What is your goal? Determine the amount of time allotted daily.
- How many days a week? Will this be 5 days a week or all 7 days?
- Who will be your accountability person *during* your thirty-day challenge? It is helpful to send a simple daily message to a friend as a way of celebrating your time with God.

We must discipline ourselves to do it. Make the Word yours! Personalize it. *God is teaching you*. He loves you! He will use the Word to instruct you and correct you because He desires your best! He will lead you in the way you should go. You will be *transformed* by meeting with Him regularly.

Let's gain ground in taking our peace back today by:

- Daily *remaining* in Him.
- Continually *planting* God's good seeds of truth by absorbing the Word.
- *Believing* His truths in our heart, which will be like pouring water on those seeds.
- *Living* out those truths, which will be like the sun (Son) shining down and making those righteous plants grow.

OUR SHARP SWORD

Bible truths are a huge factor in the *life of peace* that God intended! We will use His *truths as tools* that He has provided for us. By them we can overcome every lie that the enemy throws our way. In Ephesians 6 Paul explains that we have been given *the sword of the Spirit, which is the word of God*. This is our *only* offensive weapon. When the enemy wants to rob us of our peace, we need to utilize our sharp sword, which is the Word of God, to cut away the lies and be protected with the truth. We will keep our peace when we know who our God is and who we are in Him. His truths are powerful. *The more we know, believe, and apply His truths, the sharper our spiritual sword will become.*

In the next chapter, we will begin to overwrite the lies of the enemy with the truths of God!

Chapter 8
OVERWRITE THE LIES

HAVE YOU EVER HIDDEN BEHIND AN INVISIBLE WALL of self-protection? Our painful past can whisper *lies* into our current situations. It may murmur the lie that "*You are not safe,* or *others are not out for your good.*" Have those statements echoed through your heart and mind? These mistrusting thoughts make us feel alone and scared. They cause us to shut down or self-protect. God faithfully helps us to unravel the roots that have entangled us. We can trust that He will make clear what needs to be dealt with and removed.

> **OUR PAINFUL PAST CAN WHISPER LIES INTO OUR CURRENT SITUATIONS.**

While I was living a life full of peace, God revealed that I had a hidden but strong *weed of self-protection*. It had become a default mechanism, causing me to forfeit my peace whenever I felt that I could not trust others. If something were said during a conversation that raised a suspicion, it could cause me to pull back in caution. I would begin to build a wall of mistrust as I attempted to protect myself once again.

I sought God to find out *why* I was acting this way. I knew God wanted me to be free. He was challenging me to fully trust Him with my heart *as* I was interacting with others. But I still struggled in this area of trust. I was perplexed as to *why I was struggling to trust others.* I pleaded with God to help me understand what stood in my way. What was it that made me want to run behind an imaginary wall of self-protection instead of running to Him and feeling safe?

In the process of Reprogramming my mind, I have found that God will use anything to set one of His kids free. Amazingly, He used one line from a movie as *the key that would begin to unlock the mystery* that was keeping me stuck in self-protection. I was in a movie theater when the actor passionately spoke these words: *"You do not need to be afraid of the things you were afraid of when you were five!"*

As those words impacted my spirit, I rested back in my seat. It felt like a big seed was planted in the middle of my chest. I sensed God prompt these words: *"It is okay. I will explain what it means after the movie ends."*

When the movie concluded, I walked into the bathroom. As I closed the door, I clearly sensed God sharing these words boldly yet lovingly: *"You don't have to be afraid like when you were five and had no dad."* Surprised by those words, again they echoed, *"You do not have to be afraid like when you had no dad."* Immediately they provoked an emotional downpour.

I knew God was aware that I had a dad, but He was making it clear He also knew that I still carried a weight from not having a caring father. Over the years I had worked with God to Release the pain that my dad had caused. I had no idea of the deep emotion that was still lingering within me. I tried to pull myself together so that I could rejoin my husband. As I walked out of the restroom, he could tell that I had been crying, but he had no idea of the magnitude of what was happening.

Walking to the car, I told him what had occurred. As we began to drive, he started to talk about everyday issues. I stopped him and passionately exclaimed, *"You don't understand. I believe God is telling me that I don't have to be afraid like I was afraid when I had no dad."* The car became suddenly silent as we both pondered what those words meant.

God Revealed the Root

We proceeded up a winding hill and continued down the other side. That is when I felt God clearly pour these words into my heart: *"You don't have to be afraid like you were when your parents did not use wisdom."* I gasped. God put words to something I could never define.

He continued compassionately to clarify, and I repeated His words to my husband: *"I feel God just told me that I don't have to be afraid, like when those in charge of me did not use wisdom."* I began to sob.

Remarkably, God revealed two parts of the *root* of my self-protection. First, I did not have to be afraid like when I had no dad. The second part of the root was that I didn't have to be afraid like I had been as a child, when my parents made decisions without wisdom. God was beginning to unravel the root that was entangling me. The mystery that God unlocked exposed the fear I had as a child when my parents made unwise choices for me. Unknowingly, this fear continued throughout my life and hindered my ability to trust others.

Being Led without Wisdom

Even as a young child I knew the things that my parents were doing were not wise. One such time was when I was five. I remember my dad announced that he was running out for a minute and that He wanted to take me along. That puzzled my mom because my dad never took me anywhere. She decided to let me go. I asked where we were going, and he said to see a friend.

We arrived at a house, and my dad told me to get out of the car. As I got out, I noticed a man on the balcony. When he saw that my dad had not come alone, he became furious! The big man above us began to yell at my dad about something he owed him. My dad told him he would pay him in time. The more my dad spoke, the more enraged the man became. Without warning, the man on the balcony pulled out a gun and pointed it toward my dad. My five-year-old eyes had never seen a gun and had never seen a gun pointed at someone, let alone at my dad. I was shocked and gasped as my mind struggled to comprehend what was about to happen. My dad laughed nervously and said, *"You won't shoot me in front of my daughter."*

The man was conflicted. He said, *"Don't tell me what I won't do!"*

They continued to argue, and soon we were back in the car. I remember I spoke first. I said, *"Dad, that man had a gun and he wanted to shoot you!"*

He smugly blew it off, saying, *"No, he wasn't going to touch me."* Then he proceeded to tell me not to tell my mom anything that had happened. It was decades later when I realized that my dad had taken me with him that day so that he would not get shot.

How reckless! He did not care about me. He did not consider what I was going to see or hear, or what could have happened. He only cared about buying himself a little more time. That was one of those times when it was obvious my dad was not a loving father and did not make wise decisions concerning me.

My dad also frequently made the unwise choice to drive with us after he was drinking. I was fearful because I knew it was wrong and that we could get hurt or we could hurt others. That was a terrible way of living as I second-guessed my parents' decisions. Another example was when my single mom wanted to move to another state. I could tell it was an emotional decision and one that was not well-thought-out. I knew it was not a good idea.

I tried to convince her not to move. I pleaded with her to stay, but she would not listen.

She summoned family and friends to help us pack up our home. We loaded up the moving truck with everything that we owned, and our belongings all proceeded to the other state. That night we stayed at my mom's friend's house. My mom and her friends went out to celebrate one last time. She met a guy at the bar, and in the morning, I found out that *now* she wanted to stay in our home state but we had nowhere to live.

Our whole family was broken up. I had to live with my mom's friend until we found another home to rent. It was a very hard summer. I felt abandoned, afraid, uncomfortable, forgotten, ashamed, numb, empty, and unheard. For those many months, I hardly saw my mom since we lived in two different places and she worked. Though her friend showed me much love, it was still a very hard and lonely season.

I HAVE GIVEN YOU WISDOM
That night in the car, God continued to tell me, *"You do not have to fear those in authority over you who did not use wisdom."* These impactful statements amazed me that God knew how fearful it was being led by those who did not have wisdom. He tapped into a sorrowful well that was unknowingly deep within me.

He followed up with His truth, and it became the answer that would begin to turn the key to my freedom. *"Because I have put My Spirit in you! My Spirit is wisdom."* My heart knew He gave me His answer. God continued to assure me, *"You have My Spirit to lead you! You do not have to be led by those who do not have wisdom, because I am in you and I will lead you by My Spirit. My wisdom is in you!"* I was sobbing loudly as I relayed to my husband all that God was communicating to my heart.

OUR LOVING HEAVENLY FATHER
Stopping at a red light, my tears continued to fall. We sat quietly as we tried to absorb all that the Lord was teaching us. It was then that God gave me a vision. It was as if He stood in front of me much bigger than life. I could sense Him throw open His arms wide. With outstretched arms, He spoke these powerful words to my heart:

> *"I am the King! You are My kid. You are the King's kid. I love My kids! I am the King, and everything is at My disposal. I will protect My children."* He continued, *"As My daughter, come to Me. I am the King, and everything is at My hand. Nothing is too difficult for Me."*

Those powerful words opened the door to my freedom. In that moment I knew God was assuring me that He was my heavenly Father and He would tenderly and lovingly care for me. I also knew this truth was *not* just for me. His *heart of compassion* is for each of His children. It is His deep desire to tenderly care for His kids. He loves us. He has everything that is needed to care for us.

As my husband and I continued to drive home, one thought after another reverberated within me. I knew that my God was telling me that I did not need to be afraid because He is my loving Father. He is the King, and the King loves and cares for His children. I did not have to be afraid because I would be led by His wisdom that lives within me. All the way home I sobbed as His words continued to impact my heart and mind.

As these truths captivated my heart, my prayer became, *"Please, Lord, allow these truths to overwrite the lie that says, 'I have to protect myself because no one is out for my good.' The truth is that You are out for my good and You always will be. I entrust my heart to You."*

Psalm 5:2 (NIV)

> Hear my cry for help, my King and my God, for to you I pray.

James 1:5 (NIV)

> If any of you lacks wisdom, you should ask God, who gives generously to all without finding fault, and it will be given to you.

This encounter was amazing. But I did have to ponder those truths, mull them over, and believe them until they became true for me. So often we do not *Recognize* how many things have shaped the way we think. *Reprogramming* our mind can *overwrite* the negative events that have happened, along with the lies that we have believed and the lies we continue to believe. Reprogramming our mind takes those negative areas and replaces them with God's amazing truth.

Can you identify with an invisible wall of self-protection?

_____

Do you find it hard to trust others? If so, do you know why?

_____

Have you embraced the truth that *you are* the King's kid? If so, in what ways?

_____

_____

How would you best describe yourself regarding coming to the Father for help? Are you: *apprehensive, half-hearted, unwilling, uninterested, eager, confident, unashamed,* or *other*?

_____

_____

THE PROCESS OF REPROGRAMMING

I began to Reprogram my mind by trusting God with every step forward that I took. For example, *when* I would become afraid, instead of running behind the invisible wall of mistrust and self-protection, I would *Recognize* my fear and *Release* my uncertainty and concerns into God's loving arms. I would *Reprogram* my mind with the truth that *I can trust God with my heart.*

> **"I TRUST YOU WITH MY HEART AND I TRUST YOU TO LEAD ME BY WISDOM."**

As I entrusted my heart to Him, *I was honest.* I told Him that I wanted to self-protect, shut down, and run. I confessed that I did not want to get hurt but that I wanted to trust Him to keep me. I knew that my peace would be restored when I trusted God with my whole heart. I had to believe that His wisdom would lead me in the way that I should go. That was my answer, *"I trust You with my heart and I trust You to lead me by wisdom."* It was difficult at times, but this was where my freedom was found.

Growth was evident that my mind was being Reprogrammed when:

- I got to the point that I trusted God to be faithful *even if I did get hurt.*
- I knew that He would heal me if needed, and He would be *just* in every circumstance.
- I knew He would give me *wisdom* in life's situations.
- I knew He would *never leave me* because He was my faithful Father.

When I am faced with difficulties in this life, I continue to come back to the foundational truth that *God is faithful and I can trust Him.* This has not been a one-time decision to trust Him but *a way of life.*

I would like you to pause and reflect for a moment. Do you believe that God is faithful and that you can trust Him? If not, why not? _____

When we do not trust God fully with our heart, we can get in the "habit" of building walls of self-protection. By faith, let's take down those walls. Let's start by looking at the prior bullet points. Is there a point that stood out to you? Take a moment and talk to God about where you are or where you want to be. *Then, if needed, pray a prayer like this:*

> Lord, this is what I notice in my own life, _____. Help me to Release this to You. Reprogram my mind with the truth that *You are faithful*. Strengthen my faith to trust You with my heart and life. Remove what needs to be removed and heal what needs to be healed. Allow Your wisdom to illuminate the way through life's circumstances. I am so thankful that *You will never leave me*. Lord, help me to trust You as a way of life! In Jesus' name. Amen.

THE LIE OF NOT ENOUGH
Let's address another huge *obstacle* that many of us have struggled with at one time or another. In step one, we Recognized the negative areas where we have been bullied or where we are vulnerable to specific lies. The area of *not enough* is widely used as a stumbling block.

I find that many people are bullied with the world's way of thinking. They believe that they are *not enough* or they believe the lie that they are *not able*. *Underline* any of the following lies that you have accepted as true.

We may feel like . . . I am *not* enough, good enough, pretty enough, smart enough, wealthy enough, liked enough, loved enough, worthy enough, kind enough, or thin enough.

We get into the habit of thinking, *I am not a good enough . . . spouse, parent, friend, child, Christian, neighbor, leader, worker, or student.* Isn't that true?

We can apply the "*not* enough" to our home. It is not clean enough, big enough, or nice enough.

Striving to fulfill all the "enoughs" in our lives will restrain us from all that God has for us. These lies leave us feeling empty and without His peace. When we say we are not enough, what are we comparing ourselves to? What standard are we holding for ourselves? Is it a standard of perfection?

Do you find yourself striving to be perfect instead of just doing your best in the areas that God has called you to?

When we set *too high a standard* for ourselves and we don't measure up, *it causes us to feel unloved or not valued.* We go through the motions of life numb. We are not fully enjoying our lives because every time we turn around, we are reminded of an area where we are not "enough."

I remember a friend sharing, that when she returns from work, and if she spends more time with her kids and she sees dishes in the sink, she immediately feels, *I am not able to keep my house clean enough.* If she keeps the house super-clean, she feels guilty thinking, *I am not a good* enough *mom.*

This type of thinking will always keep us feeling condemned. Yes, there is a balance, and my friend does a great job. Anyone who knows her knows she excels in all those areas. Still *this negative mind-set is like a weed that tries to choke out the life from the good that she does accomplish.* Does that sound familiar?

I have another friend who was in college and had admitted that even though she was getting great grades, the thought prevailed that she was not smart enough. She had almost completed a very strenuous program and she continued to feel overwhelmed with the thoughts that, *I am not able; I am not smart enough!*

It is almost certain that as we go forward in the way God is leading us, we tend to second-guess our abilities. My best answer that I tell myself and I told my friend is, *"If God calls you to it, He will get you through it!"* As a side note, my friend has now graduated and is working in her field.

"IF GOD CALLS YOU TO IT, HE WILL GET YOU THROUGH IT!"

I know many who feel that they are not a *good enough* friend, which is another pitfall of desiring to be *perfectly liked*. This is the pit of people-pleasing. We can be so stuck in a rut of pleasing others that *we can lose who we really are.* We can want to please our family, friends, and others to such a degree that giving in to their desires is more important than staying true to who we are.

People-pleasing is an empty way of living. It causes us to feel we cannot do *enough* for others. This way of living can hinder us from obeying God because we are so focused on others that we are not fulfilling what He has called us to do.

Are there areas of your life where you feel as if you are not enough? If so, in which areas?

_____

Have you bought into the standard that you need to *do it all* and *do it all perfectly?* _____

Do you feel the need to be perfect, perfectly liked, or perfectly perceived? If so, in what area(s), and how has it affected your life?

_____
_____

Do you Recognize that you are a people-pleaser? Does it hinder you from fulfilling what God has called you to do? If so, in what ways?

_____

_____

WE ARE NOT ABLE
In all honesty we are *not* enough. We are not able to do it all. Today is the day we are going to Reprogram our minds!

When the bully shouts: "*You are not enough! You need to do more! You are not able!*"

Our answer is: "*I am not able, I am enabled!*"

The truth is: We must embrace not being enough. This is when we become *dependent* on the One who is enough!

- I am not enough … but He is enough. In my own strength I cannot do enough. Although, *I can do all things through Him who strengthens me.*

  Philippians 4:13 (AMP) I can do all things [which He has called me to do] through Him who strengthens *and* empowers me [to fulfill His purpose—I am self-sufficient in Christ's sufficiency; I am ready for anything and equal to anything through Him who infuses me with inner strength and confident peace.]

- I am not able! *I have been enabled* by the spirit of God that lives in me!

  2 Peter 1:3–4 (NIV) His divine power has given us everything we need for a godly life through our knowledge of him who called us by his own glory and goodness. Through these he has given us his

very great and precious promises, so that through them you may participate in the divine nature, having escaped the corruption in the world caused by evil desires.

Our lives will bring God glory when we are *not* striving to be enough and *we rest* in the fact that *Jesus is enough. His Spirit is enough* to fill, lead, and teach us the way we should go! *His blood is enough* to cover all our sins. Covered by Jesus is enough!

Knowing *Jesus is enough* must be our focus. He will see us through. Fears will shout that bad things can happen. Should we focus on the hardship that may come? No. We are to focus on our God, who created heaven and earth and knows us by name. That same *God is with us, no matter what comes.* We are never alone. He is with us and He is enough!

2 Thessalonians 3:16 (AMP)

> Now may the Lord of peace Himself grant you His peace at all times *and* in every way [that peace and spiritual well-being that comes to those who walk with Him, regardless of life's circumstances]. The Lord be with you all.

When our heart is focused on His goodness and His sufficiency in every situation, then faith is close and fear is far. We choose what we will focus on. When we choose to walk with Him, He will fill us with His peace, and by our faith we will be anchored to Him.

REPROGRAMMING EXPOSES WRONG THINKING

In this process, I Recognized that although I was beginning to know these amazing truths, I was still full of negative self-talk. Unfortunately, many of us have a horrible way of speaking *to ourselves* or *about ourselves. S*ometimes we are repeating what we have heard spoken about us. Other times we have simply adopted a negative viewpoint about ourselves. Either way it is destructive.

I have found that even though I was in the Word, and walking with God, I would still catch myself in negative self-talk. I pointed out my own flaws, inconsistencies, and past and present failures. My thinking could be harsh and critical. I knew I had to rethink how I was thinking. I began to pray this prayer:

"Lord, this is what I say about myself... but what do You say?"

I then waited for Him to speak. The first time I asked God this question, I recall being moved by His answer, which was, *"You are the apple of my eye."* That was such a sweet moment. That statement gave me a visual of looking into God's eye and seeing my reflection there. I could feel His grace covering me. It made me realize that He was tenderly and lovingly thinking about me. That was in stark contrast to the way I was feeling about myself. Can you see yourself as the apple of God's eye?

Deuteronomy 32:10–11 (NIV)

> In a desert land he found him, in a barren and howling waste. He shielded him and cared for him; he guarded him as the apple of his eye, like an eagle that stirs up its nest and hovers over its young, that spreads its wings to catch them and carries them aloft.

When we are feeling bad about ourselves, God's Word allows us to see how He lovingly cares for us! He rescues us, shields us, cares for our needs, and guards us as the apple of His eye. He teaches us to fly and catches us when we fall. He faithfully carries us when we need it.

Another time when I was afraid and I wanted to trust God, but I was struggling to trust Him, I said,

> "Lord, this is how I feel . . . but what do You say?"

He reassured me, "*I am for you. Who can be against you?*" Another time He answered me, "*I love you. I will never leave you!*" Each time, I cried out to Him, I waited for His still, small voice. His words comforted me and strengthened my heart. I knew God was reminding me of the scriptural truth that I was learning yet struggling to fully believe.

Hebrews 13:5b–6 (AMP)

> For He has said, "I WILL NEVER [under any circumstances] DESERT YOU [nor give you up nor leave you without support, nor will I in any degree leave you helpless], NOR WILL I FORSAKE *or* LET YOU DOWN *or* RELAX MY HOLD ON YOU [assuredly not]!" So we take comfort *and* are encouraged *and* confidently say, "THE LORD IS MY HELPER [in time of need], I WILL NOT BE AFRAID. WHAT WILL MAN DO TO ME?"

Through the Bible He will share His heart with you! He desires you to be comforted and encouraged. The Lord is your Helper; you can confidently trust in Him. He lovingly yet strongly declares in Hebrews that He will *never* under any circumstances desert you, nor leave you without support. He will not relax His hold on you. He will not let you down. Wow! Are you reassured by the love and support that He exerts toward you? I was encouraged then and I still am now.

We Can Hear His Voice
Asking God to weigh in on my faulty thinking truly helped me to Reprogram my mind and heart.

John 10:27 (NASB)

> My sheep hear My voice, and I know them, and they follow Me.

He is our shepherd, and as His sheep, we can hear His voice! We are *known* by God! Not only are we known by God, *we are loved as we are, where we are*! He knows our faulty thinking. We can stop and listen for His voice amid the chaos. We can then follow Him in the way He wants us to go!

Are you hard on yourself? Do you point out your own flaws? Are you critical? If so, in what ways?

___

Are you willing to ask God to weigh in on your faulty thinking?

Will you go to God and ask Him, "*Lord, this is how I am feeling, but what do You say?*" Will you share your true feelings and wait for His still, small voice?

Take comfort and be encouraged that God is with you. He will never leave you or forsake you. Believe the best of who you are *in* Christ. When you are not sure of who you are, continue to seek God through His Word. God always speaks to us through His Word. God's Word will prompt our heart or illuminate a truth that He is revealing to us. Knowing His Word is knowing His heart.

Psalm 19:7–8 (NIV)

> The law of the LORD is perfect, refreshing the soul. The statutes of the LORD are trustworthy, making wise the simple. The precepts of the LORD are right, giving joy to the heart. The commands of the LORD are radiant, giving light to the eyes.

The Lord will lead us to build on the solid ground of truth, precept upon precept. His Word is trustworthy. When we believe His truth, it brings light to our eyes, refreshes our soul, makes us wise, and replaces our faulty thinking. We will be restored, strengthened, edified, and transformed by the renewing of our mind. Peace and joy will overflow our heart.

IDENTIFY YOUR OBSTACLES
Identifying our obstacles and Recognizing the lies that we believe are key in learning to Reprogram our heart and mind. In the following sections, we will resume where we left off in step one. Do you recall the areas that you *Recognized in chapter three* as being the most susceptible to the enemy's lies? *Underline* the areas where you suspect you are the most vulnerable.

1. Not Able/Not Enough
2. Fear/Anxiety
3. Doubt
4. Rejection
5. Sin/Shame
6. Sadness/Grief
7. A Weak Relationship with God

I have provided a fuller description of the seven main areas, followed by a few of the lies associated with each obstacle.

Read through each obstacle and their lies. You will notice that the lies can be written as "You" as an accusation or as an "I" like a self-condemnation. They can be interchanged to make them more accurate for you.

Let's identify our obstacles. *Underline* the statements that are true for you.

1. Not Able/Not Enough

When we feel we are not able or not enough, it can lead to insecurity, lack of confidence, timidity, or fear of stepping out to try something new. This negative mind-set is like a weed that steals life from the *good* that we have accomplished. It tries to convince us that what we have done was *not* enough. We may battle with the thoughts that we are not able to succeed or finish what we have set out to do. We can second-guess our value. Our standard may be perfection, which will promote our falling short continually.

LIES: You are not able to do that! You will fail! You are a failure. Everyone is better than you. You will never change. Stop trying; you will only make it worse. I am not able. My best is never enough!
Added Lie: _____

2. Fear/Anxiety

Fear and anxiety can negatively affect our mind and body. They can impact our ability to move forward by making us indecisive, avoid situations, or feel paralyzed. We may even feel like "running" from our problems. Fear can prompt anger to rise quickly. We can panic and try to control what we perceive as being out of control. We can vividly imagine terrible things and quickly presume that they are going to happen. Fears do not have to be rational to make an impact. Anxiety increases when we feed fear. It can feel like a calamity about to overtake us.

LIES: Something bad is going to happen to you or to someone you love. What if this or that happens? I cannot trust anyone, including God. Nothing or no one is safe. I will never get rid of these fears. I will mess things up and I will end up alone. Anxiety is my new normal.
Added Lie: _____

3. Doubt

Doubt makes us suspicious of others' motives. We can feel uncertain, doubting if life will work out well. Doubt will try to tarnish any area of our lives by having us question everything. Doubt is like a wall that does not allow the good to enter. We doubt the goodness of others. We doubt their kind words. We doubt our value, worth, and abilities. We may even doubt God's love, power, and heart toward us. Doubt prevents anything from being perceived as solid, unchanging, or secure. Jealousy and comparison arise when we doubt our own worth.

LIES: You cannot put your hope in that; you will be disappointed. Does God really love me? Will this really work out? Will my life amount to anything good? I can't count on anyone. I know I will be let down in this relationship. Things will not work out. Why would anyone help me? What is their motive for being nice? Am I *really* loved?
Added Lie: _____

4. Rejection

Rejection can make us feel left out, empty, or jealous. Abandonment can twist how we see ourselves. Our self-worth can be greatly affected by rejection, causing us to become easily wounded. We compare our perceived flaws against others' strengths. We can feel as if we must prove ourselves. Rejection can cause us to look for the next negative incident, negative word spoken, or disappointment to occur, suspecting that pain looms around every corner. We can have high expectations of ourselves and others. We may try to manipulate a standard that will keep us from getting wounded. We can keep others out as a form of self-protection. We expect others to let us down. We may feel insignificant, unimportant, unconnected, or irrelevant, which produces loneliness.

LIES: You are different; you don't fit in. No one really wants to be in a relationship with you. No one will help you. You are not seen. You are not known. You cannot trust others. You are alone. You must protect yourself. No one wants to hear what you have to say. I will never have long-term relationships. They will leave me too. I am unlovable. I will never feel whole.
Added Lie: _____

5. Sin/Shame
Sin and shame can cause us to feel guilty and unworthy. We tend to speak more harshly to ourselves or about ourselves than we would to another person. Our own sin and shame wreck relationships. We may be hard on others, pointing out their flaws to make ourselves feel better. Past wounds and/or unhealed personal sin can be continually carried as a heavy weight. Shame can feel like a dark cloak that we wear. It covers our mind and heart, which hinders us from coming to or receiving from God. The cloak of shame desires to keep hidden what is in darkness. When we have not dealt with our sin and shame, it can perpetuate our negative behaviors.

LIES: If others knew the truth about you, they would have nothing to do with you. I am not worthy to be a part of anything good. No one can know the real me. I am too sinful. God cannot forgive *me*! I will have to pay or suffer for my past sins. I don't like who I am and no one else will like me either. I will never get it "together." I am hopeless, and my life is irredeemable. I am unworthy of love.
Added Lie: _____

6. Sadness/Grief
Sadness and grief can be caused by losses of many kinds, such as the loss of our childhood, loved ones, dreams, relationships, positions, possessions, and health. Sadness and grief can also be caused by unfairness, tragedy, or a heavy burden. Long-term illness, long-term negative circumstances, long-term issues, or disappointments can weigh us down triggering us to become

bitter or angry. We may grieve the loss of how we thought our life would be. Our losses can make us susceptible to self-pity, isolation, and loneliness. Our heart can ache or become jealous, desirous, and envious when we see others with what we have lost. It can feel as if we are wearing gray-colored glasses causing us to long for sunny days as we deeply desire "normalcy."

LIES: You will have to suffer alone. No one wants to see you cry. They do not want to hear about your pain again. God won't help *me.* God does not care if I am hurting. No one sees my pain. I may never feel better. My circumstances will never change. Loss is right around the corner. Loss *always* comes quickly and without warning. No one is safe. Misery and loneliness will be my lifelong companions. The weight of my poor choices will never lift. I have to pretend to be happy.
Added Lie: _____

7. A Weak Relationship with God
When a negative issue arises, we run to a person for help, not to God. He is the last one we seek for counsel. Trusting in God is hard for us to do. When something good happens, we get excited and tell others, but we don't think to praise God. We don't want to stop what we are doing to fully surrender our heart and life to Him. We may *want* to be closer to God, *but* we don't change our lives to make Him a priority. Life is too full to read the Bible. If we pray, we pray on the run. We dismiss the fact that we can count on God for His help, love, comfort, and wisdom.

LIES: You can figure it out. You do not need a relationship with God. You are a good person. Just keep *trying* to do good things. He is *not* a good Father, or you would not be hurting. Your family or friends are the only ones you can count on. You don't *need* God. You are smart; you can handle your own life. At least I go to church on Sunday. That is enough time for God right now. I cannot really trust God. If I say *yes* to Him, He may ask me to do more than I am willing or able.

Added Lie: _____

Can you add additional insights into any of those areas?

_____
_____

Which is the *most* prevalent area you want to overwrite *first*?

_____

Number the remaining areas that you want to deal with *next*.

_____

It may feel overwhelming to Recognize the obstacles and lies that have become barriers to God's peace. In this next section, we will begin to overwrite them! God's plan is to help us *rebuild* what has been ruined and to *restore* the places long devastated. He will even help us to *renew* the places that have been devastated for generations.

Isaiah 61: 4 (NIV)

> They will rebuild the ancient ruins and restore the places long devastated; they will renew the ruined cities that have been devastated for generations.

OVERWRITE YOUR LIES
Determine *the main obstacle* you want to address *first*.

1. Read through the "Truth is" section that applies to you.
2. Mark the scriptural truths that you will use *to overwrite your lies*.
3. You can continue through the rest of your obstacles, but *first focus on your main area*.

1. Not Able/Not Enough

Truth is: *I am not able, but God is able. He is in me and He has enabled me. He will instruct me and teach me in the way I should go. He will help me to do all that I am called to do. God will give me strength when I am weary. When I am weak, He will increase my power. My hope is in the Lord. He will renew my strength to walk, run, and even soar like the eagles. He counsels me with His loving eye upon me. By His grace I am built up and set apart for His purposes.*

1. Psalm 32:8 (NIV) I will instruct you and teach you in the way you should go; I will counsel you with my loving eye on you.
2. Isaiah 40:28-31 (NIV) Do you not know? Have you not heard? The LORD is the everlasting God, the Creator of the ends of the earth. He will not grow tired or weary, and his understanding no one can fathom. He gives strength to the weary and increases the power of the weak. Even youths grow tired and weary, and young men stumble and fall; but those who hope in the LORD will renew their strength. They will soar on wings like eagles; they will run and not grow weary, they will walk and not be faint.
3. Philippians 4:13 (NASB) I can do all things through Him who strengthens me.
4. Acts 20:32 (AMP) And now I commend you to God [placing you in His protective, loving care] and [I commend you] to the word of His grace [the counsel and promises of His unmerited favor]. His grace is able to build you up and to give you the [rightful] inheritance among all those who are sanctified [that is, among those who are set apart for God's purpose—all believers].

If this area of Not Able/Not Enough pertains to you, reflect on your chosen scripture and write out a prayer to God:

_____

_____

2. Fear/Anxiety

Truth is: *When I seek the Lord, He will answer me. He will deliver me from all my fears. He is with me and He will save me out of all my troubles. I will not fear because it is God who helps me. He is loving and He will lovingly care for me. God is in control. I will not anxiously look around, because I know that Almighty God will help me and strengthen me! He will uphold me with His right hand. I will trust in Him. The Lord has never forsaken those who seek Him.*

1. Psalm 34:4–8 (NIV) I sought the LORD, and he answered me; he delivered me from all my fears. Those who look to him are radiant: their faces are never covered with shame. This poor man called, and the LORD heard him; he saved him out of all his troubles. The angel of the LORD encamps around those who fear him, and he delivers them. Taste and see that the LORD is good; blessed is the one who takes refuge in him.
2. Isaiah 41:10 (NASB) Do not fear, for I am with you; Do not anxiously look about you, for I will strengthen you, surely I will help you, Surely I will uphold you with My righteous right hand.
3. Isaiah 41:13 (NASB) For I am the LORD your God, who upholds your right hand, Who says to you, 'Do not fear, I will help you.'
4. Psalm 9:10 (NIV) Those who know your name trust in you, for you, LORD, have never forsaken those who seek you.

If this area of Fear/Anxiety pertains to you, reflect on your chosen scripture and write out a prayer to God:

_____
_____

3. Doubt

Truth is: *I can remain in God's infinite love. I will not allow doubt to cause me to question His love for me. The Lord has compassion on me. He will never forsake me, and He will meet my needs. His lovingkindness will not be removed from me. His covenant of peace will not be shaken. The God of hope will fill me with all joy and peace as I trust in Him. By the power of His Spirit that is in me, I will overflow with His hope.*

1. John 15:9 (AMP) I have loved you just as the Father has loved Me; remain in My love [and do not doubt My love for you].
2. Romans 15:13 (NIV) May the God of hope fill you with all joy and peace as you trust in Him, so that you may overflow with hope by the power of the Holy Spirit.
3. Psalm 37:25 (NIV) I was young and now I am old, yet I have never seen the righteous forsaken or their children begging bread.
4. Isaiah 54:10 (NASB) "For the mountains may be removed and the hills may shake, but My lovingkindness will not be removed from you, and My covenant of peace will not be shaken," says the Lord who has compassion on you.

If this area of Doubt pertains to you, reflect on your chosen scripture and write out a prayer to God:

_____
_____

4. Rejection

Truth is: *I am loved by God! Although others may have rejected me, my God will never reject me. I am His child. He will never forget me. He has inscribed me on the palms of His hands. He will guide me and hold on to me. He has plans to prosper me and not to harm me. He will give me hope and a future. He will teach me His way and lead me on level paths.*

1. Isaiah 49:15-16 (NASB) Can a woman forget her nursing child and have no compassion on the son of her womb? Even these may forget, but I will not forget you. Behold, I have inscribed you on the palms of *My hands*; Your walls are continually before Me.
2. Psalm 139:7-10 (NIV) Where can I go from your Spirit? Where can I flee from your presence? If I go up to the heavens, you are there; if I make my bed in the depths, you are there. If I rise on the wings of the dawn, if I settle on the far side of the sea, even there your hand will guide me, your right hand will hold me fast.
3. Jeremiah 29:11 (NIV) "For I know the plans I have for you," declares the Lord, "plans to prosper you and not to harm you, plans to give you hope and a future."
4. Psalm 27:10-11 (NASB) For my father and my mother have forsaken me, But the Lord will take me up. Teach me Your way, O LORD, and lead me in a level path because of my foes.

If this area of Rejection pertains to you, reflect on your chosen scripture and write out a prayer to God:

_____
_____

5. Sin/Shame

Truth is: *God accepts me where I am, but He will not leave me stuck there. I will return to Him and He will set me free. By my faith in Jesus, I have been saved. Jesus is my Lord. He has forgiven and removed **all** my sins. They are as far away as the east is from the west. Jesus died on the cross, paying the penalty for all of my sin. I do not have to carry the weight of my sin and shame! God has nailed it to the cross once and for all. He has set me free! He wants a deep, loving relationship with me.*

1. Isaiah 44:22 (NIRV) I will sweep your sins away as if they were a cloud. I will blow them away as if they were the morning mist. Return to me. Then I will set you free.
2. Romans 5:6–8 (NASB) For while we were still helpless, at the right time Christ died for the ungodly. For one will hardly die for a righteous man; though perhaps for the good man someone would dare even to die. But God demonstrates His own love toward us, in that while we were still sinners, Christ died for us.
3. Romans 10:9–11 (NIV) If you declare with your mouth, "Jesus is Lord," and believe in your heart that God raised him from the dead, you will be saved. For it is with your heart that you believe and are justified, and it is with your mouth that you profess your faith and are saved. As Scripture says, "Anyone who believes in him will never be put to shame."
4. Psalm 103:12 (NIV) As far as the east is from the west, so far has he removed our transgressions from us.

If this area of Sin/Shame pertains to you, reflect on your chosen scripture and write out a prayer to God:

_____
_____

6. Sadness/Grief

Truth is: *The Lord is close to me when I am brokenhearted. He saves me when I am crushed in spirit. He will comfort me as I mourn. The light of His love will illuminate my darkness. He gives me a garment of praise instead of a spirit of despair. He delivers me from all my troubles. He will replace my grief with a crown of beauty. My mourning will be exchanged for His joy. My deep wounds will be bound and healed. He will restore those places long devastated. He will strengthen me. I will be freed. He has borne my griefs and carried my sorrows and pains. By Jesus' stripes (wounds on the cross) I am healed.*

1. Psalm 34:18–19 (NIV) The Lord is close to the brokenhearted and saves those who are crushed in spirit. The righteous person may have many troubles, but the Lord delivers him from them all.
2. Isaiah 61:1b–4 (NIV) He has sent me to bind up the brokenhearted, to proclaim freedom for the captives and release from darkness for the prisoners, to proclaim the year of the LORD's favor and the day of vengeance of our God, to comfort all who mourn, and provide for those who grieve in Zion— to bestow on them a crown of beauty instead of ashes, the oil of joy instead of mourning, and a garment of praise instead of a spirit of despair. They will be called oaks of righteousness, a planting of the LORD for the display of his splendor. They will rebuild the ancient ruins and restore the places long devastated; they will renew the ruined cities that have been devastated for generations.
3. Psalm 119:27–29 (NASB) Make me understand the way of Your precepts, So I will meditate on Your wonders. My soul weeps because of grief; Strengthen me according to Your word. Remove the false way from me, and graciously grant me Your law.

4. Isaiah 53:3-5 (AMP) He was despised and rejected by men, A Man of sorrows *and* pain and acquainted with grief; and like One from whom men hide their faces He was despised, and we did not appreciate His worth *or* esteem Him. But [in fact] He has borne our griefs, and He has carried our sorrows *and* pains; Yet we [ignorantly] assumed that He was stricken, struck down by God and degraded *and* humiliated [by Him]. But He was wounded for our transgressions, He was crushed for our wickedness [our sin, our injustice, our wrongdoing]; The punishment [required] for our well-being *fell* on Him, and by His stripes (wounds) we are healed.

If this area of Sadness/Grief pertains to you, reflect on your chosen scripture and write out a prayer to God:

_____
_____

7. A Weak Relationship with God

Truth is: *I can trust in the Lord, who showers me with His lovingkindness. I can rely on Him confidently. I do not have to understand everything, but in all things, I will know, acknowledge, and recognize Him. He will make my path straight. He will remove the obstacles that block my way. I will rejoice in God's mighty strength because He is my protector. He will help me. I can cry out to God, who accomplishes all things on my behalf. I run to Him as my safe place. The God of peace will equip me with everything good for doing His will. By abiding in Jesus Christ, He will work in me what is pleasing to Him, and my life will bring God glory!*

1. Proverbs 3:5-6 (AMP) Trust in *and* rely confidently on the Lord with all your heart And do not rely on your own insight *or* understanding. In all your ways know *and* acknowledge *and* recognize Him, And He will make your paths straight *and* smooth [removing obstacles that block your way].

2. Psalms 59:16–17 (AMP) But as for me, I will sing of Your mighty strength *and* power; Yes, I will sing joyfully of Your lovingkindness in the morning; For You have been my stronghold And a refuge in the day of my distress. To You, O [God] my strength, I will sing praises; For God is my stronghold [my refuge, my protector, my high tower], the God who shows me [steadfast] lovingkindness.
3. Psalm 57: 1–3 (AMP) Be gracious to me, O God, be gracious *and* merciful to me, For my soul finds shelter *and* safety in You, And in the shadow of Your wings I will take refuge *and* be confidently secure Until destruction passes by. I will cry to God Most High, Who accomplishes all things on my behalf [for He completes my purpose in His plan]. He will send from heaven and save me; He calls to account him who tramples me down. Selah. God will send out His lovingkindness and His truth.
4. Hebrews 13:20–21 (NIV) Now may the God of peace, who through the blood of the eternal covenant brought back from the dead our Lord Jesus, that great Shepherd of the sheep, equip you with everything good for doing his will, and may he work in us what is pleasing to him, through Jesus Christ, to whom be glory for ever and ever. Amen.

If this area of a Weak Relationship with God pertains to you, reflect on your chosen scripture and write out a prayer to God:

_____
_____

THESE TRUTHS ARE SO POWERFUL!
This is only a *small* sample of the truths that *can* overwrite our lies. God's truths will Reprogram our mind and restore our thinking. They will renew the devastated places in our heart. His scriptures will be the steppingstones to our freedom and peace.

I suggest writing down *your* truths:

- In your *notebook*.
- On *index cards* or *sticky notes*. You may want to place them in *strategic* places such as in your car, on your bathroom mirror, on your desk, in your kitchen, or next to your bed as a reminder.
- Make a *memo* called "*My Truths*" on your phone or device for easy access. When it is needed, you can quickly reference it. You can continually add more truths to your list.

Reprogramming the Lie

I created *two formats* to help overwrite the lie with the truth that you want to live by. *Choose* one or both ways, whichever makes it easier to **Recognize** the lie and **Reprogram** with the *truth* that will set you free. *(More blank copies of these two charts are in the back of the book for later use.)*

Here is the first example:

Lie: *You must protect yourself.*

Truth: "*God knows the plans He has for me. Plans to prosper me and not to harm me. Plans to give me hope and a future.*" Jeremiah 29: 11

Lie:_____

Truth: _____

_____

Another example:

When the lie *I can't do it, I will mess up*
presents itself, I will Release it and believe the truth that
God will counsel me with His loving eye on me.   Psalm 32:8

When the lie _____
presents itself, I will Release it and believe the truth that
_____

Take time to process all that the Lord is doing to set you free and overwrite the lies of the enemy. Reprogramming is not a one-day event but can be our way of life.

OVERWRITING THE LIES SOFTENS OUR HEART TO RECEIVE GOOD SEEDS

As God Reprograms our mind and heals our heart, *we are changed*. Those hardened, wounded places become soft and pliable, able to receive *good new* seeds. These new good seeds can come from some of the most unlikely sources.

As I mentioned, my dad and I had a tumultuous relationship, which caused me to have wounds of rejection, doubt, sadness, grief, fear, and feeling like I was not enough. I am thankful that God carefully cared for my wounded heart. One by one, He overwrote my pain with His love and His amazing truths. Ultimately God Reprogrammed my heart with the truth that *"I am loved by my Father in heaven."* Knowing that I am loved by God gave me the ability to hold my relationship with my dad in an open hand with no expectations.

SEEDS FROM UNLIKELY SOURCES
Shortly after I was married many years ago, my dad went into a rehab for his alcohol addiction. I felt led to write him a letter explaining God's amazing salvation and His unconditional love. Even though I was in the beginning of my walk with God, I wanted my dad to find the love and freedom that I had found in Jesus Christ. He cherished that letter. My dad later told me that He had placed his faith in Jesus that day. I was elated, even though he went back to his old way of living and he stayed stuck for decades with only little glimpses of hope of any transformation.

I knew that I could not look to my earthly father for validation, love, or *really* anything. I just *looked up to God* and I allowed Him to heal my wounded heart. I continued to work with God when any new or old pain would arise. I was amazed with the healing God did accomplish.

MY FIRST "I LOVE YOU"
God continued to restore my heart in ways that I could not anticipate. I was an adult when I heard my first sincere *"I love you"* from my dad. My heart recognized his words as new foreign seeds. I was slow to receive his words of love, but as I listened, I assessed his heart. During that conversation, my dad was *not* drinking. He was broken over the recent death of my mom, his first wife. His heart was sad, reflective, and remorseful. Sadness entwined the kind words that he spoke about my mom.

Unexpectedly, he then said, *"Dawn, you are the best Christian woman I know."* His words jarred my heart. They were followed by a sincere, *"I love you."* I remember acknowledging those words as if they were being said in slow motion. His words penetrated my ears. I allowed them to process through my mind. Then slowly and cautiously those words dropped into my *softened* heart. For the first time, I received them as seeds of love.

I remember as I heard his words, I had to sit down to take it all in. He repeated those words again and again, saying, "*I mean it, Dawn, you are the best Christian woman I know. I love you. You are a great wife, mother, sister, and daughter.*" I contemplated all that he said, barely responding.

I was thankful for the work I had done with God. I knew if my heart had still been hardened, those words may have just run right off the hard soil, not being received and not causing any new life. But because God had helped me to soften my heart, I was able to cautiously receive his words as truth. They were seeds of life that brought about another form of healing. My softened heart held on to the truth that *I am loved by my dad, no matter how imperfectly.*

New Beginnings

During that season, I knew my dad was still struggling with alcohol. I took the opportunity to offer to take him to a twelve-step AA (Alcoholics Anonymous) Bible study. He agreed, and for the weeks that he did attend, I would bring him back to my house for his favorite pasta and the Sunday football game.

Every Sunday after the study, we were met at my front door by my little one, who was overjoyed by grandpa's arrival. We would hear squeals of delight and pattering feet as we were greeted with excitement at the front door. Through the eyes of a toddler, my dad saw pure unconditional love. He felt loved deeply.

Now, during the game, my dad did not have a good hold on controlling his tongue. So many times as he yelled at the players, he would use swear words. When my older kids would hear Pap swear, their eyes would get huge and sometimes they would giggle, knowing we were not supposed to use that language. He would always quickly apologize.

Again, I did not expect him to be perfect or someone he wasn't. I did not idealize our relationship. I knew it would never be what it should be. I accepted it as it was, and I kept my boundaries when needed. This open-handed love allowed my dad to know that I loved him. When he was doing good things, I would be the first one he'd call. I had bought him a Bible, and out of the blue he would call me and say, *"I wanted to tell you that I was reading the Bible, and in Matthew I learned . . ."* With a smile, I would encourage him. I treasured those moments.

THE SUMMER MY DAD PASSED AWAY

The summer before my dad passed away, he called me to share an awesome testimony. He said, *"While I was at the local outreach church, they had a special speaker from South Africa. The guest speaker taught an amazing message and then he ended by asking, 'Is there anyone here who hates how you are living your life and you want to be free? Are you tired of living the way you are living?'"*

My dad said, *"That was me. Dawn, I hate how I am living!"* My dad continued to tell me that when the preacher told them to go up front, he was thinking, *I can't go up there. I will be so embarrassed.* But then my dad declared, *"I hated how I was living so I jumped up and went forward.* He continued, *"I walked up front and the preacher prayed for me. Everyone there was praying and congratulating me."* Moved with tears, he said, *"I thought you may want to know what I did today."*

Just a few months later, my dad passed away. The next day, I called his friend to understand how my dad had died. He explained that when he realized my dad was having a heart attack, he began CPR. He said, *"As I was giving your dad CPR, your dad looked straight up, and I saw a look of love like I have never seen."* He continued, *"I have never seen a love like the love I saw in your dad's eyes as He passed."*

God was gracious to us. He allowed us to know that during my dad's last breath, he looked toward heaven and his eyes were filled with love and amazement. I thank Jesus that my dad did hope in Him and he was not disappointed. We believe his faithful Savior came to take him home.

The day after his funeral, my husband encouraged me to go out. As we made our way down our road, in the sky God put a cross. Yes, it looked like clouds had made a cross in the sky. It was a reminder that, *"those who hope in me will not be disappointed."* (Isaiah 49:23c NIV) This picture is on my website, DawnMarasco.com/CPFree

> THOSE WHO HOPE IN THE LORD WILL NOT BE DISAPPOINTED.

When we hope in our Lord, we will *not* be disappointed! That is a huge thought. It is a choice to place *our hope* in God daily. It may feel more difficult to place our hope in God when we are hurting or when life is difficult. But when we hope in Him, our peace will be strong within us.

He can lead us and heal us. He has healed my heart. *If* I had hardened my heart and kept my dad out, I never would have been a part of leading my dad to Christ all those years ago. Neither would I have known that in his brokenness, my dad kept pursuing a relationship with God. I look forward to heaven, where there will be no more addiction, sickness, pain, and no more tears.

Revelations 21:4 (NIV)

> He will wipe every tear from their eyes. There will be no more death or mourning or crying or pain, for the old order of things has passed away.

NEW GOOD SEEDS
I do not know the wounds that God is healing in you, but remember that He is in the process of making your heart soft. *A softened heart can receive God's new seeds, which will create an abundant harvest.* He will provide new good seeds in the most unexpected ways.

As you take this step of Reprogram, allow God to rework any hardened soil, making it soft and pliable. Our God is ABLE to transform our heart. He works with us to Recognize the hardened areas, pull the weeds, remove the obstacles, soften the soil, and then replant with His new good seeds. We can water those seeds with the truths found in His Word. We entrust the growing season into His hands. Our God will make it grow into an abundant harvest in its time.

Do you Recognize places in your heart that are still hardened and need to be softened? Those hardened places can become a hindrance, not allowing the good seeds to be received.

- If so, write down those hardened places and talk to God about those areas.
- Recognize if you are vulnerable to any lies regarding that area, then write them out.
- Ask God for the *truth from scripture* that will *overwrite* those lies. Overwriting those lies by believing God's truth will soften your heart.

_____
_____

Congratulations for allowing God to reveal the areas that need to be overwritten. It will be well worth all your effort to Reprogram your heart and mind. In this process, God will make your heart soft soil *prepared* to receive the new seeds that *He has planned for you.*

In our next chapter, *we will create our Desired Harvest*. We will discuss *how to uproot* the weeds of our current harvest and learn *how to replant* with God's good seeds.

Chapter 9
Design Your Harvest

WHAT WE FEED WILL GROW
DO YOU WANT A WONDERFUL, HEALTHY HARVEST overflowing with abundant fruit? If so, we need to be watchful of the seeds that we are sowing. We must *know* for certain *that what we feed will grow and what grows will produce our harvest.*

Many years ago, I was putting this principle of *what you feed will grow* to work in my life by carefully choosing to sow *good* seeds. I was strategically planting seeds of love, patience, kindness, joy, faith, and being slow to anger. Great fruit was blessing my family and my marriage.

One day my husband and I were getting into a disagreement. Carelessly, we began to go back and forth with our words. The tension was beginning to mount. That was when a negative harsh thought came into my mind. I considered speaking it. Knowing the negative thought that I wanted to say, God prompted my heart,

> *"If you say that . . . you will invite anger in."*

I heard God clearly. I then *disregarded* His warning and spewed the negative comment. As my words hit my husband's heart, he stood up. I saw anger enter our disagreement, and by the shocked look on his face, I could see its toxic effect. It was obvious what I had done. My disobedience scared me. I was shocked that *my careless words had so much power.* I quickly said, *"I am sorry! I did not mean what I said."* And I immediately left the room.

I went out to my deck and sat on the swing wringing my hands, overwhelmed by what I had done. I began to apologize to God for not listening or heeding His warning. Even though I had repented to God, I still did not know how to make it right. I knew I had to be honest with my husband and try to mend things. I really felt bad for what I had done.

I asked God: *"How can I undo what I just did?"*

God's answer blew me away. He began to instruct my heart with statements such as: *"You just fed anger. Now it is strong within you. It will be very easy to get angry again. For days, you will tend to be quickly angered because you fed anger. It is now alive in you. You cannot give in to the anger. You must resist it. Do not feed it, and over time it will shrink and lose its power. It will become weaker and weaker every time you do not feed it."*

God led me and my husband, who did not initiate the anger, through that destructive mess. We had to reject the strong urge to get angry. We both had to resist the quick angry flare-ups by choosing *not* to give in to those temptations. It was hard at first because the anger rose up quickly when we were aggravated. As we resisted feeding the anger, *it dissipated*. It began to lose the ground that we had given it.

We realized we would have to handle disagreements differently. We Recognized how much power is in our words. I learned that I could not just say what came into my mind.

I had heard God's warning and I disregarded it!

His Spirit is in us to lead us and guide us. *Will we let Him?* Have you been careless with your words, causing others pain or enabling anger to flare up? Have you been in a situation where you have allowed jealousy, frustration, bitterness, unforgiveness, or envy to enter your heart and affect you and your relationships? Have those encounters caused you to condemn yourself?

Reprogramming begins with us Recognizing our ways that can be hurtful and negative. In that situation *I chose to learn the hard way*, by *not* listening to God's warning.

Afterward I had to:

- Recognize the wounding offense
- Release it all to God
- Repent for my actions
- Ask my husband to forgive me
- Reprogram with love

It did not stop there. I did not want to *repeat* that type of behavior, so I had to *continue* to Reprogram my mind. I went to God and asked Him to *weigh in, teach me, and instruct me in the way I should go*!

I learned that:

- I must desire God's will, trust His wisdom, and obey His warnings.
- I must quickly turn toward God and ask for help.
- I must *weigh it before I say it.* Meaning I must choose carefully what I will say before I say it. This is a lesson I must remind myself of continually and will for the rest of my life.
- It is *easier* to keep my mouth shut than it is to repair a relationship that I have carelessly injured.
- I must *place a high value on others* by pausing and considering that my words and actions have consequences. My words will either build up a relationship or they will tear it down.

- I must remember my concern or love for the other person. This always helps me to Reprogram my mind in the moment.
- I learned that *my anger would dissipate if* I did *not* feed it by giving in to it.
- Instead of saying the negative comment, my negative *attitude will change as I pray.*
- I have a choice. Will I *feed* the argument, or will I *overlook* the disagreement by not allowing it to grab hold of my heart?
- I can choose to show kindness and mercy. This will remove the opportunity to feed any anger.

Fruit Is Produced

We may wrestle with wanting to give in to our own desires. However, we must remember to remain in Him. It is *by His Spirit,* which is alive in us, *that we can choose* consistently to plant good seeds and *not* feed what is negative or destructive. *Remaining in Him* is where the *fruit is produced.*

> OUR NEW HARVEST WILL BE CREATED FROM THE SEEDS THAT WE ARE CURRENTLY SOWING.

Fruit matters. Our new harvest will be created from the seeds that we are currently sowing! Daily we can plant good seeds of love *or* we can choose to plant negative seeds from our bad attitudes and habits. We will also plant the seeds that we are accepting from others. Whether good or bad seeds, they will produce a harvest of their own kind.

We can choose to uproot the negative seeds that have been growing and embedding themselves in us.

For example:

- If we are consistently angry or bitter, it could be a bad habit of allowing and feeding anger, jealousy, negative emotions, desires, or addictions. (What we feed will grow!)
- Our anger, bitterness, and destructive behaviors can also be a sign that we are carrying current or past wounds.

If we are wounded, we need to *Recognize* and *Release* the offense, along with the anger that has entangled itself with the wound. In chapter five we more thoroughly discussed *how* to Release our wounds to God. But here let's remember it is a journey of Recognizing and letting go of our current and painful past, and seeking God for the healing that is needed. Our healing will consist of *Reprogramming* our heart and mind. We must determine to *uproot* the negatives and choose to *replant* that area with new good seeds. *This will produce abundant fruit for the future.*

This life is not easy, nor are the things that God calls us to in this life easily attained. We may feel like quitting or giving in to the negative pressures. It is then that we need to look to God and ask Him *for the strength to remain.* If we want to be fruitful and have an abundant harvest, then we need to abide in Him!

We Choose What We Will Remain In

We must choose to remain in good things even if it is harder than we thought, or it takes longer than expected. How many times have you stayed the course instead of quitting and you were thankful? We must stay the course when we are trusting in God. We can *continue* to look to Jesus for the *wisdom, life,* and *strength* that we need to take our *next right step* and *remain in Him.*

Continuous Peace

John 15:4–5 (NIV)

> Remain in me, as I also remain in you. No branch can bear fruit by itself; it must remain in the vine. Neither can you bear fruit unless you remain in me. I am the vine; you are the branches. If you remain in me and I in you, you will bear much fruit; apart from me you can do nothing.

Remain means to stay, continue, persist, wait, and endure. *Imagine that we can stay in a place with Jesus where He enables us to bear good fruit continually.*

We will be learning that as we remain in Jesus, *His life is in us, empowering us to bear much fruit.* Let's use the John 15:4-8 (NIV) to insert our name into the blanks, making it more personal.

Remain in me _____, as I also remain in you. No branch can bear fruit by itself; it must remain in the vine. Neither can you _____, bear fruit unless you remain in me. I am the vine; you _____ are the branches. If you remain in me _____ and I in you, you _____ will bear much fruit; apart from me you _____ can do nothing. If you do not remain in me, you are like a branch that is thrown away and withers; such branches are picked up, thrown into the fire and burned. If you _____ remain in me and my words remain in you, ask whatever you wish, and it will be done for you. This is to my Father's glory, that you _____ bear much fruit, showing yourselves to be my disciples.

> *"This is to My Father's glory, that you bear much fruit, showing yourselves to be My disciples."*
> John 15:8 (NIV)

REMAIN IN HIM
When we remain in Jesus, His Spirit will bear much fruit in us and through us. When we bear His fruit, we will show that we are His disciples, those who follow Him. I had a friend recently share with me how easy it is for her to see when she is not abiding in Him because her fruit quickly shrivels and she feels spiritually dry. It is not difficult to evaluate if we are remaining in Him. Just look at *the condition of our fruit.*

Let's use the Galatians 5 scripture as a guide and ask ourselves, *how is the fruit of the Spirit growing in my own life? How is my love, joy, peace, patience, kindness, goodness, faithfulness, gentleness, and self-control?* The teaching continues in verses 24 and 25: *"Now those who belong to Christ Jesus have crucified the flesh with its passions and desires. If we live by the Spirit, let us also walk by the Spirit."* (Galatians 5:22-25 NASB)

> IT IS NOT DIFFICULT TO EVALUATE IF WE ARE REMAINING IN HIM. JUST LOOK AT THE CONDITION OF OUR FRUIT.

I love that this scripture shows us how we can be living. We are told to crucify the flesh with its passions and desires. We know when our flesh is strong within us we can be angry, negative, bitter, insecure, miserable, filled with fears, and desiring to do what is contrary to God. We may also try to control or solve our own problems, not Releasing them to Him.

By trusting Jesus, we will *follow* the Spirit's leading. When we are living by the Spirit, we will *walk* in the power of His Spirit. Walking closely with Him, we will be filled with His peace. We will glorify God as we bear His abundant fruit of love, joy, patience, kindness, gentleness, and self-control in our lives, which is a wonderful way to live.

How Do We Follow the Spirit?

We follow the Spirit by remaining in Jesus every step of the way. We get to choose *if* we will remain in Jesus *thought by thought* and *day by day*. If we remain in Him, we will Recognize the negative things that rise up from within us and we can choose what we will do with them.

We choose the seeds that we will sow by the decisions we make all day long. *If we feed* our negative desires, they will be encouraged to grow and bear more negative fruit! The choice is ours.

- Will we gossip about someone?
- Will we be rude, harsh, unforgiving, or unloving?
- Will we have outbursts of anger, pout, or shut down because we did not get our way?
- Will we give in to harmful fleshly desires?
- Will we use substances or foods to numb our pain?
- Will we give in to frustration and lash out?

Feeding the negatives is like pouring water on those destructive weeds to promote their growth.

We Remain in What We Feed

> What We Continually Feed Is What We Will Remain In.

I know firsthand that what we continually feed is what we will remain in. There were years when I went back and forth feeding the negatives and then hating the results of my actions. My relationships suffered. I felt far from God and far from His purposes for my life.

If we continue in these negative ways of thinking, speaking, and living, we will remain in them. By *feeding* the negative way of living, we will *reap* the destructive fruit from those seeds. This can become a cycle of *remaining in it*. Continuing the negative cycle, we will naturally give away the caustic fruit from our harvest. This type of sowing is not what God desires for us. He wants our best. He wants us to *remain in Him* and live an abundant life.

Abundant living occurs as we continue to *plant* and *feed* the good seeds. When we *Recognize* the negative issue, we can *Release* it to God, letting go of it and trusting Him with the outcome. We can Remain in Him for the strength and wisdom to Release the fear, negative desire, or anger. We can trust Him to *Reprogram* our heart and mind. Our future harvest will be impacted every time we *reject* the negative seeds and *choose to plant* the better seeds of trust, love, and self-control. We will then produce good fruit to share with others.

The seeds we plant will create the fruit we will harvest.

On the following pages I created two illustrations to express what it looks like to remain in what we choose. I used the infinity sign to demonstrate that what we continually feed, we will continue to remain in. *Our choices will impact the trajectory of our lives.*

WILL YOU CHOOSE TO... REMAIN IN HIM?

Trust God
Know you are loved
Release negatives
Plant good seeds
Bear good fruit

Remain in Him

If we choose to Remain in Him, we will:

1. Trust God with our situations and concerns.
2. Know we are loved and He is near to us.
3. Visualize Him comforting us as we Release our concerns to Him.
4. Trust in His faithfulness as we plant good seeds.
5. Bear good fruit and receive more of Him: His love, His strength, His healing, His wisdom, and His peace.
6. Confidently walk with Him, wherever He leads.
7. Praise God for being near, knowing He will never leave us or forsake us.

If we remain in Him, we will enjoy a close relationship with Jesus, which overflows with His good fruit. This is the fruit we will have to give away!

WILL YOU CHOOSE TO ... REMAIN IN IT, THE NEGATIVE WAY OF LIVING?

If we choose to Remain in it, we will:

1. Plant and Feed fear, negative thoughts, and behaviors.
2. Lose our peace by attempting to control our situations.
3. Visualize the issue repeatedly, allowing fear, anger, worry, or unforgiveness to *step in front of* God's presence.
4. Feed and be misled by our bitter attitudes or negative desires.
5. Bear the effects of the destructive, negative fruit, which can consume our everyday lives.
6. Feel far from God, weighed down, and distant in our relationships.
7. Murmur and complain about our situation, permitting the anxious mess to become our constant companion.

If we remain in it, we will forfeit our peace and continually bear more negative, undesirable fruit. This is the fruit we will produce and give away!

Are you remaining in Him or are you remaining in it?

_____

How does it feel to know that *you can choose* what you will remain in?

_____
_____

Using both examples, which of the preceding numbers (1–7) were true for you?

_____

Which point(s) do you desire to know and live by?

_____

Which point(s) do you need to let go of or change?

_____

**We can choose how we will Respond in this life.
We choose our harvest!**

FOUNDATIONAL TRUTH
The following Scripture is a *foundational truth* for me personally. This is the principle of sowing and reaping. I love this scripture! It has taught me *how to save my harvest.*

Galatians 6:7–9 (NIV)

> Do not be deceived: God cannot be mocked. A man reaps what he sows. Whoever sows to please their flesh, from the flesh will reap destruction; whoever sows to please the Spirit, from the Spirit will reap eternal life. Let us not become weary in doing good, for at the proper time we will reap a harvest if we do not give up.

This truth can keep us from falling into a victim mentality. We may feel as if we are powerless to choose how we act or react. However, God states clearly that *we are able to* decide *if* we want to please the Spirit that lives within us or *if* we want to please our flesh. We decide! It is not happenstance. We *get to* choose what we will sow. We choose the seeds that will please the Spirit or we choose seeds that please the flesh.

EVERY DAY WE CHOOSE THE SEEDS WE WILL SOW
A few years ago, I was preparing for a dinner party. I offered to make homemade pizza dough so that everyone could create their own pizzas. When I doubled the dough mixture, I realized it would not be enough, so I doubled it again. Still being uncertain how much dough was needed for everyone to make their own personal pizzas, I doubled it again. That day making the dough created a big mess. It also took a while to rise. My miscalculation took up a big portion of my day.

Beyond providing the food, I desired to create an inviting environment. I wanted to light some candles. I had it all pictured in my mind. But then I began to feel frustration taunting me, as I realized that I would not have enough time to focus on the pretty details. I had too much to accomplish. It became apparent that I had only enough time to prepare the foods so that they would be ready when everyone arrived.

In a hurry I ran down to my basement. As I turned the corner, it was as if a wall of frustration was set before me. I felt frustration press against me as it attempted to *influence* the direction and focus of my heart.

The frustration began to remind me that *I was not* going to have enough time to do *everything* that I wanted. I was not going to be able to make my home look pretty. The thought intruded, *What will people think if you don't make things look welcoming?* Frustration wanted me to focus on impressing versus blessing.

As those thoughts grew, I could feel frustration attempting to gain ground within my heart.

That is when I stopped and Recognized *why* I was frustrated. I then Released it by saying loudly, *"No! I will not give into frustration and allow it to rob every good thing tonight!"* I began to Reprogram my mind and heart with my prayer, *"Lord, I will not allow frustration to destroy the good things that You have planned for us tonight. I don't care if I get candles lit or if the house looks pretty. I just pray that you give me a joyful heart as I prepare a meal for all of us. I pray we all enjoy our time together."* Immediately frustration left. I went about joyfully cutting up the toppings for our pizzas.

On a funny note, my son asked, *"Who were you talking to?"*

I laughed and said, *"God. Frustration was trying to get me upset over what I could not get done. I chose to have joy about what I could accomplish."* He just laughed.

Everyone came. Not one candle was lit. The house was *not* pretty, but it was clean. I was told that it was the best pizza they had ever eaten. They were thinking of giving me an award for the pizza. It's funny. That day I could have gotten frustrated over not doing *everything* that I wanted, but I chose to *remain in Him* and do what I could do that night. God blessed us all.

NOT ALL SEEDS ARE CREATED EQUAL
These principles are true! *Each seed has a given value and will produce fruit after its own kind.* We choose what we reap by what we sow. That night, I could have given into the weed of frustration and planted its destructive seeds. I would have reaped a bad attitude by *remaining* focused on what I could *not* accomplish. But by the grace of God, I knew this principle was true. I decided to go to God, Release the frustration, and Reprogram my mind with the truth that *what I could do was*

enough! I trusted Him with the outcome. He gave me the fruit of peace and joy.

God will not be deceived... We will reap either *destruction* or *life* from the seeds that we sow.

We plant seeds that have the potential of bringing life and we plant seeds that can potentially produce death. Bullies and the lies of the enemy are always used to bring death to relationships, dreams, hope, love, and to our productivity. They try to rewrite *who we are* and *what we think* about ourselves and others. Don't take the enemy's bait. Discard the negative seeds and choose to plant God's good seeds.

We choose which seeds we will sow, just as we choose *what* we are going to say before we say it. We choose *what* we will believe and *who* we will believe. Will we believe the lies of the enemy or will we believe the truths of God? We choose whether we will plant a positive seed that brings life *or* a negative seed that causes destruction.

- We must Recognize the potential of the seeds that we are planting.
- These seeds, once planted, will grow up and create a beautiful *life-giving* plant or a *destructive* weed.
- Each seed will have an impact on our lives and can impact the lives of others.
- The accumulation of seeds sown will produce a harvest!

Choose wisely! Be patient. A harvest takes time to grow. "*Let us not become weary in doing good, for at the proper time we will reap a harvest if we do not give up.*" Galatians 6:9 (NIV)

Do Not Grow Weary in Doing Good

A farmer does not plant a good seed then pull it out to see *if* it is rooted or growing. No, he waters and cares for it and waits for the plant to emerge. We plant and water, but God brings the increase. In 1 Corinthians 3:6 (NIV), Paul states, *"I planted the seed, Apollos watered it, but God has been making it grow."* It is God who makes the seeds grow.

I remember when my kids were young, and they had planted kidney beans in a pot. A few days later they pulled the seeds out. They were amazed that the shell had broken open and the *life within* the seed had begun to root in the dirt. We had a wonderful conversation. We spoke about how God created each seed with the ability to become a plant of its same kind. The seed on its own is dormant; it needs good soil, water, and sunlight. The soil and the water soften the shell so that the new life can emerge. The rootlets develop to drink in the nutrients from both the soil and the water. This brings life to the seed and encourages it to grow. The amazing seedling grows toward the light, which is another form of nutrient.

This remarkable process *takes time*, and every step is critical. If my kids had pulled the emerging seed and did not place it back in the dirt, it would have dried up and died. So we must not grow weary in doing good. We must allow the good seeds time to grow.

> *God created the growing process.*
> *He will see it through to completion.*

Our daily choices determine *what seeds* will be sown, and those seeds will produce our future harvest. Will your daily choices produce the harvest you desire? Explain.

_____

_____

A good farmer *strategically* plants the seeds that he knows will produce his desired harvest. We are also equipped to choose our desired harvest by the seeds that we will plant. But before we can make real and lasting changes, *we must first assess where we are.* Like the farmer assesses his harvest, let's take some time to assess our current harvests.

Put a check next to the areas that need peace. *Choose* the *one* area that is most in need of peace. This will be the area that *you will focus on first.*

HARVEST ASSESSMENT
My CURRENT HARVEST

I desire peace in:

- My personal life
- My spiritual life
- My marriage
- My home life
- My family
- My health/weight
- My workplace
- Other area _____

Now focus on that *one main area* that needs peace the most. Fill in the blank.

My priority area: I desire peace in my _____.

Take a moment and think about the current condition of that harvest. There are usually both positive and negative seeds that were sown to create your current harvest. Visualize both the good and the negative. First, write down the *life-giving seeds* that were sown in your main area. I have found some who find it more challenging to Recognize and write down the good seeds that have been planted. Please, allow yourself to Recognize the good and write them below.

LIFE-GIVING SEEDS
The *good seeds* that I have sown in my priority area:

_____
_____
_____

Here are only suggestions of some good, life-giving seeds that you may have sown. *Underline* the ones that apply and then *add* them to your good seeds list.

Truth, Love, Faith, Patience, Trust, Wisdom, Praise, Self-Control, Confidence, Honesty, Stillness, Willingness, Agreement, Gentleness, Humility, Comfort, Helpfulness, Kindness, Generosity, Thoughtfulness, Attentiveness, Consistency, Laughter, Hope, Grace, Mercy, Contentment, Perseverance, Encouragement, Acceptance, Caring, Serving, Enjoying, Putting Others First, Having Fun, Giving of Self, and Believing the Best.

Now go back and circle the main seeds that are *creating the most life in* your *current* harvest. Write those seeds here.

_____

NEGATIVE SEEDS
Visualize what has caused destruction in that same current harvest. Be honest! It will help you to Recognize the negative seeds that you have sown to create the weeds in your priority area. Do you Recognize any *negative seeds* or *destructive actions, attitudes, or ways* (weeds) that may be standing in the way or choking out the life of your peaceful harvest?

The *negative seeds* that I have sown in my priority area:

_____
_____
_____

Here are only suggestions of some negative seeds that may be robbing your harvest of peace. *Underline* the ones that apply and then *add* them to your negative seeds list.

Sowing seeds of: Disrespect, Doubt, Fear, Frustration, Anger, Bitterness, Lack of Love, Unforgiveness, Gossip, Jealousy, Inconsistency, Self-Pity, Cruelty and Selfishness.

Being: Rude, Mean, Unreasonable, Irrational, Irritable, Hasty, Spiteful, Discouraging, Unavailable Physically or Emotionally, Lazy, Prideful, Too Busy, Attention-Seeking, Unfaithful, Distracted.

Habits of: Tearing Down, Arguing, Blaming, Lying, Shutting Down instead of Addressing Issues, Going through the Motions, Allowing Sadness to Rule your Heart, Building Walls, Pointing Out Other's Flaws, Needing to Be Right, Negative Self-Talk, Harsh Words or Tone with Self and Others, Substance Abuse, People-Pleasing, Lack of Follow-Through, and Lack of Positive Expectation.

Now go back and circle the main weeds that are *creating the most destruction in* your *current* harvest. Write those weeds here.

_____
_____

As we assess our current harvest, it may be eye-opening. It may also be heartbreaking to *see clearly* what has been robbing us of our peace and hindering our good, fruitful harvest. Do not be concerned. Our current harvest can be enriched or uprooted and completely changed!

Design Your Harvest
A farmer maps out the type of fruit he desires to harvest. He then follows through with choosing the correct seeds to accomplish

that harvest. Likewise, when we know our desired harvest, we can *intentionally* and *faithfully plant* the right seeds to create the plentiful harvest we desire.

Be Intentional. Now, this is the fun part! Visualize your desired harvest. Pray and ask God to lead you to design the future harvest that you desire. Add descriptive words to describe it. It's your future harvest. Create it as you desire. Ask yourself, *What do I want to harvest in this one specific area?*

Psalm 37:4 (NASB)

> Delight yourself in the Lord; And He will give you the desires of your heart.

My *Desired Future Harvest* in my priority area:

_____

_____

_____

Are there specific seeds that will need to be sown to create your Desired Harvest? For example, I desired a harvest of *peace.* That meant that I needed to sow *trust and obedience to God as seeds.* They would produce peace in its time!

What are the specific life-giving seeds that you will need to plant in order to receive the harvest you desire? (You can use the examples from the life-giving seeds list.)

_____

_____

_____

God desires that we be fruitful.

Psalm 107:37 (NIV)

> They sowed fields and planted vineyards that yielded a fruitful harvest.

CONTRAST YOUR HARVESTS

Please take a moment and contrast how you described your Current Harvest and your Desired Harvest. Hopefully you wrote them down, so it is easy to assess.

- First, Recognize the negative seeds or destructive actions, attitudes, or ways that you *circled*, *revealing what is robbing you* the most in your current harvest.
- Next, *circle* the fruit you desire *the most* in your *future* harvest. *Write* them both below.

My most destructive weed _____
My most desired fruit _____

NOW CONSIDER IF THEY *ARE OPPOSITE* OF EACH OTHER.

What I have found is that usually the very thing we want the most in our desired harvest is being robbed regularly by the negative weeds that we are currently feeding. For instance, I wanted peace more than anything, yet fear was my inseparable companion. Every time I gave in to fear, it grew stronger and easily robbed me of the fruit of peace that I desperately desired. Do you see how our desired harvest can be robbed by our current choices?

Here is another example of someone who was assessing their current harvest in the area of their health/weight. The main fruit in her desired harvest was *self-control*. Yet the weed that she was continually sowing in her current harvest, which was robbing her the most, was *inconsistency and lack of follow-through*. Do you see that what she desired was self-control and what she was sowing was inconsistency? They were the exact opposites of each other.

We are not reaping our desired harvest because we are consistently sowing seeds that overrun our current harvest. When we plant the negative seed, we are choosing not to plant the life-giving seed. We have a choice of which seeds we will sow.

REVERSING A NEGATIVE HARVEST
It is amazing that once we Recognize *what* is robbing our desired harvest, we can *reverse* it! We can reverse our negative harvest by Recognizing what needs to go! We can choose not to feed the negative weed that is creating destruction in our current harvest. We can uproot it and choose to *replace it* with good, life-giving seeds. We can remain in Him for the strength and wisdom to continue to plant good seeds consistently.

We can remove the harmful weeds when we:

- *Recognize* the negative seeds that created the weed.
- *Repent* for *our part* in the negative harvest.
- *Release* the painful truths to God.

We can prepare for our desired harvest by:

- *Reprogramming,* which prepares the soil as we renew our mind through the Word of God.
- *Resisting* destructive seeds and determining what we will sow.
- *Replanting* with good seeds by remaining in Him.
- *Rejoicing* knowing the new harvest is on its way!

This will produce a harvest of life as we choose to work with God and do the hard work of reversing the negative harvest.

Here is an example that helped me reverse the negative harvest in my life. *(More blank copies of this chart are in the back of the book for later use.)*

My most desired fruit I wanted to harvest was: *peace in my life*.
I had to stop feeding or sowing: __*fear and doubt.*__
I must consistently sow: __*trust and faith in God.*__

Another example: I have a sweet friend who wrote that she desired more love and laughter in her marriage. She had to decide *what* she could sow today to reap a harvest of love and laughter. After praying about it she decided:

My most desired fruit I want to harvest is:
__*love and laughter in my marriage.*__

I will have to stop feeding or sowing:
__*busyness and marriage as a low priority.*__

I must consistently sow:
__*15 minutes to talk and connect daily,*__
__*also try to add a date night once a week.*__

Now fill in the following chart with your answers.

My most desired fruit I want to harvest is:

_____

I will have to stop feeding or sowing:

_____

I must consistently sow:

_____

Now that we can visualize our desired harvest, it should be easier to Recognize which weeds we need to uproot and which seeds we need to plant. When we Recognize a negative seed is about to be planted, it becomes a warning that blares loudly. We can be keenly aware that if we plant that negative seed, it will produce a destructive weed. This warning gives us a moment to consider which seed we want to plant. *We must choose wisely.*

EVERY SEED HAS A VALUE
Every seed will produce fruit after its own kind. I cannot sow a tomato seed and expect to reap an apple tree. Neither could I scatter dandelion seeds and hope to receive squash in return. Likewise, I cannot sow the seed of rudeness and expect to receive love. I must sow a seed of kindness, which will produce love in its proper time.

Even though fear was my main weed producer, I also Recognized the weed of *lack of love* that was robbing my harvest of peace. In the early days of Reprogramming my mind, I knew very little about loving God and loving others as God wanted me to love. I had to learn *what love was* and *what love was not* if I was going to thwart the weed of lack of love from choking out my harvest of peace.

WHAT IS LOVE AND WHY DOES LOVE MATTER?
The Word of God is awesome to teach us!

1 Corinthians 13:4–8a (NIV) establishes what love is.

> Love is patient, love is kind. It does not envy, it does not boast, it is not proud. It does not dishonor others, it is not self-seeking, it is not easily angered, it keeps no record of wrongs. Love does not delight in evil but rejoices with the truth. It always protects, always trusts, always hopes, always perseveres. Love never fails.

God is loving! He has a heart of love and kindness toward us. Do we realize that God is patient with us? He is not easily angered, and His love never fails. This simple yet profound scripture *shows us how* to live a life of love and *how* to reap a harvest of love.

Let's add love into the harvest chart.
My most desired fruit I want to harvest is: _____LOVE_____

I will have to stop sowing: _envy, being boastful, proud, dishonoring, self-seeking, easily angered, keeping records of wrongs, and delighting in evil._

I must consistently sow: _patience and kindness, rejoicing with the truth, and choosing to always protect, always trust, always hope, and always persevere because love never fails._

THE MOST EXCELLENT WAY
1 John 4:19 (NASB)

> We love, because He first loved us.

Knowing we are loved and knowing that God considers love the *most excellent way* to live, I realized I had a lot to learn. Over the years, I have used the scripture in 1 Corinthians to teach myself and my children what love is and what love is not. When one of us would act in an unbecoming way, I would ask, *"Was that loving?"* By knowing these truths, we could easily Recognize *if* we were acting in an unloving way.

I knew *if* I wanted to harvest love, I had to present the scripture in a way that made it easy for us to remember. I also had to be the example of love. I had to do the hard work of *living* in accordance with what love is and what love is not. So I created a visual reminder using 1 Corinthians 12:31b, 13:4–8a (NIV)

"I will show you the most excellent way."

LOVE IS . . .
  Love is patient.
  Love is kind.
  Love rejoices with the truth.
  Love always protects.
  Love always trusts.
  Love always hopes.
  Love always perseveres.
  Love *never* fails!

I also had to be on the lookout for what love is not:

LOVE DOES NOT . . . LOVE IS NOT . . .
  Love does not envy.
  Love does not boast.
  Love is not proud.
  Love does not dishonor others (by being rude).
  Love is not self-seeking.
  Love is not easily angered.
  Love keeps no record of wrongs.
  Love does not delight in evil.

CHOOSING TO PLANT SEEDS OF LOVE
When we began to live this way as a family, it was easy to Recognize if we were rude, selfish, or easily angered, each of which was *not* love. This was an eye-opening way to live. It was obvious when we were planting seeds of love. When we were planting negative seeds, we *repented* and *apologized* quickly. We then followed up with *sowing* good, life-giving seeds.

When I plant a negative seed, which will happen, I now Recognize it. I immediately pull that seed out of the soil by repenting to God and to the individual. I may pray, *"Lord, forgive me. I desire to be loving, and what I just said was rude. Please heal this relationship."* Then I turn to the individual and say, *"Please forgive me for speaking rudely. I am sorry. I really love you and I do not want to hurt you. Do you forgive me?"*

Recognizing and Releasing the truth of what I have done to God and then repenting to Him and the person immediately pulls that negative seed from the soil. When we are quick to repent, we pull that destructive seed before it gets rooted and grows. By pulling the seed immediately, it stops the growth of bitterness, resentment, or lack of love from developing into a strong weed. We can *replant* new seeds of reconciliation, respect, and love. *Love is God's most excellent way to live!*

Loving as God wants us to love will create an abundant harvest of peace.

Our family keeps it lighthearted, knowing we all want to be loving. We give each other grace, knowing we are a work in progress. When I am not loving, my family laughingly calls me out by saying, *"Mom, was that loving?"* We all laugh. We know our goal is to love. Once we Recognize what love is, it is apparent when we witness our or others' lack of love being planted.

A few years ago, a friend had called me to tell me that her daughter is catching on to my teaching on love. She shared that after another family member had lost their temper, her daughter asked kindly, *"Was that loving?"*

My Friend said, *"I had to laugh."*

STOP THE PROGRESSION
A key to producing our desired harvest is to stop the progression of negative seeds from being sown. This can be challenging because sometimes our thoughts can feel so strong within us that we feel we must spew out what we are thinking! But trust me: *we will not combust* if we do not say that negative or rude

comment. *We must weigh it before we say it.* So in the midst of the internal pressure, we can pause and think before we speak instead of saying the first thing that comes to our mind.

WE MUST WEIGH IT BEFORE WE SAY IT.

When we refrain from feeding anything negative, we prevent its growth. When we do not entertain the thought by either dismissing it or Releasing it to God, that negative thought will shrink and lose its power. This will destroy the negative seed along with the impact it could have had. This allows us to keep God's peace continuously.

WHO TO LOVE AND HOW TO LOVE

Without the Word of God, we would not know that God considers love the greatest commandment. The Bible is amazing, and with it we can Reprogram our mind with the truths about His love. In the Word, He even tells us *who* to love and *how* to love them.

Matthew 22:36–39 (NIV)

> "Teacher, which is the greatest commandment in the Law?" Jesus replied: "'Love the Lord your God with all your heart and with all your soul and with all your mind.' This is the first and greatest commandment. And the second is like it: 'Love your neighbor as yourself.'"

Deuteronomy 6:5–6 (NASB)

> You shall love the LORD your God with all your heart and with all your soul and with all your might. These words, which I am commanding you today, shall be on your heart.

Jesus knows if we allow the truths about *who* to love and *how* to love to penetrate and Reprogram our heart and mind, we will be living in a loving relationship with Him. Our relationship of love will overflow our hearts and become the love we can give away! We are to love the Lord our God with all our heart. We are to love Him with all our soul. We are to love Him with all our mind and might. We are to love others as we love ourselves.

Loving with all seems unattainable to me, until I break it down.

LOVE THE LORD WITH ALL OF OUR:
- **Heart** — *Protecting* what we lift up, believe, and hold on to.
- **Soul** — *Guarding* what our *mind* thinks on, what our *will* desires, and what our *emotions* attach to.
- **Mind** — *Setting* our mind on Him and His truths, no matter the circumstances.
- **Might** — *Determining* to love God and love others, which will include rejecting anything destructive in our thoughts, feelings, and the way we are living.

The Holy Spirit will empower us to keep God first in our heart and in our lives. He will prompt us to live a life of love. *I have learned not to ignore His promptings,* for they produce life. By loving Him and loving others, we will be *living* in His love, *building* with His love, and *promoting* the love of God. Loving like this multiplies our peace. These seeds will create a harvest overflowing with peace, love, and joy.

Let's Wrap Up Step Three!

REPROGRAM IS THE STEP WHERE WE ARE TAKING our life back! We are trading in the life that has been tossed back and forth by every scheme of the enemy. We have already begun to overwrite the enemy's lies with the light of God's powerful truth.

Continuous peace will become our calm way of living!

God has empowered His Holy Spirit within us to guide us as the "rudder" of our lives. It is small tweaks by the rudder that can redirect a large ship. He can easily prompt our heart to direct our way, tweak our course, or help us to make major corrections when needed. We can trust our God to lead us in the way we should go. Stay connected to Him.

Remember, when you are frustrated with your progress with God, be willing to give Him *your cup*, no matter the condition of the contents. Our life in Him is a lifelong journey. We will grow, develop, and mature day by day. A surrendered life . . . is a life that He will fill and overflow with good things.

WE CHOOSE OUR HARVEST!
- *Know* your desired harvest.
- *Plant* seeds to increase your fruitful harvest.
- *Uproot* anything that will entangle or choke out all the good God has in store for you!
- *Choose* to live a life of love.

My concern is that in this life, *we will get busy*. We will get sidetracked. We will begin to focus on the immediate and get frustrated by what is pressing. We may miss the most important.

Let's Wrap Up Step Three!

The most important aspect of this step of Reprogramming is that we are to *stay connected to God*. Daily we are to continue to seek Him, well beyond the 30-Day Challenge. We can choose to become deeply rooted in His peace through a daily decision to draw close to Him, rely on His love, and remain in Him.

We will remain in what we are planting! We can continually plant good seeds even in the storms of life. Storms will come. But as we remain in Him, He is our strength to help us to continue forward. He is with us no matter what we face. When we invite Him to weigh in, He will speak specifically to our hearts about our situations. In Him we can be confident that we are loved, cared for, known, and accepted. These are awesome seeds that we can plant!

The truth is that the closer we are to Him day by day, the less we are moved by the storms of life.

Step 4 is our final step. We will learn how to *Respond faithfully for a continuous life of peace*. Let's finish strong. In the next chapter, I will share a storm that hit while editing this book. It was a devastating storm. I will reveal how in Jesus we can Respond faithfully. I am looking forward to you crossing the finish line and entering into the life of peace that God intended for you!

Remember John 15:4 (NIV)

> Remain in me, as I also remain in you. No branch can bear fruit by itself; it must remain in the vine. Neither can you bear fruit unless you remain in me.

4 Steps to Continuous Peace:

1. RECOGNIZE the Obstacles That Rob
2. RELEASE the Barriers That Confine
3. REPROGRAM My Heart & Mind with Truth
4. **RESPOND Faithfully for a Continuous Life of Peace**

Step 4 Respond

Respond Faithfully

Chapter 10
HOLD ON. HOLD ON TIGHT.

HOPE SPRANG UP WHEN PEACE WAS MY WAY OF life! I was amazed that applying these four steps could bear such amazing fruit. I remained in His continuous peace as I became more skilled at *Recognizing* what was robbing me of God's peace, quickly *Releasing* it to Him, and repenting if necessary. By *Reprogramming* my mind and overwriting the lies with God's truth, those good seeds continued to enrich and expand my harvest. I was able to *Respond faithfully* by *choosing to trust my faithful Father as a way of life*.

This step is where the abundant life is developed. We will take our Christian life to a new depth. We will grow and become stronger. We will bear much fruit. We will explore many ways in which we can grow, develop our faith, become deeply rooted, and be anchored to the life that God has called us to. We will continue to uproot the weeds and continue to plant the seeds of truth, *but in this* step, we will be *living them out* by Responding faithfully.

Psalm 1:3 (NASB)

> He will be like a tree *firmly* planted by streams of water, which yields its fruit in its season. And its leaf does not wither; And in whatever he does, he prospers.

Being firmly planted in God, we will yield an abundant harvest. I know from past experiences that we can continue to prosper, keeping our peace even amidst terrible storms. We are not prepared for all that we will face in this life. *This life can be very difficult*, but knowing that we are journeying with Almighty God, we are able to keep our peace. We can rest in Him every step of the way, and especially in the extremely severe seasons of life. It is then that we will need to hold on tight to Him, *knowing He will keep us no matter what the circumstances.*

"Hold On. Hold On Tight."
Those were the words I sensed recently as I began to walk on my treadmill. I felt God was telling me to *"Hold on. Hold on tight."* There was no fear associated with it, just a strong impression for me to hold on tight. I also felt He instructed me to *keep my eye on His eye and He would lead me through.*

By faith I held on to the bar of my treadmill. I said, *"By faith, God, I will hold on."*

I hoped and even assumed that it had to do with finishing this book. I thought that perhaps it would go so well that I would have to hold on to Him as He led me in the way I should go. I was wrong. Two days later as I was proofreading the grief section of this book, I received an emotional call from my family informing me that my brother had just attempted suicide.

As those words penetrated my heart, immediately from my soul a deep cry came rushing out. I screamed so loudly that my piercing shrieks scared my dogs and everyone in the house. The anguish from within came from a depth of pain I did not know existed. As I hurried to get out of my house, the pain became so heavy that I could not take one more step. I fell to the floor and cried out in excruciating sorrow. Pushing myself to regain a little strength, I jumped to my feet to get over to his house.

When my family and I arrived, the police and the homicide units were already there. Seeing the homicide van in front of his house made it evident that he was gone. He had ended his own life. We were all in utter shock. It was so hard to believe. I had spoken to him the day before and he had seemed fine.

He had an ongoing illness that he had dealt with for decades. He had been getting worse. He had ongoing pain, but He also had really happy days. He loved deeply, and he was deeply loved. He knew God, but he also struggled in this life. I had watched my brother hit some very low lows with his illness and with some poor choices. I also had watched the way that God cared for him and his needs, and it made my faith grow stronger. I saw God do amazing things for him.

My brother knew how to pray. He believed in God and knew that God hears our prayers. When he would hear that I had a need for myself or a need in my family, he made it his personal mission to pray until God heard. I have told many that he could pull down heaven with his prayers. His prayers were an awesome gift that he had given to me.

The day after his death, I reread the two scriptures that I had received from God the morning prior to this happening. These scriptures were a reassurance of God's love for my brother, and for us all.

John 10:27-30 (NIV)

> My sheep listen to my voice; I know them, and they follow me. I give them eternal life, and they shall never perish; no one will snatch them out of my hand. My Father, who has given them to me, is greater than all; no one can snatch them out of my Father's hand. I and the Father are one."

Luke 14:15 (NASB)

> When one of those who were reclining *at the table* with Him heard this, he said to Him, "Blessed is everyone who will eat bread in the kingdom of God!"

These scriptures reassured me that life here on earth is not everything. We have eternal life, or better stated, we will live with our God in heaven for all eternity. We will not perish, and we are assured that nothing can snatch us from our Father's hand. Nothing! Not even my brother taking his own life could snatch him from God's hand because God is faithful.

The second scripture was a wonderful picture of us being blessed to eat in God's kingdom. In the past when I had wanted my brother to come over, I would entice him with good food. I would say, *"Why don't you come over?"* Then I would list the different foods that I was making, such as chicken parmesan, wedding soup, chili with cheesy cornbread, or pasta with hot and mild sausage and peppers.

He would always say, *"Mmmmm!"* Then he would laugh and add, *"You don't have to twist my arm."* Many times, when he slept over, I would be awakened around 2 AM to the hum of the microwave. In the morning he would say, *"Your wedding soup or your chicken parm was calling my name. I had to get some more. I hope I did not wake you."* I just smiled. I enjoyed making him the foods that he loved.

I am thankful that we will be blessed to eat together again in heaven. Our God is good, and heaven is a place of blessing. I am also *sad* that my brother chose to forfeit the plans that God had for him. My brother will not be a part of the everyday events that he enjoyed, nor will he be a part of the special occasions or "firsts" that are to come. Sadly, he will miss out on *making the impact* that *only he could have made*. I think if he could look back on that moment, he would choose differently. If he had seen the devastation this one decision created, it would have broken his heart. I believe he would have reached out for help.

Unfortunately, we cannot change the past, but we can learn how to Respond faithfully as we entrust our shattered hearts to God. While we are here in this life, we will face difficult times. My brother's death is one of those painful, dark places that was filled with deep sorrow and the ache of loneliness. My heart was pierced by the loss of not seeing him, hearing his voice, or enjoying his contagious laugh. *(My mom and my brother could make me laugh as no other. They are both now in heaven.)*

> WE CANNOT CHANGE THE PAST, BUT WE CAN LEARN HOW TO RESPOND FAITHFULLY.

RESPONDING FAITHFULLY STEP BY STEP
The evening that my brother died, as everyone else was asleep, I could feel the shock that had been like a shield protecting my mind begin to lift. I felt fear begin to push in and the shadows of terror trying to envelop me. Fearful thoughts tried to convince me that *no one was safe.* I was threatened by the *truth* that *loss can come quickly and without warning.* Those threats turned the truth into the lie that *I would never be safe and that no one will ever be safe.*

That is when I knew I had to *Respond faithfully* because this type of fearful thinking would lead me into a dark pit of despair. I immediately went to the ***four steps*** in order to keep my peace. I **Recognized** fear's tactics. I asked God to help me as I **Released** my honest and heartfelt fears to Him. I knew that I had to fill up with God's Word, but physically and emotionally, I was not strong enough to seek truth for myself. I chose to pull up a recording of a woman I could trust to lead me. I began to

Reprogram my mind with the truth that she shared. As I listened to her words, God's promises comforted my heart and began to replenish some hope, faith, and strength within me.

As I lay in the darkness, I was reminded of this truth, which penetrated my heart and Reprogrammed my mind: *"My God is the same yesterday, today, and forever."* I held on to that truth knowing that my God who faithfully stood with me yesterday was the same God who would stand with me today. He will be with me forever. *The fear was silenced* as I Reprogrammed my heart with the truths that I knew. *God is good! God is with me. He will never leave me. He will get us through.*

Hebrews 13:8 (NASB)

> Jesus Christ *is* the same yesterday and today and forever.

Deuteronomy 31:8 (NIV)

> The Lord himself goes before you and will be with you; he will never leave you nor forsake you. Do not be afraid; do not be discouraged.

By tightly embracing the truth that God is faithful, I was able to **Respond** *faithfully*. While my insides were shaking with grief, I Released all my cares to God. I *trusted* Him with my brother, who was now with Him in heaven. I intentionally *trusted* God with my own wounded heart and my family's broken hearts and lives. The weight of their sorrow weighed heavily upon me. I knew I had to *trust* God to care for all those whose hearts were devastated by my brother's death.

I continued to remind myself to trust in the truth that *my God was faithful before. He will be faithful today. He will be faithful forever because that is who He is*! As I resisted the continued taunts of fear by holding on to God and His truths, I could feel the comfort of His peace lightly covering me. Continuing to listen to those teachings, I was able to fall asleep. As I woke up, I would tell my heart to *hold on tight to Him*. Again, I put on another biblical teaching to allow my mind to be filled with God's truth. This happened for the next two hours, and then I shut off the TV and peacefully fell asleep for the night.

That was supernatural. There is no way that it makes sense that I could fall asleep with peace on the night my brother committed suicide. God helps us when we stay close to Him during our times of need. I am thankful that God told me to *hold on tight* and *to keep my eye upon Him and He would lead me*. Starting that night and every day since, I knew I had to keep my mind focused on Him and focused on what is good in order to maintain my peace.

THINK ON WHAT IS GOOD
Philippians 4:8–9 (AMP)

> Finally, believers, whatever is true, whatever is honorable *and* worthy of respect, whatever is right *and* confirmed by God's word, whatever is pure *and* wholesome, whatever is lovely *and* brings peace, whatever is admirable *and* of good repute; if there is any excellence, if there is anything worthy of praise, think *continually* on these things [center your mind on them, and implant them in your heart]. The things which you have learned and received and heard and seen in me, practice these things [in daily life], and the God [who is the source] of peace *and* well-being will be with you.

Trust me, it was a choice as to *what* I would think on. It was imperative that I focused on what was good and what would bring me peace. I knew that any negative thoughts would fill my mind and implant themselves into my heart, which would quickly rob me of my peace. I was careful to keep my *focus* on God who is *my source* of peace.

I had to be diligent to Respond faithfully when it came to my thoughts about my brother's death. As the troubling images would try to enter my mind to have me *focus* on *how* he ended his life and *what* had happened, I immediately felt my peace being robbed. I acknowledged the truth of what happened, but I chose to think on the good. I reminded myself that he is with God and that God will faithfully see us through. It was then that my peace remained as an anchor that kept me secure.

In our difficult days, we must stay focused on what is good and the good that God is doing in our situation. During our trials we can choose to allow fears to rule our hearts and minds, enabling sorrow to weigh us down. This can easily happen if we do not diligently focus on what is good. *When I concentrated on God, His truths, and His past faithfulness, my peace was restored.* He comforted me.

When the storms of life arise, we need to cling to the rock. As we hold on to God, we find Him to be the rock we can stand on. He is the rock we can trust in. He is the rock that we can throw ourselves upon when we have no answers or we need wisdom, strength, and guidance.

> Every time I have run to Him or clung to Him,
> I have found Him FAITHFUL!

He Is Faithful

I remember *a few years ago* I went through a two-month storm. It affected our whole family. One of my children needed a sudden surgery. Another son was in two serious accidents, both resulting in concussions (and one in which his truck was totaled). I also was helping an extended family member's marriage as it was abruptly unraveling. It was one traumatic and emotional circumstance after another. I was exhausted after those two months of trials.

It was during worship at church when I asked God if this storm was almost over, because it was so difficult. I felt Him ask me this question: *"Look back. What do you see?"* I thought back over the last two months and every difficult situation, and then I burst into tears.

I cried out, *"Lord, I found you faithful! You were faithful in every situation!"*

We will know Him to be faithful to the depths we need Him to be. I needed Him every step during that two-month trial. I clung to Him and He gave me His peace. Sometimes it is not until we look back over our experience that we fully know *Jesus is faithful to keep us through the most difficult storms of life.* That is when our faith grows immensely.

> JESUS IS FAITHFUL TO KEEP US THROUGH THE MOST DIFFICULT STORMS OF LIFE.

This two-month trial gave me a deeper understanding of God's faithfulness. By my own personal experiences, I now knew that *God is faithful.* The night my brother died, I pulled from my past understanding of God's faithfulness, and that brought me life. Every experience with God can be drawn upon when we need it the most. It always amazes me that we *get to* have this type of intimate relationship with our God. He knows what we need and when we need it. He is faithful. That is who He is!

Write down a specific time when you have experienced the faithfulness of God.

_____
_____

How did it feel when you found God faithful in that situation?

_____

_____

Can you name areas or situations where you are *having a hard time* believing that God will be faithful?

_____

_____

HE IS THE ROCK IN WHOM WE CAN TRUST

It is in trusting God that we Release our control and place our faith in Him and Him alone. We take our next step, knowing that *God causes all things to work together for good to those who love Him.* (Romans 8:28 NASB) We must trust Him, desiring His will to be done. That means that we may not understand it all completely, but we trust the One who does. Having a close and personal relationship with Jesus has become a foundation for my peace.

Another account when I had to cling to the rock was when, amidst a "normal" day, a negative situation arose suddenly. I remember feeling overwhelmed by the scope of the situation. I cried out to God, saying, *"Lord, I need You! You are the rock I have stood on. You have been so faithful to me. You know the situation. You know I am so concerned that it will continue to go badly. Today Lord, I throw myself on You, my solid rock. Lord Jesus, I am praying for Your favor, wisdom, and insight."*

I told Jesus that I was throwing myself on Him until the storm passed. I trusted in His ability to keep me. I prayed that He would work it out and give me wisdom for the steps I needed to take.

It was amazing that as I was trusting Him with all my concerns, He was behind the scenes working on my behalf. When I got word of a new door of kindness and understanding opening, I knew He was already working in ways that I never could.

He was changing hearts. I had to walk through another door by faith, and sure enough, I encountered more favor, understanding, and help. It was so evident that my God was working.

We have a choice every day. Will we trust in God? Will we trust His plan? *Trust is the foundation that keeps us in His peace.* It can be hard to trust in Him for everything we need. In that moment when I was "throwing" myself upon Him, I was expressing that, *"I am not able to figure this out. I am not able to do anything to make this work out. I choose to cling to Your mercy and Your goodness to care for us in this situation. You are my only help."* There is no rock like our God.

> **TRUST IS THE FOUNDATION THAT KEEPS US IN HIS PEACE.**

Psalm 18:1–3 (NLT)

> I love you, LORD; you are my strength. The LORD is my rock, my fortress, and my savior; my God is my rock, in whom I find protection. He is my shield, the power that saves me, and my place of safety. I called on the LORD, who is worthy of praise, and he saved me from my enemies.

Isaiah 26:3–4 (NIV)

> You will keep in perfect peace those whose minds are steadfast, because they trust in you. Trust in the LORD forever, for the Lord, the Lord Himself, is the Rock eternal.

I love how Isaiah states that God will keep in perfect peace those whose minds are steadfast. How were their minds steadfast? By trusting in the Lord. He instructs us to, *"trust in the LORD forever, for the Lord, the Lord Himself, is the Rock eternal."*

This rock will not crumble or disappear. The Lord Jesus is our strong rock now and for all eternity.

Are you able to trust in the Lord? Does He keep you in perfect peace because your mind is steadfast?

> **Steadfast** means: unwavering, unfaltering, resolute, persistent, committed, dedicated, firm, loyal, faithful, constant, devoted.

Is your trust in Him unwavering, resolute, dedicated, firm, and constant? Are you committed to trust in God no matter what you face? I know many who trust God *until something in their life goes wrong.* Then they blame Him for the negative issue and withhold their trust. When things go wrong, that is when we need to hold on to Him even tighter. If we keep our minds stayed on our God, He will keep us in His perfect peace.

HIS PERFECT PEACE
Twenty-four hours *after my brother's death,* so many were praying for us. My pastor called me, and he prayed for my whole family. That is when I became aware of God's peace becoming so strong. One hour went by with no tears. Two hours, no tears. I thought, *I think God has lifted my grief.* To my amazement I started to witness His peace covering my whole family. I could see a difference in all of us. The best way I can describe it was *His peace came and lifted the deep sorrow* that we were all feeling.

As confirmation, shortly after I noticed God's peace covering us, my youngest son came up to me and said, *"Mom, I feel guilty because I do not feel sad right now. I feel like I could actually go play. Is that okay?"*

Smiling, I reassured him and said, *"Honey, we are experiencing the grace and mercy of our God. His peace has come in and is carrying us. This is the peace that surpasses all understanding."* I explained that he should not feel guilty but thankful for the gift that we have been given.

Philippians 4:7 (AMP)

> And the peace of God [that peace which reassures the heart, that peace] which transcends all understanding, [that peace which] stands guard over your hearts and your minds in Christ Jesus [is yours].

I am so thankful that we held on tightly to our Lord, *trusting Him to keep us* during this great loss. By the grace of God, He filled us with His peace. His peace is a perfect peace. In the natural there was no way we should have had peace, but our God is our refuge, our place of safety. He guards our hearts and minds. He is our rock and our strength. His peace protected us, and over time God gave us the strength to process our loss and heal more deeply.

We have a choice. *Will we allow* Jesus to be the One we trust in to keep us ... so that we can Respond faithfully?

BUILD ON THE ROCK
Matthew 7:24–26 (NIV) The Wise and Foolish Builders

> Therefore, everyone who hears these words of mine and puts them into practice is like a wise man who built his house on the rock. The rain came down, the streams rose, and the winds blew and beat against that house; yet it did not fall, because it had its foundation on the rock. But everyone who hears these words of mine and does not put them into practice is like a foolish man who built his house on sand.

Continuous Peace

Jesus is our solid rock. We have been building on this rock, from the beginning of this book. Every time we believe God's truths and put His Word into practice, we are building on the solid rock! He will keep us when the storms of life come. Our Rock, Jesus, is strong enough to keep us no matter what we encounter! We must determine not to build on the sand by only hearing His Words and *not* putting them into practice. *Sand erodes and cannot keep us in times of storms.* We must know the truth and live by the truth.

If we don't fully trust Jesus, His timing, His plan, or His way, we will continually try to figure things out for ourselves, which is like building on the shifting sand. Our minds will get bogged down with our many problems, emotions, and disappointments. We will try to accomplish all things in our own strength by not going to the Lord for help. By not trusting Him, we carry the weight of our burdens. This can feel like we are in sinking sand, which frustrates us even further.

The truth is *often we want what we want when we want it.* That lifestyle is building on the shifting sand of self-effort, self-confidence, and a self-directed way. When we trust in God, we Release our control over to Him. It is like saying, "*Your way is best. I trust You to lead me.*" We build on the rock when we know His truth and trust Him to carry out His will. As we trust Him to keep us, He will lead us and strengthen us. Building on the rock is building on solid ground.

We are blessed that we *get to* trust in Him. We *get to* run to Him when the storms of life come, and they will come. He will be a shield to all who take refuge in Him. It is God who arms us with strength and keeps our way secure. We get to come to Him and receive the benefits of Him being our Lord, Savior, and our Rock eternal.

Our relationship with God is ever growing. The greater we pursue a relationship with our God, the deeper we will know

Him. The better we know Him, the broader we will trust Him. This relationship that we get to have with our God never ceases to amaze me. It is ever deepening and ever growing.

> We can continue to grow daily
> by choosing to do the next right thing.

2 Thessalonians 3:13 (NIV)

> And as for you, brothers and sisters, never tire of doing what is good.

DO THE NEXT RIGHT THING
How many relationships, jobs, and lives would be impacted if we just did the next right thing? We need to Respond Faithfully even when we don't feel like it. It is easy to persuade ourselves into going back to bed, holding back from doing a good thing, or just staying stuck and not proceeding forward. It is then that we must *choose* to do what is good. Doing the next right thing becomes a safety net for our life, and it will be greatly rewarded.

> DOING THE NEXT RIGHT THING BECOMES A SAFETY NET FOR OUR LIFE, AND IT WILL BE GREATLY REWARDED.

We find God faithful to meet us right where we are as we do the next right thing, even if everything within us protests loudly. After my brother's death, although I had miraculous peace, there were times when I felt like my spirit was swirling with many heavy emotions. Thoughts would come and go as I was processing through the grief.

Continuous Peace

On one specific occasion, I had an uneasy feeling that was not lifting. After my Bible time, I wanted to go back to bed, throw the covers over my head, and ignore the churning emotions. The weight of the emotions robbed my strength. I wanted to escape, hide, or ignore all that I was feeling.

I knew I had to do the next right thing, which was finish my time with God in worship and prayer. I pushed myself to obediently worship God on my treadmill. It was within the first few minutes that I began to cry out with literal tears. I poured my broken heart out to God and Released all the emotions that were holding me captive. He met me there, and amazingly, He lifted the sorrow and removed the swirling emotions. I felt relieved as my spirit was renewed.

He lifted me up. I am so thankful that I Responded faithfully when I really did not feel like it. I can guarantee if I had gone back to bed, the negative emotions would have intensified.

I thank God that we can trust Him to lead us to do the next right thing!

Do You Respond Faithfully by Doing the Next Right Thing?

Sometimes we are staying stuck because we won't do the next right thing.

What is the next right thing that God is calling you to do? Many times, it is right in front of us. Perhaps it is finishing what we started. It may be apologizing, forgiving, letting something go, believing a specific scripture, praying, talking to someone, finding a faithful counselor, writing it out in order to get it out. It could be working, doing that chore that you've put off, finding a good church, joining a small group, trusting God, or letting others in. *Sometimes we are staying stuck because we won't do the next right thing.*

When I feel stuck, not knowing what I should be doing, I start by praying for wisdom. I pray for God to show me what to do next. This may sound very basic, but God is faithful to lead us in the way we should go.

My prayer may include these points:

- Lord, I feel stuck. I feel like I don't know how to go forward.
- I don't want to take steps backward.
- Please, give me wisdom and show me what I should do.
- Reveal my next step and equip me to do it.
- Thank you! I want to do what is right. Please, lead me.

I then wait and listen for His still, small voice. Sometimes I will be able to visualize my next step, which makes it easier to faithfully follow through.

I can also refer to a list I made of *my responsibilities* and *my desired want-to-dos.* It has been helpful to keep my goals written down and before me so that if I get sidetracked, I have a good visual to pick up where I left off. I update my list so that when I get stuck, I can recall the list and do the next right thing. I can also show myself grace concerning the things that still need to be done, because I know that I am focusing on what I need to do.

Just by doing the next good thing in our lives (God's good things), we can keep our peace.

What is the next right thing that you know that God has called you to do?

_____
_____

LIFT UP YOUR HEAD
Psalm 24:7,10 (NIV)

> Lift up your heads, you gates; be lifted up, you ancient doors, that the King of glory may come in.
>
> Who is he, this King of glory? The Lord Almighty—he is the King of glory.

When we Respond faithfully, we are to *look up* to the One who is able to lift us up. He is the One who will come in and give us His peace. He is Almighty God. Looking to Him we will be lifted up!

When God first taught me this powerful lesson, I was experiencing a terrible fear that was rooted in a real concern that I was facing. Immediately as I was about to lose my peace, I got on my knees and began to cry out to God. I voiced my concern to Him. I told Him I needed a truth to hold on to. I prayed, *"Please, Lord, speak to me through Your Word."* I felt Him prompt my heart, *"Psalm 24:7."*

I quickly opened my Bible and read Psalm 24:7. As I read the words *"Lift up your heads,"* I actually looked up. With my head lifted, I took a deep and calming breath. With my focus now upon my faithful Lord, I felt spiritually lifted up. I felt the heavy weight lift from within me.

God prompted my heart, *"How often are you to lift up your head and take your eyes off of your circumstances, fixing your attention onto Me?"* I was amazed when I realized the scripture is Psalm 24:7. What a great reminder that twenty-four hours a day, seven days a week we are to look up to God.

In that moment God showed me that He knew where I was and what scripture I needed. He knew that I was beginning to focus on my circumstances, which was causing me *to lose sight of His presence in my life.* Focusing on my negative circumstances produced fear and was beginning to rob my peace. When I focused on the Lord Almighty, He lifted my fear and gave me faith to trust Him and a clear understanding that He wants me to look up to Him 24/7 so that I may be lifted up!

Our lives give us many opportunities *to look to God*. Even in the devastating circumstances in life, we are to look up to Him. I hope that you are not going through a situation like the one I did with my brother, but I know *if* we look up to God, we will *be lifted up*. He will take our greatest pain, disappointment, or sorrow and saturate those depths with His peace, comfort, and love.

I am in awe of the faithfulness and ability of our God. He truly is strong and mighty. I know that *according to the depth that we need Him, He is there*. To the depth of our emptiness is to the depth that He faithfully fills us. There are no all-time lows that His love and peace cannot penetrate and fill. To the degree that we need Him, we find Him faithful. He can keep us, heal us, and even bless us beyond measure. Our God is always with us. In His presence we have His peace. He is amazing!

> ACCORDING TO THE DEPTH THAT WE NEED HIM, HE IS THERE.

LOOKING BACK OVER THIS CHAPTER
Do you lift your head up to the Lord Almighty? Have you ever experienced being lifted up by Him? If so, what was that experience like?

_____

_____

Are you trusting in Him with a steadfast faith? If not, in what areas do you desire to have an unwavering faith in Almighty God?

_____
_____

If you are *not Responding faithfully* to the circumstances in your life, will you:

- *Remember* God is your (rock, shield, refuge ...)?
- *Recognize and ask* God to reset your focus on Him?
- *Think on* those things that are good and the good that God is doing in your situation?
- *Do the next right thing* that God is calling you to do?
- *Look up to God* 24/7, knowing Almighty God will lift you up?

Chapter 11
RUN YOUR RACE

RUN YOUR OWN RACE
WHEN WE RESPOND FAITHFULLY, WE WILL BE RUNning our own race. When we run our *own* race, we will be fulfilling God's plan for our lives. The Bible instructs us *how to run and what to watch for while we run*. We have been called to run *with* endurance and *without* comparing.

Hebrews 12:1–3 (NASB) Jesus, the Example

> Therefore, since we have so great a cloud of witnesses surrounding us, let us also lay aside every encumbrance and the sin which so easily entangles us, and let us run with endurance the race that is set before us, fixing our eyes on Jesus, the author and perfecter of faith, who for the joy set before Him endured the cross, despising the shame, and has sat down at the right hand of the throne of God. For consider Him who has endured such hostility by sinners against Himself, so that you will not grow weary and lose heart.

Each of us runs our own specific race. We run on different tracks. We are called to certain individuals and groups. We each have unique callings. God has given us specific talents, gifts, desires, hopes, and dreams that equip us to run our own race. We cannot run our friend's race. We are only called and equipped to run the race that God has set before us.

Do not compare the plans that God has for you with another's! Do not compare your family with any other's. Do not compare your way of raising your kids or living your life with other's way of living. Be free! There is *only one you*, and you were *called* and *entrusted* with the race God has *designed* for you! We are called to run our race with endurance, fixing our eyes on Jesus as we run!

We are to:

- Lay aside every encumbrance.
- Set aside the sin that so easily entangles us.
- Run with endurance the race that is set before us.
- Fix our eyes on Jesus, the author and perfecter of our faith.
- Look to Him and His example to endure, so we don't grow weary and lose heart.

I am thankful that we are told how to run. We are to run with endurance . . . in *what?* The race that is set before us. *How?* By laying aside *every* encumbrance and the sin that so easily entangles us. *How are we to do that?* By fixing our eyes on Jesus. He is the One who authored our race and the One who will perfect our faith as we run. He is our example of fulfilling God's call with endurance so that we will not grow weary and lose heart.

RUNNING WITH ENDURANCE
When I have run on a track, I notice that the first lap is the hardest. When my legs begin to burn, I want to quit every time. I literally try to talk myself into quitting on lap one! I say to myself, *"Why did I think running today was a good idea? What makes me want to do this? I really don't like running! I want to quit!"*

I know my answer is that God has called me to pray and worship while I exercise. Knowing God has called me to this, I tell myself *what* I am going to do. *"You are running! You are going to finish! You are not a quitter! Talk to God out here on this track! Focus on Him and He will meet you as you run. He will speak to your heart!"*

When I focus on my achy legs and my body that wants to quit, I am focused on the circumstances. But when I change my focus to God and remind myself of *why* I am running, then I can run with endurance. I look to Him and I complete what He has given me to do.

> **The meaning of *endurance*** is to have continuance, patience, fortitude, durability, strength, persistence, steadfastness, stamina, perseverance, and staying power.

Just like when I was on the track and wanted to quit, in my life I had to choose to run *with* endurance. It is too easy to quit when life gets hard. There will always be *many* reasons to quit running our race. There may be distractions that sideline us and disappointments or circumstances that can stop us in our tracks. Many situations in our lives can be difficult. We may need times or even seasons of grace to deal with a certain issue. But if you know God has called you to something specific, don't allow the daily pressures to weigh you down and tempt you to quit. You can come to Him. Ask Him to *help you* with the endurance to run your race. This is not about your performance; it is about you choosing to continue to fulfill what God is calling you to do daily without sinking under the pressure from life's stresses.

> **DON'T ALLOW THE DAILY PRESSURES TO WEIGH YOU DOWN AND TEMPT YOU TO QUIT.**

We are called to run in the state of continued and committed steadfastness. We are to run with our focus on Jesus. We are *not* called to run aimlessly. We are *not* to compare. We are *not* called to run our neighbor's race, our brother's race, our friend's race, or even our spouse's race. *We are only equipped to run our own race.*

ENDURANCE IN ALL SEASONS
Endurance is also needed *in the waiting* seasons. Many times, we feel as if God has put us on a shelf. In those times we may *feel* like we want to give up or stop believing. God has used my waiting seasons to give me a physical rest and to refuel me spiritually. I have found that *what I have learned in the waiting seasons has benefitted me in the seasons that were to come.* These seasons of waiting are for our own good. We do not have to understand *why* we have to wait. We only need to endure as we *trust Him in the waiting season.*

Our God is good! *If He has called us to it, He will get us through it!* We must fix our eyes on Him. He will perfect our faith as we go through. Nothing will be wasted. He will use every failure and hardship to make us stronger, wiser, and more compassionate. His Word will empower us to run our daily race with endurance. Let's not give up or give in! Joy comes when we run our race.

What is the race that God has called you to (as a child of God, spouse, parent, child, friend, helper, worker, mentor, etc.)?

_____

_____

Are you consistently running your own race? Do you glance at others, which causes you to stop, compare, become jealous, prideful, lose heart, or despair? Explain.

_____

_____

In what areas would you like to have more endurance?

_____

_____

There are times when we may realize that we have been running the wrong race, and the correction that needs to take place can be painful. If we are not willing to *embrace the pain* and *correct our course*, we will continue to run aimlessly.

EMBRACE THE PAIN

A course correction is worth the effort to remove every encumbrance.

Can you envision me showing up to the track with my heavy backpack on my back and beginning to run? I would become exhausted and be a spectacle on the field. Can you imagine how much harder it would be for me to run? My whole body would be impacted by the weight of my backpack. My heart, lungs, and legs would have to work much harder.

When we deal with our wrong behaviors, wrong thinking, and sins, it can be painful. Unpacking our backpack full of wounds and undealt with issues or shame may be hard to Release, but *by embracing the pain, we allow God to heal us*. Every effort to embrace the pain and not run from it will bring us more freedom and more of God's peace. Pain wants to demand that we stop, but we must press on with endurance to fulfill what God has called us to.

When I began to run, the pain in my legs yelled for me to stop. In a similar way, pain tries to dictate our quitting while we are removing the obstacles or sins that so easily entangle us. That is when we need to choose to *embrace the pain* because it leads to the *continuation of our transformation*.

When we Release our pain, God heals us. Remember while our God is healing us, we will experience some pain. But *the pain of transformation is temporary*. God is an amazing healer. He will be faithful to complete the good work He began in us.

Years ago, my wonderful friend confided in me that she was an alcoholic. It was hard to believe because she had hidden it so well. In those first few months of sobriety, our phone calls were difficult because she was in a lot of pain: *physical pain* of withdrawal, *emotional pain* of regret and shame, and *mental pain* of changing her ways and her engrained habits. I remember many times saying to her, "*You have to embrace this pain.*" She hated to hear that statement because she hated pain. She acknowledged that the reason she probably drank was to numb her pain.

HERE IS HER ACCOUNT OF THAT SEASON OF HER LIFE:
>When I first got sober, I was a nervous wreck. I would go to AA meetings because I was told they would help me. After weeks and then months of sobriety, I still shook like a leaf. I literally trembled inside. I would cry out to God, "Why Lord, why do I still shake? I haven't had alcohol for __weeks, __ months. This feels unfair." I wanted to FEEL better.
>
>I saw people in AA who were happy, carefree, but I did not feel that way. I met with a dear friend, Dawn, who told me to embrace the pain. "What??!!" I thought that was one of the most ridiculous things I had ever heard. I CAN'T EMBRACE the pain. I am afraid of pain. I am afraid to hurt. I run from pain.
>
>What Dawn meant by embrace the pain was choosing not to run from whatever is hurting me and letting God handle it, so that I would be renewed.
>
>If I chose to keep running from pain (and sometimes, I still do today) nothing gets fixed. Nothing heals. It's the same old pathetic story of timidity and fear. But if I choose to open my mind and my heart to Christ, He can dissolve the pain. He will help me deal with the source and pull it out by its roots. I did not learn

this overnight. Actually, it took me years to honestly and genuinely kneel down and FULLY surrender to God and allow him to dig deep and pull out all the stuff that was causing me fear, doubt, insecurity, and lack of confidence.

I would hear people say in recovery that they would NEVER change a thing in their recovery process. They would even go through the pain all over again because it helps them to be the person they are today. The truth is, I wholeheartedly agree.

My friend is beautifully living a life of freedom and peace as never before. There is freedom in embracing our pain! Course correction may be painful, but we can choose our response. Will we *ignore* our old or current issues, or will we Respond by *embracing* what God shows us? We can choose to put our desire to be *free* and *full* of His peace ahead of hiding from the painful issue.

Course correction may be painful,
but the pain of transformation is temporary.

When I face a course correction, I will Respond by:

_____
_____

Knowing We Get To
- We *get to* bring God all our concerns and Release all our anxiety to Him because He cares for us.
- We *get to* have a close relationship with God and be filled with His peace.
- We *get to* be taught what is best for us and be directed in the way we should go.

- We *get to* draw near to God as we are. He will fill us with His love and every good thing.
- We then *get to* give away the overflow of what He has poured into our lives.

A life of peace fully Recognizes that we get to Respond to the Father's amazing love moment by moment. With the Holy Spirit in us, *we get to* participate with Him in fulfilling His will for our lives. We also *get to* join Him and become a blessing to others.

I Get To

I have instructed married couples and moms for years to view their relationships not as I have to but that I get to. *"You don't have to care for your spouse, children, or home; you get to!"* That is my heart. We have been blessed in many ways and *we get to* care for *who* and *what* God has *entrusted* to us.

> **We can replace "I have to" with a heart Response "I get to."**

This principle can bring life to each of us as we replace *"I have to"* with a heart Response *"I get to."* We *get to* care for those who have been entrusted to us. Getting to do what the Father has called us to do is very fulfilling. Let's not overlook the beautiful everyday things that we get to do in our lives.

We will lose our peace if we *fret* over tending to the many routine things of life such as changing diapers, making meals, cleaning bathrooms, and doing other household chores. We may also get overwhelmed with working outside the home, instructing children, or caring for, helping, and encouraging others. It may feel like these things will never end. Remember that this season can quickly pass or change, so *let's make the most of it.* Peace and joy come when our heart Response is, *"I get to."*

Our lives have many daily blessings. Sometimes we may take those blessings for granted. We should be humbled by knowing *there are those who would love to step in and care for what we call ordinary or mundane.* Many times others can view our lives more easily as the great blessings that they are. Let's be thankful for what we get to do!

Is there an area in your life that you need to change your perspective from "*I have to*" to a heart response of "*I get to*"? If so, name that area. _____

Then fill in the following statement.

Thank You, Lord, that in this season, I get to:

_____

WE GET TO REST
We get to sow rest into our own lives. Yes, add in time to *rest*, times of *refilling*. Each one of us requires "downtime." We need time to be *renewed* and to *replenish* our own spiritual, physical, and mental strength. We need to be *intentional* with our times of rest.

I remember when I was busy seven days a week with no day to rest. I began to resent my home and become frustrated with the mess I always had to clean up. God taught me the incredible blessing called a Sabbath rest. I would choose one day a week, usually Sunday, to go to church and then rest. I did not do what I did the rest of the week. I still cared for my children, but we all knew we would *not* be shopping, cleaning, or going places. We usually ate leftovers. It was a day to enjoy. If we had to be at an event, I would try to choose another night to rest.

My Sabbath rest was not a law that I lived by but a heart desire to honor God and obediently slow down. I needed downtime, a time to rest. This immediately took away the resentment that was robbing me of my peace. After church, I learned to enjoy my Sunday nap or just "hang out" with my family with no agenda.

> A DAY OF REST HELPS US TO ENJOY OUR GOD AS WE SLOW DOWN TO HEAR HIS VOICE AND APPRECIATE HIS BEAUTY ALL AROUND US.

Sabbath is also meant to be a special day of refreshing, a day to *fill up* with *more of God.* It is a day to spiritually renew our heart, perhaps by lying down and reading a good book, watching a favorite preacher, or reading through a portion of the Bible.

A day of rest helps us to enjoy our God as we slow down to hear His voice and appreciate His beauty all around us. When rested, we can better enjoy and cherish those He has entrusted to our care.

How will you renew yourself? Do you have a little bit of time for daily rest? Can you create one day a week to replenish your spiritual, physical, and mental strength by resting? (If needed, you can *be creative* by choosing one evening and another portion of time on another day.)

_____

_____

> Just by slowing down and *enjoying* our relationship with our God and those He has *entrusted* to us, we will *shield* our harvest from the *weed of regret*!

BE THANKFUL
1 Thessalonians 5:16–18 (AMP)

> Rejoice always *and* delight in your faith; be unceasing *and* persistent in prayer; in every situation [no matter what the circumstances] be thankful *and* continually give thanks *to God*; for this is the will of God for you in Christ Jesus.

In Christ Jesus we are to continually give thanks to God. In our relationship with Him, we get to be thankful! We get to rejoice always. We get to delight in our faith. We get to pray to our loving Father.

Rejoicing, praying, and being thankful is God's will for you!

Imagine if we were joyful always… if we were quick to pray and not worry or complain. What if we looked for the good that God is doing in every circumstance? Would your life be different? Would your walk with God be enriched? Would others see a difference in your *response* to life's circumstances?

THANKFUL FOR WHAT WE HAVE

I remember praying for a bigger home. We had a two-bedroom home and a growing family. We prayed and searched for a bigger home, then prayed and searched some more. I was getting frustrated. We did not have a lot of money, so it was hard to find a home. This went on for three years. Somewhere in the process, I remember God put on my heart, *"I will not give you another home until you are thankful for the one that you have."*

Wow! While that was hard to hear, I had to realize that I was getting frustrated with the lack of space in our home. With two little ones, I had off-season clothes stored behind dressers and under beds. I felt like we were bursting at the seams. I hadn't realized until then that *I had stopped being thankful for what I did have!*

I Recognized how that was *disrespectful* to God, who had provided this home for us and had given us the means to afford it.

My *focus* was diverted to what I did *not* have, which was enough room. God wanted to change my heart to be thankful rather than increasingly frustrated and ungrateful. From that day forward, I became appreciative for all that I did have! I genuinely thanked Him for everything. My thankfulness gave me the ability to really enjoy our home and make the most of it.

Being thankful was one of the ways that God began to transform my heart. When we can become *thankful while frustrated*, it leads the way to being thankful in all things.

OUR PEACE REMAINS AS WE ARE THANKFUL
Our *peace remains* as we thank Him for all that we have. We can rejoice for the big and small blessings in life, being aware that everything good comes from God! We can be thankful even in the *waiting seasons* knowing His timing is perfect. We can be thankful in the *challenging seasons* discerning we can become more like Him. When we look, we will find many reasons to be thankful!

- Thankful for our growing relationship with our God
- Thankful for our salvation, our life blessed by Jesus now and for all eternity
- Thankful that in Christ He forgives *all* our sins and restores us
- Thankful for His comfort, especially during turmoil or trouble

- Thankful for our daily provisions—our food, our home, and our work
- Thankful for our loved ones—family, friends, neighbors, and community of believers
- Thankful for all we get to do
- Thankful for our purpose in this life

- Thankful for the sunshine that warms our face
- Thankful for the rain that will make things grow
- Thankful that God surrounds us with His splendor
- Thankful for His love, care, and covering

When we focus on all that we can be thankful for, we will be Reprogramming our mind to look for the good. Being thankful will *transform* our mind, *soften* our heart, and *produce* His peace and joy in our lives.

What are a few things that you are currently thankful for?

_____
_____

In what areas of your life do you want to be more thankful?

_____
_____

Can we even be thankful for our trials? If we Recognize that our trials lead us into an even deeper understanding and depth of our relationship with God and others, then we would be thankful.

THANKFUL DURING TRIALS
James 1:2–4 (NIV) Trials and Temptations

> Consider it pure joy, my brothers, and sisters, whenever you face trials of many kinds, because you know that the testing of your faith produces perseverance. Let perseverance finish its work so that you may be mature and complete, not lacking anything.

Trials can make us mature if we allow them to *finish* their work. When a trial arises, we may quickly *resist* it by becoming negative, blaming others, or pulling away. When I first started this journey for peace, God began the cleansing process within me. Every week a different past issue would arise for me to deal with. Each exposed issue felt like a trial or hardship because it was still wrapped in its initial pain. It was a difficult season. I remember early on asking friends to pray for me because it felt like the enemy was dredging up one negative mess after another.

As I earnestly cried out to God, I felt Him say, *"Why do you give credit to My enemy for the things that I am doing in your life?"*

Shocked, I responded, *"YOU . . . are doing this?"*

I determined if God was revealing these negative painful places, *it had to be to heal me*. My new understanding changed how I perceived my trials. Consequently, when a trial would arise, I would pray, *"Okay, God, what can I learn?"*

God was doing a new work in me and I wanted to joyfully work with Him. Similarly, when He revealed a negative place within me, I would pray and ask Him, *"What do you want me to Recognize?"*

This way of handling my trials has strengthened my relationship with God, matured my faith, and produced more peace in my life. Even now when I encounter various trials, I still go straight to God and work with Him until I can Respond faithfully. This response to trials has taught me to trust God with everything in my life.

If God has us recall a past painful memory or walks us through a trial, it is to heal us or to mature us. We can allow the testing of our faith to shape our heart, which will affect our behavior and the way we live.

Our trials can help us to become more like Him.

We can consider it pure joy by knowing the trial will test our faith and produce perseverance. When perseverance finishes its work, we will be mature, complete, not lacking anything. We can be *confident* that He works *all* things together for good for those who *love* Him!

Romans 8:28 (AMP)

> And we know [with great confidence] that God [who is deeply concerned about us] causes all things to work together [as a plan] for good for those who love God, to those who are called according to His plan *and* purpose.

When a trial arises, will you be able to consider it all joy because you are *confident* that God is working in you to *mature* you, and to *work it out* for your good? (If not, why not?)

_____
_____

God is deeply concerned about us. He is working all things together for good for those who love Him. It is through thankfulness and persevering in our faith that His joy and peace will overflow our hearts.

Chapter 12
FINISH WELL

GROWING DEEPER
CONTINUOUS PEACE IS CULTIVATED THROUGH A rich relationship with our heavenly Father. God has established the church to be a place where we can become *deeply rooted* in our faith. God's "A" plan is for believers to join together and create a rich church community. We are God's children and we are to grow with our spiritual brothers and sisters. I know that God has allowed many people in the church to shape me into who I am today. Through these relationships I have come to understand God's love and His truths in ways I never could have on my own.

Hebrews 10:23–25 (NASB)

> Let us hold fast the confession of our hope without wavering, for He who promised is faithful; and let us consider how to stimulate one another to love and good deeds, not forsaking our own assembling together, as is the habit of some, but encouraging *one another;* and all the more as you see the day drawing near.

We grow when we are in a great Bible-believing church. This is where we can be fed spiritually. Then if we join a small group we can continue to mature in our faith, be stretched, supported, known, and loved. A church is supposed to be a big family that we *get to* love, worship with, learn from, know more deeply, and nudge one another into good deeds.

I will forever be grateful for those who have come alongside to sharpen me, correct me, challenge my thinking, and encourage me. Growing with others makes the Word come alive. Each one brings a new perspective and vantage point. When we apply what we have learned, we are transformed.

I have friends who were willing to journey together until we experienced spiritual freedom in certain areas. Still others were willing to dive into Bible studies so that we could grow deeper in our relationship with God. It is a gift to have a community of friends who are willing to process life together.

I have a fond memory of a Bible study that we had one summer. It started with my strong desire to understand the *holiness of God*. I had a book that I was reading, and as I asked some of my closest friends what they knew about the holiness of God, we all became interested in learning more. We decided to get together weekly for dinner and to dig deeper into that topic. Those discussions could last for hours. I recall one evening that it was midnight when we remembered to pull out our refrigerated baked goods. We laughed as we joyfully consumed our late-night chocolate éclair dessert. We were having so much fun. It was a unique study with close friends. We all grew that summer. Friends are God's awesome gift.

FRIENDS ARE UNIQUELY DIFFERENT
In community we will build friendships. It is a gift to walk with a godly friend and a blessing to have someone you can connect to, be real with, lean on, pray with, and enjoy. We are *not* supposed to look for a perfect friend. No one is perfect. We are *all* quirky, and unique, and see life differently. That is what makes friendships great. We get to *cherish* our quirkiness, *treasure* our similarities, and *celebrate* our differences.

With each friendship we can add value to each other's lives. We can support, encourage, and be there for one another. I have enjoyed being able to journey together through different seasons with my friends. We were the hands of love, care, and encouragement to one another. We have come alongside to carry each other's heavy burdens. We have met each other where we were and supported one another in our own unique ways.

FRIENDS CAN STAND IN THE GAP

I recall a time a few years after I lost my mom when my heart still felt empty and void. I longed for the fun that my mom and I could have doing everyday, ordinary things. My mom could make me laugh harder than anyone else. She could make me laugh so hard that all of life stood still. I really ached for those moments.

During my season of grieving, I truly tried to enjoy my life with God and those He had entrusted to me as family and friends. One summer day, I took my children and a friend to an amusement park. As my friend and I sat and ate ice cream, my teenage son joined us. Sitting across the table from me, he loudly exclaimed, *"Wow, look what I found over on that table . . . a barely eaten ice cream cone!"* With that he pulled the cone to his mouth to lick it. Appalled that he would eat an abandoned ice cream cone, my "mama ninja" skills went into full power, and with lightning-fast speed, I reached across the table and slapped that ice cream cone out of his hand. It flew many tables away from us. Thankfully, it did not land on anyone. The look of shock on his face as he yelled *"I was kidding! That was my ice cream cone!"* produced an immediate explosion of laughter.

None of us expected me to react that way, not even me. So when I slapped that cone away only to find out that he was kidding, my friend and I roared with an uncontrollable laughter. We laughed so hard that I could feel something inside me heal. It is remarkable how it wasn't until I experienced that kind of deep laughter that *my heart could reassure me that I was going to be okay.*

My healing grabbed hold that day . . . the day I hilariously laughed with my friend. Friends can stand in the gap and become a stitch in the ripped fabric of our heart.

HEALING THROUGH FRIENDSHIPS
James 5:16 (NASB)

> Therefore, confess your sins to one another, and pray for one another so that you may be healed. The effective prayer of a righteous man can accomplish much.

God does amazing *healing* through friends. I had a friend who called me one day and said, *"Dawn, I need to confess my 'uglies' to you."* She went on to confess how she had reacted that morning. We spoke and then we prayed. When she hung up the phone, she was a happy woman. Why? Because she took the weight of how she had acted and we Released it, and then we prayed. She was healed. She did not condemn herself any longer. Her heart was right with God, and she was going to make it right with others. It was beautiful.

God's plan for us is to be *real* with each other. That is so powerful. I love having people in my life that I can be real with, knowing that I am loved and not judged. It is awesome to be known for *who* you are and loved *where* you are. In these friendships we can build each other up, and we can speak the truth in love, and it can be received.

HINDRANCES TO FRIENDSHIPS
Unfortunately the pain from our past can interfere with us reaching out to others. We may try to go it alone, and alone is what we become and feel. Other times *the weeds of mistrust entangle us*, and when we speak with someone, we tend to keep it surface-deep. We do not share who we are, what we desire, or our personal struggles at any level because we do not trust.

We are afraid of getting wounded once again. Our undealt with past wounds impede us from engaging and from moving forward. If we allow the weeds of mistrust to remain, they will rob our peace and hinder our relationships.

When we have been hurt, we tend to build walls. Our walls actually wall us in. I came across a woman who I wanted to be friends with; however, when I walked over to her, she put up a wall. I did not know why. Regrettably, I responded by putting up a similar wall to protect myself. We exchanged niceties, but the friendship did not take off.

I went to God and asked Him what I should do. He put on my heart that she had been hurt before and that it was hard for her to truly trust. He then reminded me that He called me to love. In order to love her, I had to be *vulnerable* and reach out to her. I had to first choose to bring my wall down and choose to love her where she was. I did. I texted a sweet message, and then immediately she responded back with a similar message. I could see that my texts were making a difference.

With each genuine encounter, I saw her open up a little more. The next time I saw her, it was evident that she was starting to take down her wall. She began to love and trust me. The relationship continued to strengthen one genuine encounter after another.

We are all a work in progress. We can all build walls of self-protection and keep others surface-deep. But if growing in community is God's "A" plan, then we need to jump in and find those we can invest in and trust. God will care for our heart.

Lower Our Expectations
It is extremely helpful to *lower our unrealistic expectations*. We *will* get hurt. We are *all* fallible humans. We will mess up. We will not find a perfect friend, nor will we be a perfect friend,

but we can *entrust our heart* to God, trusting that He will heal us if we need it.

God has taught me:

- to be hard to offend
- to think the best of others
- not to assume the worst

These mind-sets have kept me from having an easily wounded heart. Difficulties, misunderstandings, frustrations, and disappointments will come, but what will we do with those situations? We cannot change another person. *We can only change how we Respond* to those hurdles. Are you hard to offend? Do you think the best of others, or do you assume the worst?

When we are offended, we can Release the wounding offense to God. The light of His love will shine in those dark places, bringing healing. Good friendships are worth our effort to restore.

SEASONS OF FRIENDSHIPS
Don't grow weary. Don't lose your peace. Friends sometimes come and go as the seasons. Realistically it may be through circumstances or through difficulties that a friendship may only last for a season. I have mourned over the loss of friends. *If* we need to let go of a friendship, let's make sure *our heart is right.* We need to let go of all the pain, disappointments, unforgiveness, negative thoughts, and any bitterness. Then we can hold on to some of the good memories.

Recently, after a friendship became distant, my heart was encouraged with the thought that *in heaven we will be friends.* Other friendships have been restored and become blessings once again. As we entrust our heart to Jesus, He will be our constant companion. He will stick closer than a brother. But since we were created for community, pray *for* a great friend, and pray *to be* a great friend. The blessings of friendship can enrich our lives with much happiness.

Learning to Be a Good Friend

It is through others that we can learn how to be a wonderful friend. A friend texted me that her daughter was sick with the flu and I texted that I would pray. I did pray and text her to make sure she was well. The following week, my son got sick and she texted me that she was praying and asked if I needed anything from the store. She offered to buy it and drop it off for me. In that moment, I saw an example of an amazing friend! I grew from her loving gesture of kindness. We need each other to grow.

Serving Together

We grow while we serve God. In church we have many opportunities to serve God by serving others. We all are called to serve in one way or another. As each one does their part, we will strengthen the church.

It is through serving side by side that we get to know one another. *This is where great friendships can begin.* Most churches have areas in which you can serve. Do you like to welcome others, lead a small group, serve communion, cook meals, pray, worship, teach or care for children?

Serving becomes a multifaceted blessing. First and foremost, God will use our gifts *to glorify Himself* and *to bless* others. Next, we will discover more of our God-given talents as we use the gifts that we have been given. God can also open doors of many kinds just by us being available and ready to serve. We will be filled with peace as we are using our gifts.

> GOD WILL USE OUR GIFTS TO GLORIFY HIMSELF AND TO BLESS OTHERS.

Another bonus is that we can develop deep friendships when we serve together.

It is very satisfying to grow while we serve God. *Ask God if there is an area where He wants you to serve.*

BE A MENTOR
As a body of believers, each one of us will have our own strengths and weaknesses. We all have areas in which we can grow. At times I found it hard to grow on my own. I love how a circle of friends can glean from one another's insights. Desiring to grow, together we can study, learn, and strengthen one another.

I remember the first few times I met with two of my friends. They had asked me to teach them from the Bible. That was before I was really growing in the Word. I reluctantly agreed. I was concerned that I would have *nothing* to teach. But do you know what happened? God showed up. He took our feeble attempts to grow in our spiritual walk, and by the grace of God, I shared what He was teaching me, and we *all* grew.

Mentoring can be leading a person or a few people who have common spiritual interests. I have also led groups that utilized Bible study books. At other times we ordered a video series to watch and discuss. I have had younger women visit me at my home, and as we spent time together, we would discuss the questions that they had about their lives. It was always good. It doesn't have to look any certain way, and *you do not need to have all the answers*!

We need to have a:

- Heart for God
- Desire to know His truths
- Heart of kindness to love others *where they are*
- Heart of wisdom to be led by God as we lead others

Mentoring is giving away what Jesus has already given to us. The more we grow in Him, the more we will be able to give away! You can share your godly wisdom and pass on the lessons you have learned as you process life together.

Be *vulnerable* as God prompts your heart to share the *real* you. It's in our vulnerability that people are drawn to us as friends. As we share our heart, others will be more deeply connected to us, and we will be drawn to those who are real. Be authentic. Pray for one another. Confess your sins when needed. God brings healing through mentoring.

Is there a friend or a few friends with like needs or interests who you could join for a study? Do you have an area such as marriage, parenting, or having more peace that you would like to grow in? You could choose a book in the Bible or a Bible study to go through. You could ask others to join you to start this book again with the intention of growing deeper in your peace. Perhaps you could order a video series that you could watch and discuss.

We will be blessed as we share our lives and grow with one another. God meets us where we are! Pray and ask God if there is someone you could grow with.

I want to ask _____ to join me for a study.

FIND A MENTOR
When I was a young Christian, I wanted to live the life that God had called me to, but I was so broken I did not understand basic spiritual principles. I thank God for the two mature older women from church who played an important role in my development. Even though I did not spend a lot of time with either, I was blessed by their encouragement and the love they showed me. Their wisdom and maturity in Christ and their knowledge of His Word have impacted my life forever.

I WANT TO BE LIKE HER WHEN I "GROW UP"
The first woman was so kind and patient. She would invite me, my friend, and our children to her home. Our little ones smeared the glass on her front door as we sat on her couch and asked her *one big spiritual question after another.* I remember her diligently and effortlessly leafing through her Bible, coming to a scripture, and reading it to us. She answered every one of our questions with the Word of God. I was in awe. I think my mouth hung open the whole time. I remember writing on my heart, *"I want to be just like her when I grow up!"*

I was a grown woman, but I had never experienced anyone who knew her Bible so well. She used her Bible and spiritual knowledge to answer *all* of *our many* questions about life, family, or even the Bible. It was awesome how we felt loved and encouraged as she *shared* her love for God and her love for His Word. She was a wonderful example of living His way. *We wanted it.* We wanted it all!

Her life was a great demonstration of how to live as a Christian. *She purposely taught us to love* God, our husbands, and our children. In her we witnessed a love that was deep, respectful, and caring. She encouraged us to *read* our Bible, to *know* God, and to *pray.* She taught us to pray the Word of God and when appropriate to insert our name, our husband's, or our children's names into the scriptures to make them even more impactful. *(I had you do this with the John 15:4–8 scripture about Remain in Me, in chapter nine.)* It is very powerful to personalize or pray the scriptures.

When I was bound by fear, she was the one who I would persistently go to after church to ask her to pray. She never grew tired of my besetting fears. She met me where I was. She lovingly yet boldly prayed for me time and time again. The compassion and spiritual strength that she demonstrated toward me I have learned and shown to others. That is the power of a mentor.

I also remember a few times I called inviting her wisdom into different situations. She always seemed to have the right way of seeing the circumstances and the right answer. I am forever thankful for my friend.

As I grew, she pointed out some of God's gifts in me. She urged me to step out and teach. She would come to my studies and enthusiastically listen and encourage me. She always envisioned more for me than I could see for myself. I hoped in the positive things she saw for my future. Over the years, every chance I got I would tell her *what an amazing influence she was in my life*. She would continue to reassure me in the plan she saw God had for me. Her impact is still blessing me today.

I Saw Love Walking

My second mentor was a true example of love walking. I remember when I saw her walking with her arm around a woman who was hard to understand, *my heart took a snapshot of that moment and said, "That is love walking."* She was my example of God's love in action.

She was incredible at calling many to encourage them; thankfully I was one. She always inquired about my family and me and let me know she was praying for us. She would then share with me the scripture that she felt the Lord wanted her to give. It never failed; it was a Word in due season. Her encouragement and love always had a positive impact. I was blessed to see her speak and teach. She shared about her own prior heartache and about how God had healed her. She also blessed women in her small group with her teachings for years. She was a wonderful example of what God can do in our lives if we are *willing* and *available* to Him.

As the years went by, we would encourage one another. Many times, she would say, "*I called to encourage you and you have encouraged me!*" We were blessings to one another. We were able to confide and pray for each other. I was able to have lunch with her recently, and we lit up when we saw one another. She still calls God's gifts out of me, encouraging me to teach and write and to lead a women's ministry. She always said, *"Hurry up and get your book written. You will help so many women with your love for God."*

The lessons learned through my mentors so many years ago are still life-giving for me today. These two mentors showed me things in God and in His Word that I could not see. They both were a picture of the Savior in their own way. They later confirmed in me what God had spoken to my heart. They were God's hands for me in a season of my life when I deeply desired to grow. God blessed me with their friendship and their mentoring. I remember other seasons when God gave me mentors who were on the TV and the radio. I gleaned and grew from their teachings as well.

Ask God if He has a mentor for you. Is there one who is more mature in your church who you can get to know better, ask questions of, and together sharpen each other's faith as you grow in your walk with God?

_____

What could hold you back from asking someone to coffee to get to know them better?

_____

WHY BE MENTORED?
You may be asking, *"But why?"* Why would we want to be mentored and grow? What is the point?

When someone comes alongside and teaches, leads, or encourages us, it enriches the soil for our spiritual life to develop and grow. They can share truths or life lessons that will continue to impact our future harvests. We are God's children, and He is preparing us for good works. Being mentored strengthens us to walk in Him and fulfill the plans that He has for us.

Colossians 2:6 (NASB)

> Therefore as you have received Christ Jesus the Lord, *so* walk in Him.

WE ARE THE WORK OF GOD'S HANDS
Ephesians 2:10 (AMP)

> For we are His workmanship [His own master work, a work of art], created in Christ Jesus [reborn from above—spiritually transformed, renewed, ready to be used] for good works, which God prepared [for us] beforehand [taking paths which He set], so that we would walk in them [living the good life which He prearranged and made ready for us].

Amen! We want to grow and be mentored because *we are God's work of art*. He is preparing us *to fulfill the plans He has for us*. It can be exciting and scary to know that God has plans that He has prepared specifically for each one of us to do. We can allow many things to hold us back from growing with God. Fear of the unknown, desiring control, and preferring our own comfort can halt God's plans. But in this last step of Responding faithfully, we are determined to be spiritually transformed, renewed, and ready to be used for God's good works. *We want to be prepared for the life that God has for us!*

> **WE WANT TO BE PREPARED FOR THE LIFE THAT GOD HAS FOR US!**

Responding faithfully is rooted in a deep desire to live for our Lord and become all that He created us to be. Every day, all day, we choose *if* we will Respond in love or react out of our flesh or our fears. Desiring to Respond rightly, we can stop and ask God, *"Please, teach me to do Your will in this situation. Allow Your good Spirit to lead me in the way You want me to go."* This is the walk.

PURSUE PEACE
1 Peter 3:11 (NIV)

> They must turn from evil and do good; they must seek peace and pursue it.

God's way is awesome! First, God wants us to live a life of peace because He loves us and wants our best. Second, His peace becomes *evidence* that His Spirit is bearing fruit in and through us. The fruit of the Spirit does not grow by accident. We must seek peace and pursue it daily *by turning away from what is not good, turning toward God, and doing what is good.* As we turn to God, His Spirit will continually bear much fruit and we will produce an abundant harvest. This way of living will impact our future harvests.

SURRENDERING MY HEART AND MY MOUTH
If I am going to walk in a manner worthy of the Lord, I know I must have both my heart and the words that I speak right. My prayer has been for *God to continually transform my heart and my words.* If my heart is far from God's will, so will my words be. I pray often the Psalm 19 prayer.

Psalm 19:14 (NASB)

> Let the words of my mouth and the meditation of my heart be acceptable in Your sight, O Lord, my rock and my Redeemer.

I ask God to help me with the words of my mouth because they can get me into trouble and cause me to lose my peace. I know how quickly a negative thought can pollute my heart and easily be spewed out through the words that I speak. Negativity can affect everyone it hits.

My prayer has become, *"Please, God, allow the meditations of my heart and the words of my mouth to be acceptable in Your sight. I want to please You, love You, and love others. You are my immovable rock and the One who redeemed me. You will empower me to live a life that is pleasing to You."*

PLACE YOUR LIFE BEFORE GOD
Romans 12:1–2 (MSG)

> So here's what I want you to do, God helping you: Take your everyday, ordinary life—your sleeping, eating, going-to-work, and walking-around life—and place it before God as an offering. Embracing what God does for you is the best thing you can do for him. Don't become so well-adjusted to your culture that you fit into it without even thinking. Instead, fix your attention on God. You'll be changed from the inside out. Readily recognize what he wants from you, and quickly respond to it. Unlike the culture around you, always dragging you down to its level of immaturity, God brings the best out of you, develops well-formed maturity in you.

Respond faithfully for a continuous life of Peace by placing your everyday, ordinary life—your sleeping, eating, going-to-work, and walking-around life—before God. By fixing your attention on Him, you'll be changed from the inside out. Embracing what God does for you is the best thing you can do for him. God will bring the best out of you. He will develop well-formed maturity in you.

Can God Use My Everyday Life?

Many years ago I remember listening to a teaching and learning to ask God to make a difference with my everyday life. Moved by the message, I prayed, *"God I'm on the way to the grocery store with my little ones. How can I make a real difference? But God I desire to! Make a way for me if it be Your will."* I remember I pulled into a parking spot and walked around to the sliding door on the van to get the kids out, when a gentleman in a truck pulled in next to me. I paused to allow him to get out of his vehicle. He kindly gestured that I continue. I told him that I had children and it was going to take me a little while to get them out. He warmly insisted that I go first, so one by one I got my children out.

Holding my youngest, I thanked him for his kindness. He reflectively spoke these words: *"No need to thank me. I love seeing families together. I just lost my twenty-five-year-old son in a car accident last winter."*

> GOD ORCHESTRATES INCREDIBLE MOMENTS WHEN WE LAY OUR EVERYDAY LIFE INTO HIS HANDS.

My eyes widened and I knew that God had just made a way for my ordinary life to intersect with a man who was deeply hurting. He confided some of his heart and I was able to share about the pain of losing my fiancé when I was younger. I told him how Jesus had helped to heal my broken heart. We had a heartwarming conversation. As I walked into the store, I was amazed how God orchestrates incredible moments when we lay our *everyday* life into His hands.

Fulfilling God's Plans

I think that it surprises us that God fulfills His call in our lives through our everyday circumstances. But it is true. It is through our everyday lives that we will be taught by God. Daily we can make a difference in God's kingdom and in the lives of others. Our everyday lives can be used to bring God glory by fixing our attention on Him and doing what He has called us to do, no matter how big or how small it is. *As we continue to love Him and love others as a way of life, we will fulfill His plan for us every day.* It is simple.

God usually speaks to our heart by giving us a *deep desire* to fulfill the plans He has for us. So many times we dismiss it as our own desire and not God's plan. Especially if we are good in a certain area, we can second-guess it as not a calling because usually it comes so easily. We can consider it mundane or ordinary and not a call of God.

- Is there something that you are good at?
- What fills you with joy when you think about doing it?
- Has God put a dream in your heart?
- What do you feel you are led to do or pursue?

As I just mentioned, often we discount what we are good at because it feels too easy. We assume because we love it or enjoy doing it, then it can't be what we are called to do. The opposite is true. Our areas of calling and giftedness usually do come easier to us.

It is important to Recognize areas where you have received compliments, such as, *"You are so good at that!"* This often points to a place of giftedness.

I remember when I was young and walking to school, I would encounter another girl, and as we walked together, we would talk. If she was struggling with some issue, I shared my thoughts. I remember her saying, *"Every time I tell you something, you always give me good advice."* I smiled and thought it was no problem. I enjoyed it. It energized me to help someone else, and it felt effortless.

Our gifts and talents are freely given by God, and it feels natural. It is helpful to know where God has gifted us. This understanding can help us to be aware of ways that God can prompt us to fulfill the plan He has for us. We will each receive joy as we utilize our gifts, allowing our lives to glorify God and bless others.

What have you been told that *you are so good at?*

_____

_____

Your answer may reveal a place where God has gifted or called you.

OUR EVERYDAY LIVES
Do not underestimate who you can impact
by just loving God in your everyday life.

When I was a young girl probably about nine or ten, I deeply desired to have a family that was intact and whole. Coming from a dysfunctional family, I noticed that my friend's mom had placed God at the center of her life. I watched as their family went to church together every Sunday. One day while sitting on my friend's steps in her home, her mom became overjoyed about a magazine that had come in the mail. She was obviously delighted, so I asked her what kind of a magazine it was. She responded, *"It is a Christian magazine. It is about God. It teaches me how to raise my family."*

I remember writing in my young heart, *"When I grow up, that is the kind of family I want to have. I want to have a good intact family with God at the center of it."*

Although my life took many twists and turns, it is amazing to think that God could use an ordinary day at a friend's house when I was so young to impact my future and the future of my own family for decades to come. My neighbor did not know that she was my first example of this type of Christian living.

My number one dream remained to have God as the center of my marriage and parenting. From a young age, I knew I felt called to stay at home and raise my children. It was my God-given desire, and I thank Him profusely for allowing me to fulfill that call. I am especially thankful because *I did not know how* to achieve a God-centered home, *but I desired it.* I trusted God, and over the years, *He led me one slow step at a time.* He taught me through marriage and parenting books. He always used the Bible and Bible studies to lead my heart. He later gave me mentors to show me the way. He will equip us for what He calls us to do.

TEMPTED TO FORFEIT
Even amidst doing the very things we love, we can become frustrated. I was happily raising my family and leaning on God for wisdom. I believed that marriage and motherhood were the highest callings in my life. Nothing else seemed to matter as much. While raising my young children, I had surrendered my wounded life for the life that God had planned for me. Even though I had a lot of healing and maturing to do, I felt that God had placed another call on me to lead a ministry *in the future.* This was somewhat overwhelming because I was still such a mess inside. I felt He had called me to share *what He had done* and *was doing* in my life. I knew if God were going to prepare me, I would need to be reading the Bible more thoroughly.

In that season I found it hard to even find time to unload the dishwasher. I desired to read my Bible, study the Word, and seek God, but my everyday life was so full of activity, I was thankful if I got to read at all. God was fulfilling my deepest desires to be a stay-at-home mom, and *I was unquestionably happy.* But one night as I rocked my sweet little one, I could feel the weight of my own frustration growing in my heart because *another* day had passed, and I was not able to seek God as I *wanted*.

As I prayed and rocked my baby, I felt these sneaky, quiet, yet very intense words *infiltrate* my mind. The thoughts boldly whispered, *Just leave! Leave these kids and your everyday responsibilities. Go follow the ministry that God has for you. Go! Leave your family. They are holding you back!* When those thoughts registered and I realized how evil they were, I gasped in shock. I Recognized that the enemy was tempting me to abandon my children, my husband, my home, along with my everyday life. He offered *the lie* that I could fulfill the call for ministry *if* I would leave everything.

It scared me that the enemy knew I was frustrated with not having enough time to seek God as I desired. In Response, I yelled out, "*No! I will not leave my family! I will become who God wants me to be . . . right here, no matter how long it takes!*" I embraced my little one even *more tightly*.

That still brings tears to my eyes! It still shocks me at how slimy the enemy was to attempt to capitalize upon my frustration to know God better and try to entice me with a life that seemed free. *The enemy always tempts us with short cuts.* God's focus is on our maturing day by day. We mature as we continue in the way God has set for us!

We know the enemy comes to lie, kill, and destroy, but our God comes to give us life and life more abundantly. We need to hold on to Jesus when we are frustrated. I have learned to place my life and frustrations into God's hands.

John 10:10 (AMP)

> The thief comes only in order to steal and kill and destroy. I came that they may have *and* enjoy life, and have it in abundance [to the full, till it overflows].

TOOLS OF TRANSFORMATION
God desires that we have and enjoy life. His plan is that our life will *overflow* with spiritual abundance. He will *strengthen* our walk with Him and *deepen* His call within us through the circumstances of our everyday lives. God will use our everyday responsibilities, frustrations, wounds, and times of seeking Him to mature us spiritually. He skillfully uses those opportunities to heal, teach, and grow us.

> God uses His Word, others, and our everyday life as tools of transformation.

GOD'S CALL CAN SEEM IMPOSSIBLE!
When we Recognize the God-sized call on our life, it can overwhelm us and be hard to believe. We may doubt that we can accomplish His will. Trust me when I say, *He will equip us for what He calls us to do.*

When God first put on my heart that *I would be a speaker and a writer someday*, I literally laughed out loud! I responded skeptically, *"Yeah, right! What would I write about and who would even listen?"* In my mind and heart, it was an impossibility! I had strong evidence that for me to be a speaker and a writer would be unattainable. To start with, I had *nothing* to say. I was broken. I had *failed* English. I had written one pathetic story in my lifetime. I could *not* write well, and I hated to read. A panic would even come over me if I were asked to read out loud.

With all those deficits, what I did not understand was that *God was going to transform my life!* He would over time take all my sin *and* immaturity *and* teach me to surrender. It was then that I learned to trust and love Him deeply. His plan was to bring His best out of me and develop well-formed maturity in me. God transformed my thinking, living, and loving. I was able to Recognize the negative way I once had lived and write about the lessons God was teaching me. I shared those life lessons with small groups. He brought me life and I could now give it away.

I became excited to share the truths that I was learning. I loved to help others grab hold of the same life change I was experiencing. My fear of speaking left me as I stood up equipped to share what God had put on my heart. I had no way of knowing at the beginning all that God would do to prepare me to fulfill His call.

God had put that call on my life when I was a brand-new Christian. Even though that was many years ago, I am *still* watching God fulfill that initial call in me to be a speaker and a writer. I can see clearly how *every step* with God is ordered by Him to help us to grow and develop. Each step is so important. It is a comfort to know, that if He calls us to it, *no matter how impossible it seems*, He will be faithful to fully complete it.

> OUR CALLINGS IN THIS LIFE CAN *FEEL* TOO BIG FOR US, BUT THEY ARE NOT TOO BIG WHEN ALMIGHTY GOD IS WORKING *THROUGH US*.

I want to encourage you! Our callings in this life can *feel* too big for us, but they are not too big when Almighty God is working *through us*. If God has called you to a God-sized step in your life, He is faithful to equip you. Trust Him. Wait on Him and His timing as you obediently take your next step. He will prepare you as He leads you to fulfill His plan.

God's Timing Is Not Our Timing

Our timing is not God's timing. I share this to bring hope to those who have been waiting for God to fulfill a specific call in their life. Some of God's calls can be realized quickly and others may take many, many years. Let's be careful not to only hope in something specific that God has spoken and discount everything else. He desires to use our everyday lives to love Him and to love others. As we embrace what is in front of us, He will teach, mature, and prepare us. Our peace can be continuous knowing that we are in His timing.

WHAT AN EXCITING JOURNEY
Recognize what He wants from you, and quickly *Respond* to it.
(Romans 12:2 MSG)

Responding faithfully takes many little steps, one by one. As we keep our eyes on Jesus through the seasons of our lives, we will fulfill the plans He has for us. Our paths will be filled with many little *but significant* purposes all along the way. Spending time with God, caring for others, pausing to listen, pray, and love one another are always our daily purposes.

Every season is different and even unique. I think it helps to Recognize that a season can quickly pass and determine to make the most of it.

Have you sensed a calling from God?
_____

What has He written on your heart about His daily purposes for your life?
_____
_____

Just by being aware of His call, you can *intentionally pray*, dig in, and *plan* out your steps according to His leading. Trust His timing and outcome. Remain *willing* and *obedient* to take the next step He reveals.

FINISH WELL

COURAGE ON THE FIRE TOWER

More recently, during the week following my brother's memorial, my family and I were able to get away for a few days. After a day of resting, my family wanted to find something to do in the area. They learned about an old fire tower that overlooked the nearby mountainous forest area. It was once used as a high vantage point to spot any forest fires. Now it was described as *an old fire tower that shakes with any movement*. I thought, *Who would* ever *go on that?*

They all insisted that it would be fun! We drove to the forest area and walked through the woods until we came to the tower. Immediately my husband and our kids—except for my youngest, who helped me hold the two dogs—proceeded up the tower. I read the posted sign: 6-PERSON LIMIT. My heart sank and I was glad to be on the ground.

When they reached the top, they were in awe. Trying to convince me to join them, they began describing the beautiful sights they were seeing. I was very content on the ground just imagining its beauty.

Looking at the ominous tower was overwhelming to me. It was made up of thin metal. It was narrow with see-through steps that led to a platform, followed by more see-through steps, then another platform for as high as I could see. I do not like heights, so it was an easy decision to stay on the ground with the dogs.

But what I did not expect was that as they shouted down to me, explaining its beauty, *my heart* would begin to scold me. The questions from within followed:

> *"Why are you content on the ground?*
> *Don't you want to see from their vantage point*
> *what they can see?*
> *Don't you want to experience this beauty?"*

Those questions resounded from the depth of my new hurt, which was the loss of my brother. The thought quickly arose, and I was reminded that, *"Life is short!"*

I was left pondering . . . *Are you going to be content to sit on the sidelines or are you going to go enjoy all of God's beauty?*

Those thoughts penetrated my heart. I wanted to enjoy the beauty, but *fear* and *comfort* kept me on the ground. The thought that *Life is short. Enjoy it!* flooded my being. As I was contemplating what to do, some of my family returned. I did not want to miss the beauty they described. That is when I decided to take a few *faithful* steps toward the tower. As I began to walk, the most amazing feeling came over me. It was as if I walked straight into a heavy robe of courage. I had never felt courage like that. It was awesome.

I knew God was giving me a new bravery as I approached the tower. Quickly I took my first few steps, and then I walked onto the first platform. Next I climbed up a few more steps and onto the next platform. I learned that if I walked lightly, stepping easily and staying close to the inside railing, then the tower did not shake. I kept my eye on the very next step.

I was amazed at how quickly but carefully I could walk without shaking the tower. I continued to stay focused on the step right in front of me. I could not look up or down for any length of time. I just focused on the next step and kept climbing.

I was about halfway up and suddenly the tower began to intensely shake and sway. I immediately crouched down, held on tight, and began to look around at what was causing the commotion. That was when I noticed a young man running up the steps, causing the entire tower to shake. It did not faze him. He ran right by me as I held tightly to the railing. He got to the top and the shaking stopped. At that point I had to choose.

Would I continue up the tower *or* would I come to my senses and go back?

The thoughts returned: *Life is too short; just continue.* At this point my family began cheering me on and encouraging me loudly to continue. I stayed the course set before me, each step another step of faith. The higher I climbed, the more the tower shook. I wanted to quit so many times! Trembling I continued to advance. I looked out to see that I was almost as high as the tall trees. Wanting to stop, I set another goal for myself. I decided that I wanted to go high enough to see over the massive trees into the distant valley below.

As the steps were narrowing and the tower was moving now with my every step, I did reach the top of the trees and I got to see the most magnificent view of the tree-covered mountains stretching far and wide. It was beautiful. I had pushed myself to get to this height, although I was still a few platforms from the tower's highest peak. I thought perhaps I will return with some of my family and we will climb this early one morning, sit, and watch the sunrise. We could capture its beauty with our cameras, which is one of my favorite things to do. I then descended, but we were amazed at how high I had climbed. *May God be glorified* because He gives us the courage to take our next step in Him.

Psalm 16:11 (NIV)

> You make known to me the path of life; you will fill me with joy in your presence, with eternal pleasures at your right hand.

Psalm 31:14–15a (NIV)

> But I trust in you, Lord; I say, "You are my God." My times are in your hands.

Finish Well

OUR TIMES ARE IN HIS HANDS
Will we be satisfied with staying on the sidelines or will we join Him on *His path of life*? We can choose to take our next right step with God. Life is too short. Let's live a life that glorifies God!

In our adventure with God, we must first *choose to begin*.

Ask God for *the courage, strength, and wisdom to plan your course*. We must stay focused on the very step in front of us. Focus on the next step and keep on climbing. Know that the tower will shake and sway, but *we can hold on tight*. We determine to continue, remembering that our times are in His hands. This life is so short. We do not want to forfeit the full life God intended for us by living sidelined in fear, distractions, and disillusionment.

During my *journey to peace* and during my climb on the fire tower, *I wanted to quit so many times*! Wanting to stop, I set another goal for myself. I stayed the course set before me. Each step became another step of faith.

Our journey to peace may be hard and scary at times. We will feel vulnerable, but if we choose to stay the course, we will experience God in ways we never could have imagined. When we choose to set our course and persevere, taking one step of faith after another, God will journey with us and we will be blessed beyond measure.

BLESSED BEYOND MEASURE
Ephesians 3:20-21 (AMP)

> Now to Him who is able to [carry out His purpose and] do superabundantly more than all that we dare ask or think [infinitely beyond our greatest prayers, hopes, or dreams], according to His power that is at work within us, to Him be the glory in the church and in Christ Jesus throughout all generations forever and ever. Amen.

God has a continuous life of peace in store for each of us. This is His gift to us who believe in Jesus Christ as Savior. His work in our lives will be beyond measure, meaning we won't even be able to measure it. God is faithful. He will carry out His purpose for you! *He will do more than all that you can dare to ask and infinitely beyond your greatest prayers, hopes, and dreams, according to His power that is at work within you!*

Honestly, when I look back at my life of fear, it is like a distant gray memory. In those days, fear had me stuck with no hope of ever living by peace. Now it is crystal-clear to me that this life of peace has resulted from my deep walk *with* God. By His powerful Holy Spirit that lives in us, He will help us to see, think, walk, and live in a way that will bear His good fruit. This *way of living* will produce His prosperous harvest *in* and *through* us. His presence and peace will overflow our lives.

CONTINUING TO FLOURISH
God's peace continues to flourish as we encounter Him with confidence. As we continue to seek the One who created us, our relationship with God is constantly enriched. His presence fills us daily if we will allow it. Our daily time in the Bible is not a task that we check off but an honored meeting with Almighty God through His Word. *Some days it may feel like we receive only a drop in the bucket* of wisdom, understanding, or love. But other days the Word overflows our cups with good things. Please press into Him! He is our best gift ever!

Join Him for this *great adventure called life.*
Don't sit on the sidelines.

This last illustration, Respond faithfully, indicates the fourth arrow of the heart, which completes the steps. Yet it also reveals that *this is a continuous process*. Once we have found peace in a certain situation, we will have freedom in that area. Although as life continues, obstacles *will* arise that will *attempt to rob* our peace. This does not mean that we have failed, but it reveals that *keeping our peace is a lifelong process.*

As new issues present themselves, we can process those issues through the four steps. These steps will become a very *quick* and *powerful* way of keeping our peace. They help to protect our lives from being redirected to paths of destruction.

I have been living this way for more than two decades. God has faithfully blessed me with peace every time I have *Recognized* an obstacle, *Released* the barrier to Him, and *Reprogrammed* my heart and mind with His amazing truths regarding that situation. Trusting Him continually equips me to *Respond faithfully*. Throughout this process, He will bless you with an abundant and continuous life of peace!

Continuous Peace

I want to thank you for journeying with me. *Pray and ask God to* seal all that He has spoken to your heart. Let's rejoice and give Him praise for all that He has done, and all that He is yet to accomplish! I will continue to pray for you. May your life continually bring God glory!

Congratulations on finishing strong!
May you live the life of peace that God intended.

Matthew 5:14,16 (NIV)

> You are the light of the world. A town built on a hill cannot be hidden. In the same way, let your light shine before others, that they may see your good deeds and glorify your Father in heaven.

4 STEPS TO CONTINUOUS PEACE:

1. **RECOGNIZE** the Obstacles That Rob
2. **RELEASE** the Barriers That Confine
3. **REPROGRAM** My Heart & Mind with Truth
4. **RESPOND** Faithfully for a Continuous Life of Peace

Conclusion

My conclusion cannot be expressed any better than Paul has conveyed in Philippians as he addressed his dear brothers and sisters. I have shared portions of this amazing scripture throughout the book. I thank God for His Word, which continually reveals our answers. I have bolded key words.

Philippians 4:6–9 (NLT)

Don't worry about **any**thing;
instead, **pray** about **every**thing.
Tell God what you need,
and **thank Him** for all He **has** done.

Then **you will experience** God's peace,
which exceeds anything we can understand.
His peace will guard your hearts and minds **as you live in** Christ Jesus.

And now, dear brothers and sisters, **one final thing**.
Fix your thoughts on what is true, and honorable, and right, and pure, and lovely, and admirable.
Think about things that are excellent and worthy of praise.
Keep putting into practice all you learned and received from me—everything you heard from me and saw me doing.
Then the God of peace will be with you.

CHART YOUR COURSE: The following *four blank sections* can help you to create your plan for peace.

<u>My takeaways regarding *Continuous Peace*:</u>

My Prayer:

My plan for a continuous life of peace:

My victories and my transformation:

Acknowledgments

This book would *not* be what it has become without the input of many amazing people!

God told me before I ever put pen to paper that He would meet all of my needs. I am forever grateful to God for beautifully providing *everyone* who has poured into this project and refined this material. I am thankful for *each* and *every* one of you!

I am most thankful to my husband for the innumerable things he has done to help me. He and my children have given me their total support, encouragement, and understanding. I have turned to each of you and sought out your advice and been blessed continually by your valuable input and wisdom. I appreciate you jumping in and helping to make our lives run so smoothly. I could not have done this without you! Each of you has blessed my life in immeasurable ways!

I am so thankful to the early readers of my rough drafts. As you read through the four steps, each of you offered unique encouragement, inspiration, and helpful critique. Listening to your hearts, I was able to understand how my material was going to impact my future readers. Your insightful feedback helped to shape the entire book.

Thank you to all those who have graciously read through my manuscript and expounded on what you found to be unclear or impactful. It helped my writing to grow, and I appreciated all your critiques. They assisted me in creating more clarity, which strengthened the book. Thank you for your excitement and continued encouragement.

Thank you to those who have sharpened my material with your technical and analytical expertise. I am so thankful for your help with formatting, grammar, and general overview. Your added attention to detail has been my delight. What a gift it has been to be able to process this material together! I treasure your insight and knowledge. All your encouragement while writing this book has been a blessing to me.

Thank you to all who have taken my course on *Continuous Peace*. I was encouraged by your great interest, enthusiasm, and growth. I appreciated the opportunity to present the material in person because it has reinforced and made more concrete the concepts throughout the book. I was inspired by how you received and applied these principles and allowed them to transform your lives. I was blessed to see you flourish!

Thank you to my amazing pastors. Over the years, I have been very blessed by each of you. Your own diligence in pursuing a loving and strong relationship with the Lord has illuminated God's path in my own life. Thank you for transparently sharing your life lessons, Bible knowledge, and amazing stories, which have helped me to continually grow and develop my relationship with God. Thank you for every opportunity that you have permitted me to teach and connect with others. Those seasons have been a true blessing and a vital step in my preparation and maturity.

Thank you to all who have prayed for me while I was writing this book. Your prayers have been a covering and a place of blessing. God heard your prayers and has impacted me with more wisdom, insight, and joy as I wrote. Thank you for joining me in praying for those *who will read* this book. May God *bless us all* as He continues to answer our prayers long into the future.

Acknowledgments

I am *thankful* for *all who will read Continuous Peace*. I have prayed for you for decades. You were always on my mind. I am praying that in Christ you will have the most abundant life that overflows with God's amazing peace. I know that what God has done for me, *He will do for you!*

Most importantly, THANK YOU, Heavenly Father. Without You this book would not exist. I am thankful that You have continued to pour into me as I poured into this book. So many times, as I would reread my manuscript, Your Spirit would uplift, motivate, or bless me as I read. Lord, may YOU BE GLORIFIED throughout this book. Create Your transformation in each of us. BLESS us all with a deep walk with You!

May we all Live the Life of Peace that God Intended!

BONUS MATERIAL *You can also download this material at* DawnMarasco.com/CPFree

Your 30-Day Challenge (Chapter 7)
Underline what your next step will be.

- Read your Word consistently.
- Write down the scripture that impacts you the most.
- Write any insight that you receive, or a prayer to Reprogram your mind.
- Worship the Lord.
- Pray and confess your sins.
- Be still. Listen for God's small still voice.
- Apply what you are learning from God's Word into your everyday life.
- Tell a friend. Ask to be kept accountable. Encourage each other to grow.

Chart Your Course
Visualize and write what your time in God's Word will look like. Where would you sit? What would you need: a Bible, devotional, notebook, pens, highlighters, a blanket, a basket or container to keep it all together? (Coffee/tea/water?)

_____
_____
_____
_____
_____
_____
_____

TAKE A MINUTE AND PERSONALIZE YOUR TIME WITH GOD.

Devise a plan: set your daily goal—*not a law* that you are under but *a goal that you desire!*

- When to read? Morning before your day begins, lunch time, or at night?
- Where to read? Select a place in your home, deck, bus, etc. (a place with few distractions).
- What to read? Choose a book in the Bible, a Bible study, or a devotional.
- What journal or notebook will you use to capture your thoughts?
- When will you start? Mark down the date and time.
- What is your goal? Determine the amount of time allotted daily.
- How many days a week? Will this be 5 days a week or all 7 days?
- Who will be your accountability person during your thirty-day challenge? It is helpful to send a simple daily message to a friend as a way of celebrating your time with God.

We *must discipline* ourselves to do it. Make the Word yours! Personalize it. *God is teaching you.* He loves you! He desires your best! He will lead you in the way you should go. You will be *transformed* by meeting with Him regularly.

REPROGRAMMING THE LIE CHARTS (CHAPTER 8)

I created *two formats* to help overwrite the lie with the truth that you want to live by. *Choose one* or *both* ways which ever makes it easier to **Recognize** *the lie* and **Reprogram** *with the truth* that will set you free.

Here is the first example:
<u>Lie</u>: *You must protect yourself.*

Truth: *"<u>God knows the plans He has for me. Plans to prosper me and not to harm me. Plans to give me hope and a future.</u>"* Jeremiah 29: 11

Lie:
_____
_____

Truth:
_____
_____

Lie:
_____
_____

Truth:
_____
_____

Lie:
_____
_____

Truth:
_____
_____

Another example:

When the lie _I can't do it, I will mess up_ presents itself,

I will Release it and believe the truth that _God will counsel me with His loving eye on me._ Psalm 32:8

Now fill in the following chart with your answers.

When the lie _____ presents itself,
I will Release it and believe the truth that_____
_____.

When the lie _____ presents itself,
I will Release it and believe the truth that_____
_____.

When the lie _____ presents itself,
I will Release it and believe the truth that_____
_____.

When the lie _____ presents itself,
I will Release it and believe the truth that_____
_____.

Take time to process all that the Lord is doing to set you free and overwrite the lies of the enemy. Reprogramming is *not* a one-day event but can be *our way of life*.

Notes or prayers:

REVERSING A NEGATIVE HARVEST (CHAPTER 9)
Here is an example that helped me reverse the negative harvest in my life.

My most desired fruit I wanted to harvest was:
_____*peace in my life*_____

I had to stop feeding or sowing:
_____*fear and doubt*_____

I must consistently sow:
_____*trust and faith in God*_____.

Now fill in the following chart with your answers.

My most desired fruit I want to harvest is:
_____

I will have to stop feeding or sowing:
_____

I must consistently sow:
_____

My most desired fruit I want to harvest is:
_____

I will have to stop feeding or sowing:
_____

I must consistently sow:
_____

Reversing a Negative Harvest Chart

My most desired fruit I want to harvest is:

_____

I will have to stop feeding or sowing:

_____

I must consistently sow:

_____

My most desired fruit I want to harvest is:

_____

I will have to stop feeding or sowing:

_____

I must consistently sow:

_____

My most desired fruit I want to harvest is:

_____

I will have to stop feeding or sowing:

_____

I must consistently sow:

_____
_____

Continuous Peace

Reader Bonuses

FREE GIFTS FOR YOU!

As a thank you for your book purchase, I would like to offer you some *free resources* to help you continue to grow.

Go to: DawnMarasco.com/CPFree

Reader bonuses include downloadable:

- Treasured scriptures and quotes from the book
- The photo of the cross in the sky mentioned in Chapter 8
- Your 30-Day Challenge
- Reprogramming the Lie Charts
- Reversing A Negative Harvest Charts

Also look for our **quiz** and other **resources** to keep you in ***God's Continuous Peace.***

Looking forward to continuing the journey,

Dawn